A Child's Learning of English

THE LANGUAGE LIBRARY
EDITED BY DAVID CRYSTAL

Australian Aboriginal Languages	*Colin Yallop*
Children's Writing and Reading	*Katharine Perera*
A Child's Learning of English	*Paul Fletcher*
A Companion to Old and Middle English Studies	*A. C. Partridge*
A Dictionary of Linguistics and Phonetics	*David Crystal*
A Dictionary of Literary Terms (revised)	*J. A. Cuddon*
Early English (revised)	*J. W. Clark*
Early Modern English	*Charles Barber*
English Dialects (revised)	*G. L. Brook*
The Foreign-Language Barrier	*J. A. Large*
A History of the English Language	*G. L. Brook*
A History of Foreign-Language Dictionaries	*R. L. Collison*
How Conversation Works	*Ronald Wardhaugh*
An Informal History of the German Language	*W. B. Lockwood*
John Donne: Language and Style	*A. C. Partridge*
Language and Class in Victorian England	*K. C. Phillipps*
The Language of 1984	*W. F. Bolton*
The Language of Walter Scott	*Graham Tulloch*
Languages of the British Isles: Past and Present	*W. B. Lockwood*
Modern Englishes: Pidgins and Creoles	*Loreto Todd*
Non-standard Language in English Literature	*N. F. Blake*
Puns	*Walter Redfern*
The Pitcairnese Language	*A. S. C. Ross*
Scientific and Technical Translation	*Isadore Pinchuck*
Sense and Sense Development (revised)	*R. A. Waldron*
Speaking of Chinese	*R. Chang and M. Scrogin Chang*
The Study of Dialect	*K. M. Petyt*
A Survey of Structural Linguistics	*G. L. Lepschy*
Thomas Hardy's English	*Ralph W. V. Elliott*
The Treatment of Sounds in Language and Literature	*Raymond Chapman*

A Child's Learning of English

PAUL FLETCHER

Basil Blackwell
in association with
André Deutsch

First published 1985

Basil Blackwell Publisher Ltd
108 Cowley Road, Oxford OX4 1JF, UK
in association with André Deutsch Ltd,
105 Great Russell Street, London WC1B 3LJ, England

Basil Blackwell Inc.
432 Park Avenue South, Suite 1505,
New York, NY 10016, USA

British Library Cataloguing in Publication Data

Fletcher, Paul
A child's learning of English. – (The Language Library)
1. Language acquisition
I. Title
401'.9 P118

ISBN 0-631-14281-9
ISBN 0-631-14282-7 Pbk

Library of Congress Cataloging in Publication Data

Fletcher, Paul J.
A child's learning of English.

(The Language library)
Bibliography: p.
Includes index.
1. Language acquisition – Case studies. 2. English language – Acquisition – Case studies. I. Title.
II. Series.
P118.F56 1985 420'.1'9 85-1244
ISBN 0-631-14281-9
ISBN 0-631-14282-7 (pbk.)

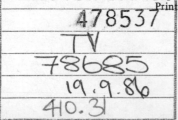

Typeset by Unicus Graphics Ltd, Horsham, West Sussex
Printed in Great Britain by Page Brothers Ltd, Norwich

For Helen, Lisa and Daniel

Contents

Tables and Figures

TABLES

FIGURES

Preface

The language of young children has always fascinated parents. It has also, in the last two decades, become a subject for serious academic enquiry, most notably within the disciplines of linguistics and psychology. This academic interest, and practical applications of the knowledge derived from it, has produced a deluge of journal articles on topics as diverse as the infant's perception of speech sounds, and the older child's understanding of metaphor. Studies span an age-range from birth to the threshold of adulthood. There are also books. In 1973, Roger Brown's *A First Language: the early stages* provided an integrated account of children's language development up to the age of about 3 years. It was a considerable achievement, and remains an invaluable source-book. More recent texts (for example, Dale 1976; Eliot 1981; Clark and Clark 1977) also inform us about theories of language development, about the variables that may shape it, and about the experiments or data analyses that illuminate it. But very rarely is the language itself – what children actually say – quoted at any length. If we want to examine a child's utterances in detail, particularly as they develop over time, we have to go back 40 years to W. Leopold's incomparable four-volume study, *Speech Development of a Bilingual Child* (1939–49). This provides broad phonetic transcriptions, and background information and comment, on the developing language of Leopold's daughter, Hildegarde. She grew up in the mid-Western United States in the early 1930s, and her father, a linguist, kept as accurate a record as he could of what she said. In the era before tape-recordings, this meant instantaneous transcription of her output. It is no surprise (and certainly no criticism) that the material on the period from Hildegarde's first words (at about 10 months) until she was about $2\frac{1}{2}$ is much more detailed than her later development.

Apart from Leopold's diary study, there is no longitudinal account of a child learning English which includes detailed exemplification of the child's speech. There are published transcripts of conversations. Wells (1975) provides transcripts of 32 children, all at the age of 3;3, talking to their mother. Each extract is of a recording (about 25 minutes in length) of the child in his or her home environment. Transcripts of the spoken language of older children are provided in a large-scale cross-sectional study of 6–12-year-old children (Fawcett and Perkins 1980). Thirty children were sampled at ages 6, 8, 10 and 12 (for a total of 120 children). However, neither of these sets of materials provides any discussion of the children's language which was transcribed.

The purpose of this book is to fill a gap for the student, academic or professional, interested in language development by providing four lengthy samples of one child's utterances, in conversations, when aged between 2½ and 4 years, and providing consistent analyses and commentaries on the first three samples. (The fourth sample is included in an appendix, with guidelines for the reader's own analysis.) The samples are taken at roughly six-month intervals, in order to maximize the possibility of demonstrating change in the child's language. For the period between samples 1 and 2, and samples 2 and 3, however, we have detailed information on the child's development in the form of twice-weekly samples. We will supplement the comparison between successive samples with information from the intervening period. We will also use the commentaries to make comparisons between the development of the child we are studying and that of other children described in the published literature. The advantage of examining one child in detail is that it affords a picture of systemic language growth, in the record of her linguistic change. The disadvantage is that the picture revealed may not be typical. We cannot know whether it is or not, until we have a larger sample of accounts of overall development which are at least as detailed. But the comparisons we are able to make with descriptions of the language learning of other English-speaking children suggest that her pattern of development shows many similarities to theirs.

The first part of the book provides a background to the samples and commentaries on them, in terms of a discussion of methodology and explanation in modern language development studies. The second part of the book contains details of the analyses performed on the samples, and the samples themselves. The first three of these are followed by a commentary, with standard headings. The commentaries pick out salient features of the samples, and link them to relevant studies. No commentary on a language sample can be exhaustive, and no analysis definitive in our present state of knowledge. It is hoped that the sample analyses and commentaries here will not only provide useful information for those interested in children's language, but also provoke them to analyses and commentaries of their own.

It would be impossible to list and thank all the teachers, colleagues and students who have, directly or indirectly, contributed to the appearance and content of this book, and the naming of those most immediately concerned does not mean that any of the others have been forgotten. I would like to acknowledge the editorial influence and support of David Crystal during the long gestation of the book; I owe a particular debt of gratitude to him. And the book could not have been written without the Yorke family agreeing to the initial invasion of their privacy by a tape-recorder, and to the publication of the transcripts of their conversations. To Sophie and Fran, in particular, but also to Hester, Griselda and Vin, my grateful thanks. The other family which should be acknowledged is my own, which has endured with equanimity the rigours of living with someone who is trying to write a book.

The project which provided the samples of conversations used in this book was supported initially by SSRC grant no. HR 9674. The text was typed and revised with care and (inexhaustible) patience by Barbara Barnes. My thanks are due to her also.

Phonetic Symbols Used in this Book

CONSONANTS

p	pet	[pɛt]	s	sit	[sɪt]
b	bed	[bɛd]	z	zoo	[zu]
t	tub	[tʌb]	ʃ	ship	[ʃɪp]
d	do	[du]	ʒ	measure	[mɛʒə]
k	cat	[kæt]	h	hat	[hæt]
g	gap	[gæp]	m	men	[mɛn]
tʃ	chin	[tʃɪn]	n	nag	[næg]
dʒ	jam	[dʒæm]	ŋ	sing	[sɪŋ]
f	fell	[fɛl]	l	let	[lɛt]
v	vat	[væt]	r	red	[rɛd]
θ	thin	[θɪn]	j	yes	[jes]
ð	then	[ðɛn]	w	wet	[wɛt]

VOWELS

i	read	[rid]	ɜ	bird	[bɜd]
ɪ	rid	[rɪd]	ə	the	[ðə]
ɛ	bed	[bɛd]	eɪ	say	[seɪ]
æ	bad	[bæd]	oʊ	so	[soʊ]
ɑ	calm	[kɑm]	aɪ	high	[haɪ]
ɒ	cot	[kɒt]	ɑʊ	how	[hɑʊ]
ɔ	caught	[kɔt]	ɑɪ	toy	[tɒɪ]
ʊ	good	[gʊd]	ɪə	here	[hɪə]
u	mood	[mud]	ɛə	there	[ðɛə]
ʌ	hut	[hʌt]	aɪə	fire	[faɪə]

1
Method and Explanation

The major contribution of the linguist to the study of language acquisition has been in the provision of analytic frameworks for organizing the data. If we want to make sense of the mass of data that children's spoken output presents us with, and characterize change over time, we must somehow summarize the information contained in the utterances we collect. The response of the linguist to a corpus of language data is to account for it in a grammar - an explicit statement of the structural principles underlying the utterances which make up the corpus. That this response might raise problems when addressed to children's language was foreseen by Chomsky at an early stage of modern language development studies:

> the attempt to write a grammar for the child raises all of the unsolved problems of constructing a grammar for adult speech, multiplied by some rather large factor. ... This study must be carried out in devious and clever ways, if any serious result is to be obtained. (Chomsky 1964: 35, 36)

It would not occur to anyone who has spent time studying children's language to argue with Chomsky's expression of this view. In particular, estimating a child's linguistic ability in the absence of linguistic intuitions (from the pre-school child, at any rate) is a daunting, though not impossible, task. The linguist writing grammars for the adult language has access to native-speaker judgements about their language, in addition to a corpus of utterances. It is thus a relatively straightforward matter to check, for example, whether a particular utterance is a representative of a structural type or not. If a sentence like *she put the cat out* turns up, we can find out from a speaker whether other sentences like *she put the fire out*, *the doctor ran a bill up*, are acceptable. In addition, by determining that *she put out the cat*, *she put out the fire*, *the doctor ran up a bill* are allowable, we can define a structural type containing verb (e.g. *put*) plus particle (e.g. *out*) sequences, where the particle can occur immediately after the verb, or separated from it, following the object. We can tap the adult speaker's linguistic capacity directly, to dramatically enrich our data base. With young children, however, such procedures are difficult, if not impossible, and our data are restricted to the corpus of utterances. We cannot assume, in the absence of intuitional data from the child, that an utterance token in the corpus is a representative of a structural type. This is a profound and possibly insuperable limitation so far as writing descriptively adequate grammars is concerned, as Chomsky recognized. Since he drew attention to these problems, a variety of methods for investigating and explaining children's language and language abilities have been tried. As a preliminary to our detailed data analysis, we need to review some of the methodological and theoretical concerns evinced by modern child language researchers. We will begin with practical matters - the data base, its collection and transcription - and then move on to consider ways in which the data have been explained. Historically, the initial explanatory hypothesis was in terms of what came to be referred to as the 'innateness hypothesis'. This was the idea that the child came to the language-learning task equipped with a rich set of specific language-learning mechanisms. An alternative hypothesis was reductive; the child's learning of language was to be explained in terms of his cognitive development. More recently, attention has shifted to the relevance of linguistic input to the child as an independent variable in language development.

All these theoretical positions have taken as data the child's linguistic output. Since this book will for the most part continue that tradition, it is appropriate to recognize, before examining methods for collecting and organizing output data, that the child is hearer as well as speaker. We will begin therefore by considering comprehension.

COMPREHENSION AND PRODUCTION

The primary source of information on the child's language has been his spontaneous speech, and our data are no exception. Production data are both plentiful and accessible. Provided appropriate recording techniques are used, there is no limit to the amount of data available. By contrast, the assembling of information about comprehension is a painfully slow and piecemeal process. In addition, the study of comprehension usually involves experimental techniques,[1] which may be problematic with young children, while spontaneous production in conversation, in the child's home environment, is arguably the most natural and representative form of language use. There is little doubt that these are the main practical reasons for the choice of spontaneous speech as the primary data base for studying acquisition. This choice means generally that comprehension - an equally important part of language-learning - is not investigated in any detail. In fact, it is often assumed that comprehension does not need to be investigated directly, since understanding is in advance of production: to get some picture of comprehension, we simply have to look at production data. However, inferring comprehension ability from production data is a risky enterprise, unless we are extremely careful about how we analyse the data. Because comprehension is so important both as a skill and as a primary source for the child learning about his language, we should take a closer look at what it is, its relationship to production, and how it is assessed.

In her account of comprehension strategies in children, Chapman (1978) begins by emphasizing the importance of the situation in which a sentence is uttered: 'It is the relation between sentence and situation rather than the sentence alone that determines what one understands and how easily one understands it.' Full comprehension for adult listeners requires a matching between a recognized signal, the utterance context and prior knowledge. The child is in the position for a good deal of the time of having only partial linguistic and knowledge systems to bring to bear on the signals he gets. We should expect, then, particularly between the ages of 2 and 4 years, imperfect comprehension, just as we expect imperfect production.

There are two sources of information on comprehension: comprehension tests, which generally use picture materials (for example, Lee 1971; Miller and Yoder 1973; see Rizzo and Stephens 1981 for review), and experimental studies, which viewed as a whole cover a wide range of grammatical or lexical contrasts, though individual studies tend to be highly specific. If we were to attempt a generalization for these studies, it could be that the appearance of a particular structure in production does not guarantee the comprehension of that structure.[2] That is, production is in advance of comprehension. As the rest of the discussion in this section should make clear, however, the superiority is only apparent. It would after all be very strange if Sophie, the child whose language is analysed later in the book, can produce an utterance like *me want daddy come down* at 2;4 (see sample 1: 1.53), but is not able to understand a similar adult sentence (for example, *you want daddy to come*). To try to resolve this problem, let us consider in broad outline what comprehension involves.

We can begin with a pair of utterances from Sophie and her mother that immediately follow *me want daddy come down* (for transcriptional conventions, see p. 58):

M. 'Daddy is wòrking sweetie/
S. nò/
nò/
'find her chèque-book/

Sophie's first task is to recognize her mother's utterance as speech, as opposed to a non-speech signal, the most basic kind of acoustic discrimination required of her. She next has to recognize unit-patterns;[3] in this case, match *he's* and *working* with pre-existing lexical representations in her memory, if possible. This pattern-matching is a skill that has to be learned. In absolute terms, the fundamental frequency (F_0) of the speaker's voice, and hence the formant frequencies of her vowels, which depend on the F_0, will be quite different to those of Sophie's father, if he were to pronounce the same sentence. The child has to learn to allow for F_0 differences and to determine, for example, that it is the formant *structure* - the relationship among the formants - and not the absolute frequencies at which each formant occurs, which is crucial to vowel identification (see Fourcin 1978). Assuming that this recognition is successful, the child proceeds to make a unit-to-meaning match, which is the third step. She can then go on to act appropriately, linguistically or otherwise. In this case, we can infer from the child's response that Sophie has (a) recognized her mother's utterance as speech, (b) completed successful unit-pattern recognition and (c) extracted an appropriate meaning from the utterance in context. What we do not know are the exact units identified under (b), and it is in this area of unit identification that all our problems in relation to comparisons between comprehension and production ability lie. It is here that we can accommodate the finding that production is in advance of comprehension, if we consider the nature of the units required by the child for successful comprehension. The criterion for success in this case is responding appropriately. In the sequence above, we infer this from the child's denial of her mother's assertion, and her description of an alternative activity that her father is engaged in. But this kind of success, impressive though it is, does not guarantee that the child has identified all the *possible* linguistic units in the input sequence. We can identify for the mother's utterance four units:[4]

he	*'s*	*work*	*-ing*
3rd person	3rd person	Main-verb	Progressive
Subject	contracted	stem	inflection
Pronoun	auxiliary		
Masculine			

Such a segmentation presupposes a considerable basis of grammatical information. But for successful comprehension purposes, the child only needs to recognize the pronoun and the main-verb stem as part of the units *he's* and *working*; it is not necessary to segment either of these further in order to respond appropriately at this point. Sophie does not need adult-like unit-pattern recognition to be able to proceed to the stage of extracting enough meaning, in the context, to be able to cope perfectly well in the conversation. Her future language-learning will, however, depend in some measure on her ability to perform more precise segmentations. We can see at once how the more stringent criteria of a test or experimental situation might show up gaps in the child's comprehension. If in her mother's utterance Sophie is recognizing *work* but not *-ing*, she may fail one of the items from Northwestern Syntax Screening Test. Figure 1.1 shows the four pictures from which she would have to choose in this test in response to a test item *The girl is drinking*.

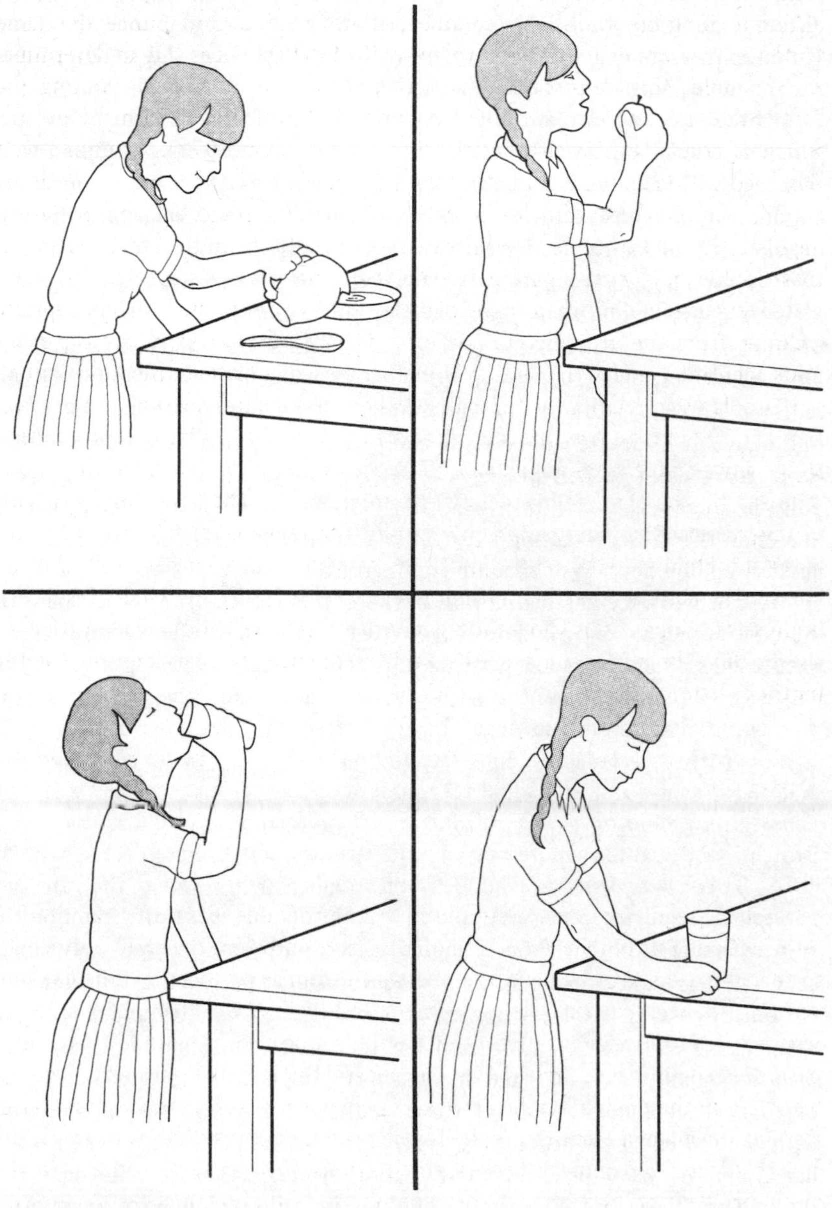

Figure 1.1 An item from the Northwestern Syntax Screening Test
(after Lee 1971)

The child has to choose, in response to this stimulus, the bottom left picture (the others represent, from top left, the girl pouring, the girl going to eat, and the girl going to drink). Successful performance here will depend on the child's understanding of the progressive form (*is* plus the *-ing* suffix on the verb) and appropriate picture identification.

It becomes clear that we are using the term comprehension in two rather different senses. In the first case, in conversation, we were concerned with what we will call comprehension for understanding (C_u). In the second case, in the test, we construct a situation in which we are checking quite specific grammatical or lexical contrasts, by asking the child to choose an appropriate picture for a description. We will call this kind of grammatical comprehension C_g. (Of course picture comprehension is not the only way to approach this ability, nor are these tests the only arena in which the ability is used. Comprehension tests simply happen to be a convenient way to point up the difference.) In the case of C_u, it should be clear that partial analysis of the full linguistic structure will be quite adequate, in conjunction with contextual cues, for a child to perform appropriately. The criterion of coping successfully in a conversation with his mother may be a much less stringent one for the child than discriminating pictures in response to a sentence stimulus in a test for comprehension of specific grammatical contrasts.

We can reinforce the distinction between the two kinds of comprehension by considering an experimental approach to children's understanding of the significance of active and passive word-orders (Bridges 1980). In a variety of tasks, children were presented with reversible active and passive sentences in four comprehension-test settings.[5] In a 'construction task', they were asked to act out with toy cars a sentence like *the red car is pushed by the green car*. A detailed analysis of individual responses across age-groups revealed different behaviours according to age and individual preference. Up to 2;6, a child in Bridges' study would ignore one car and push the other himself (cf. Chapman 1978: 314). Between 2;6 and 3;9, one child might assume that the car nearest his hand when he hears the instruction is the agent of the action the verb refers to. Another child of similar age would move the first-mentioned car. After 3;9 children tend to respond appropriately. What is relevant here for our discussion is the possibility of the child between 2;6 and 3;9 apparently giving evidence of C_g in relation to a particular stimulus, although a comparison of his correct and incorrect responses will indicate that he has only a partial understanding of the stimuli he is hearing. If he is presented with *the red car is pushed by the green car*, and the green car is nearer to his hand, and he uses the 'near car as agent' strategy, then he will appear to respond appropriately. The strategy he is using to cope will become apparent only when he responds incorrectly to the same stimulus when the red car is closest to him. The example emphasizes that for the young language-learner the comprehension process may be based on partial linguistic knowledge. It also makes clear that his performance, in matching this partial knowledge and contextual cues to arrive at linguistic or behavioural responses, can be impressive. It is often only by careful investigation that we can pick up discrepancies between C_u and C_g.

Corresponding to the distinction we have made between C_u and C_g is a production distinction which also depends on the nature of the units the child is operating with, and which we might conveniently refer to as P_u (production for understanding) and P_g (grammatical production). Again, the distinction is between different kinds of successful performances. Consider once more *me want daddy come down*. Apart from a pronoun error and the omission of the infinitive marker *to*, this seems to be an appropriately constructed grammatical string. Its structural basis - the grammatical units employed by the child in constructing it - is unknowable simply by considering this one string. We do not if this is a stereotype of the child's (a learned routine appropriate for the context, but not generalizable in whole or in part), if it is a construction with word-level elements, or something in between. Each of these will be equally successful in the conversation - will achieve P_u - whatever their unit-basis. But it is only the construction of sentence types with different lexical items in them, in a variety of contexts, that is the mark of syntactic productivity (P_g). The full mobilization of the syntactic resources of the language will require the child to analyse fully the lexical items in *me want daddy come down*, and their syntactic relations.

Table 1.1 summarizes the different senses of comprehension and production that we have discussed. The various possibilities for units the child may use

TABLE 1.1 Criteria and possible unit bases for types of comprehension and production

<table>
<tr><th></th><th>Criterion</th><th>Unit basis</th><th>Unit basis</th><th>Criterion</th><th></th></tr>
<tr><td>C_u</td><td>appropriate behaviour and/or response in conversation</td><td>|he's working|
or
|he's|working|
or
|he|s|work|ing|</td><td>|me want daddy come down|
or
|me want|daddy come down|
or
|me|want|daddy|come|down|</td><td>production in appropriate context</td><td>P_u</td></tr>
<tr><td>C_g</td><td>as above, plus discriminating responses in test and experimental situations</td><td>|he|s|work|ing|</td><td>|me|want|daddy|come|down|</td><td>production of this and similar tokens in appropriate contexts, with lexical differentiation</td><td>P_g</td></tr>
</table>

for C_u and P_u, indicated by vertical segmentation lines, indicate that the analytical basis for successful performance on the child's part may vary from a holistic 'chunk' to a string of minimal meaningful elements.[6] For C_g and P_g, on the other hand, the requirements are much more stringent. For C_g, the child will have to analyse minimal units like *-ing*, and employ knowledge of the systems in which such elements have contrastive status. To attribute P_g to the child, we will require productivity – lexical variation in utterances of the same structural types: *me tell daddy come down*, *you ask Hessy come down*, *me ask the lady go out*, etc. as well as *me want daddy come down*. It should now be apparent that the problem raised earlier, of production being in advance of comprehension, is a pseudo-problem resulting from the ambiguity of these terms; although it may seem unreasonable for production to be in advance of comprehension, it seems quite plausible for P_u to be in advance of C_g, once we have these terms at our disposal.[7]

In the data we consider later in the book, it is possible to address both C_u and P_u, directly, by considering maternal and child utterances and their contexts. We can make only an indirect approach to C_g via the P_g information we extract. Provided that this account of P_g is detailed and accurate, it can serve as a conservative estimate of C_g, in the absence of C_g tests that are comprehensive enough to cover the range of grammatical structures relevant to the $2\frac{1}{2}$ to $3\frac{1}{2}$-year-old child.

PRODUCTION DATA

We now turn to some general considerations relevant to production data – the kind of data available, the conditions under which data are collected, and the way data are transcribed. Where possible we will make explicit the effect, or possible effect, of the methodology on explanation, since in language acquisition research, as in other areas of enquiry, the two are inevitably linked.

Diary studies

The earliest records of children's speech come in so-called 'diary studies', of which Leopold's (1939–49) is the most detailed and famous example for (American) English. Other languages are represented in similar linguist-parent records: for example, Gregoire (1939) for French, Keyneres̀ (1926) for Hungarian, Stern and Stern (1928) for German. But the diary method is not limited to the era before the tape-recorder. A recent study of phonological development (Smith, 1973) uses procedures not dissimilar to Leopold, as these quotations indicate:

The observations were written down as they were made, usually in daily entries. From 1;7 on, they became too numerous for this procedure; they were then entered on slips in my pocket and transferred in systematic order into the diary at infrequent intervals. (Leopold 1939–49: vol. 1, 14)

All the data analyzed were taken down in phonetic transcription on index cards. A tape-recorder was used occasionally ... but most of the description is based on non-recorded material. ... Data was recorded systematically from 2 years 2 months to age four; sometimes at intervals of a week, sometimes every day. (Smith 1973: 9–10)

Despite being more than 30 years apart, these studies have (in their data-collection procedures) a great deal in common. They provide longitudinal information on the speech of a single child, at frequent sampling intervals, in a natural situation. The observer, who is almost always a parent, *selects* data thought to be of relevance:

After the middle of January, 1932 (1;6), words which she repeated on demand were no longer taken into consideration, but only such as had become an active part of her vocabulary. Otherwise every word was recorded through 2;0. After that, progress became so rapid that the entries had to be restricted to new acquisitions of typical importance, still rather detailed, but no longer complete. (Leopold 1939–49: vol. 14)

Smith's criteria for inclusion of data depended 'partly on the instability of his [the child's] system, partly on the time available'. Coincidentally, in both studies there was a gap of six weeks in the data collections. Leopold taught at a summer school in July-August 1932 (beginning when Hildegard was 1;11);[6] Smith collected data only sporadically during a six-week family visit to India when Amahl was 2;2. Despite such gaps, and their inevitable selectivity, records like these have formed the only published detailed longitudinal records, and are hence invaluable. One index of their importance is the frequency with which they are used as data bases for either comparative purposes or hypothesis-testing by other scholars. Leopold's data are extensively referred to in works such as Barrett (1978), Brown (1973), Fletcher (1979), Griffiths (1979) and Ingram (1976). Even Smith's much more recent work has provided the data base for an alternative explanation of aspects of phonological development (Macken 1980). The strength of the diary study is that it allows the tracking of language growth, of systematic development within one individual, on the basis of data collected at very short sampling intervals. However, it generally provides a better data base for assessing phonological development than syntactic; once the child's output increases dramatically in the third year, the recording of utterance tokens has to become much more selective, and a full picture of syntax development is hard to achieve.

Recorded speech samples

The best-known corpus of children's speech is that collected and analysed by Roger Brown and a talented group of associates in the 1960s (see Brown 1973, for a full account). For the best part of a decade, this corpus and the results of its analysis dominated the field of child language studies. There were three children in the study, known as Adam, Eve and Sarah. They were selected in the first place 'because they were just beginning to speak multiword utterances, had highly intelligible speech, and were highly voluble'. All were the only children in their families at the start of the study. They furnished data in the form of samples of spontaneous speech amounting to at least two hours every month: 'For Adam and Eve a two hour visit every second week was the basic schedule. For Sarah it was one half-hour each week.' This basic recording schedule was augmented 'when interesting things seemed to be happening fast'. The child's mother and two members of the research team were present at the recording sessions, held in the child's home. For two of the children a microphone was visible in a fixed position; the other child had a microphone sewn into a piece of the clothing she always wore during recording sessions, by which her speech was transmitted to a tape-recorder. These details may seem trivial: they do, however, relate to important questions about the methods of child language study. How many children should a study involve, and how 'typical' of the population should they be? What should the sampling interval between recordings be? Does the presence of observers affect the character of the data we are seeking to obtain? We will deal with these questions in turn.

Sampling size and sampling interval

Most child language researchers have followed the lead established by Brown and operated with small numbers of children. The collection, transcription and analysis of child language data are time-consuming, labour-intensive and hence very expensive, if large samples are involved. To transcribe, code and fully analyse a one-hour tape can take up to a full day or even longer.[9] There thus tends to be a trade-off between sampling size and sampling interval - the more frequent the sampling, the smaller the sample size in terms of number of subjects. Since most investigators have wanted to sample language output frequently, the number of children involved has generally been between one and five (see, for example, Bloom 1970; Clark 1974; Fletcher 1981; Griffiths, Atkinson and Huxley 1974). The radical alternative to such studies is the large-sample project on British children by Wells and his associates (see Wells 1974, 1981). Theirs is the first attempt to chart the development of a *repre-*

sentative sample of subjects, and it involves 128 children. Two groups of children (64 in each group), one aged 15 months and the other aged 39 months at the start of the study, were sampled from the population of Bristol children. There were equal numbers of boys and girls, and equal numbers of children in each of four socio-economic groups. Each child was studied for a period of two years three months, giving a three-month overlap between the two groups (from 39 to 42 months) and an overall age-span from 15 months to $5\frac{1}{2}$ years. The sampling interval for recordings of the children's language was three months, each sample comprising about half an hour's material.

There are advantages and disadvantages of both large-sample and small-sample approaches. We are enjoined, in human behaviour research, to use random samples that are as large as practicable for reasons that have to do with the relationship between sample statistics and population parameters (see, for example, Woods, Fletcher and Hughes 1985 ch. 6). If we compute a mean or any other statistic from a sample, a population value is being estimated. The larger our sample, the less likelihood there is of the estimate derived from our sample being in error. Other things being equal, it would seem sensible in language acquisition research to plump for the large-sample study. Our findings will then represent more closely our target population. But other things are not equal. In particular, there is a developmental axis to take into account. Since we have *a priori* no reason to assume that the only relevant changes in the child's language will take place at three-month intervals, the broadening of the sampling interval necessitated by our large sample size may involve a loss of information about the developmental axis. In reality, we have two sampling requirements – the provision of a representative sample of children, and the provision of representative current samples of utterances from any one child. Since important changes can take place in a matter of days and since for practical reasons it is generally impossible to satisfy both sampling requirements, it might be argued that we should initially concentrate on the developmental axis and sample frequently from a small number of children. This inhibits generalization, but does not prevent us from bringing together case-studies or small samples at a later date. If we concentrate on representativeness with respect to numbers of children, it is impossible (given, say, a three-month sampling interval) to recover the language of any of these children at intermediate stages. We can illustrate the potential importance of this point with an example from Sophie.

At the time of the first recording of Sophie, on 14.11.79, when she was 2;4, she used virtually no regular verb forms other than the unmarked form. That is, she would use *play* as in *our play that* (where *our* is used in place of *we*), but not *playing*, *played*, *plays* or *can play*. She would also use a very few irregular past-tense forms. If from this point we focus on the development of past-time referring forms, and pick another sample as near as possible to three months after this date (12.2.80), we find more extensive use of irregular past tenses, and in addition the occurrence of two *-en* forms, *taken* and *given*, which refer to (recent) past time. On the basis of these correct forms, we are unable to tell whether the child is using the *-en* inflection systematically.[10] As it happens, the recording schedule for Sophie allows us to see that three days later, on 15.2.80, the child uses two overgeneralized past participles, *boughten* and *builden*. A three-month sampling interval which just happened to light on the 12.2 would have missed this important piece of information, which suggests that the child is using a rule of past participle formation productively (see below p. 121) for a fuller discussion of this phenomenon). If, in addition, the period during which the past participle was overgeneralized happened to be less than three months, significant information about this aspect of the child's language learning would be lost.

So the sample which is representative of the population can be unrepresentative of the individual; equally, one individual's temporary strategy for past-time referring may be irrelevant for most children. In the absence of corpora which are representative both ways, the best compromise is to use the study with the large number of children (see Wells 1981) as a check and comparison for extensive data from a single child or a small group.

Role of the observer

In investigating the characteristics of casual speech styles, sociolinguists have made the point that it is very important *who* collects the data of interest, and in what circumstances. Labov formulates an Observer's Paradox: 'we want to observe how people talk when they are not being observed' (1971: 461). For the sociolinguist who wants to describe not the language of Chomsky's ideal native-speaker hearer', but vernaculars spoken in everyday situations, this uncertainty principle raises considerable problems. The presence of the middle-class, adult academic will inevitably pose a spurious formality on the speech of a working-class teenage group, for example, and render the investigation of causal speech patterns difficult, if not impossible. Do similar difficulties attend the child language researcher, with the presence of outsiders changing the nature of the phenomenon to be described? Apart from anecdotal evidence, there is little or no hard information on the effect of the presence of adult observers on the child's language (although there is evidence that the child is able from a relatively early age to tailor his speech style to different listeners (Sachs and Devin 1976)). There is, however, an intriguing discrepancy in relation to *maternal* language between Brown's study and that of Wells, which is worth briefly examining.

Those studying the language of Adam, Eve and Sarah had noted the occurrence of what they called grammatical expansions in the mother's speech, when she produced a gloss that (incidentally or otherwise) yielded those items missing from the child's utterance, as the following pair of utterances shows:

Child:	Eve lunch
Mother:	Eve is having lunch

The mother's response maintains the child's basic proposition, but adds a lexical verb and the appropriate auxiliary and inflection. In Brown's data, expansions tended to be rather common in the early stages of children's learning. For two of the three children at stage I - at the time, that is, when they were producing utterances with an average length of 1.75 morphemes - expansions appeared about 30 per cent of the time. Such immediate parental responses to the child's utterance provide grammatical information in a transparent way, and were initially considered a potentially valuable training technique, since they 'confirmed [that] everything [the child] said was appropriate to the circumstances, and they set a learning target only slightly advanced beyond his performance'. It is, of course, impossible to demonstrate the efficacy of expansions for syntax training using only conversational data.[11] A comparison of Brown's data with Wells's data makes the hypothesis that expansions are primarily a training technique rather less plausible.

In a study of adjustments in adult speech and their relation to linguistic growth in the Bristol project children, Wells (1980: 46) reports a generally low frequency of occurrence of expansions - much lower than Brown. More significantly, Wells indicates that in his data expansions 'only occur with any frequency when a stranger is present - a situation which has occurred in other studies when a researcher has been present during the collection of the data'. In other words, the differences in maternal style between the two studies, with respect to expansions, could be explained with reference to the research methodology. We have already seen how Brown collected his spontaneous speech data - a technique that involved the presence of observers on every occasion that data were collected. Wells, by contrast, made every effort to exclude observers from the data-collection procedure. Each recording of the child's spontaneous speech was obtained by means of a radio-microphone (inserted in a garment the child wore); this microphone was controlled by means of a timing device that was preset to take 24 90-second samples at approximately 20-minute intervals between 9 a.m. and 6 p.m. No member of the research team was present while the recording was being made, and neither the mother nor the child was supposed to know when a recording was being taken. The size of Wells's sample, together with the change in frequency of expansions when an outsider is present, make his conclusions about the role of the observer in affecting maternal speech style plausible. It seems as if the expansions in some cases may not be used to provide grammatical information for the child, but to provide a gloss for the observer on the meaning of the child's incomplete utterance. Such a link between methodological procedures and the data obtained (even though in this case not the child's data) is instructive.

TRANSCRIPTION

Once the data are collected, they have to be represented in an appropriate way for syntactic analysis. Occasionally the transcription will be phonetic (see Brown 1973: 52). More usually, it will be orthographic, perhaps supplemented with phonetic data where necessary. There is, of course, no automatic procedure for getting from an acoustic signal to the written word, and the transcriber's rendering of the conversation he hears is subject to a number of decisions, which can affect the interpretation of the sample transcribed. Since transcription is so often taken for granted, it is worth while making clear how much information selection, loss or bias there might be in an orthographic transcription, if it is not supplemented.

Some grammatical examples

The abstraction involved in orthographic transcription and its relevance for a linguistic assessment of the child can be underestimated. As an example, consider the auxiliary *have* when it occurs following a modal, as in *he might have finished*, *she must have heard him*. Children of primary-school age (8 and 9-year-olds), in common with adults, generally pronounce the *have* as [əv] in pre-main-verb position. There is some evidence that children do not interpret this [əv] as a form of *have*. First, in sentence-final position, for example, in *she might have*, where (under stress) we might expect [hæv], the children not uncommonly produce [əv] – which adults would not normally do. Second, it is common for these same children to make the mistake of spelling *have* as *of* in their writing. These two pieces of evidence suggest that the children do not necessarily identify the *have* of *might have left* with the *have* of *I have finished*, which the linguist at least would certainly want to do. Quite what the verb system of these children is like is difficult to say without more extensive data; it looks at least possible that they do not organize their auxiliaries in the same way as adults. What is clear is that if we represent occurrences of [əv] and [ɒv] as *have* in an orthographic transcription of speech from children of this age, we are likely to overlook an interesting stage in their development. The example suggests that a sensible compromise in transcriptional practice would be the phonetic transcription of 'suspicious' elements such as *have* in an otherwise orthographic transcription. With this example in mind, we can look at some other aspects of orthographic transcriptions, indicate some possible limitations, and suggest how they should be interpreted and, where necessary, supplemented.

As a more widespread example of potential idealization resulting from writing conversation, we can instance contractions like *he's*, *what's*, *haven't*, *their*, *I'm*, etc. The child's pronunciation of *what's that* may be exactly the same as that of an adult, on a particular occasion. For the child under 3 years old, however, the contracted element may equally well be omitted on another occasion. This variability in marking for a contracted copula or auxiliary would indicate that the child has not come to grips with the syntactic status of the form, and may not associate the 'contracted' element with its appropriate full form. Since a number of distinct full forms have contractions signalled in the same way in English, the learning of these relationships may take some time. The form *'s* on *what's*, for example, can be interpreted as a contraction of four distinct full forms as follows:

what's that	contracted copula *be*
what's he doing	contracted auxiliary *be*
what's he done	contracted auxiliary *have*
what's that say	contracted auxiliary *do*

It is only by observing and interpreting the co-occurrence relationships of this form that the child will eventually determine its place in the grammatical system. In the meantime, we might expect variability in use, as a reflection of the child's lack of connection between contracted and full form. It follows that the conventional orthographic representation of [wɒts] as *what's*, which automatically assigns a grammatical status to the final [s], is potentially misleading. If variability exists in the 3-year-old's pronunciations of such forms, it would seem appropriate to transcribe them without apostrophes as a reminder of their doubtful status.

This attitude towards contractions is a specific instance of the general point that it is illegitimate to assume that a form used by a child has the same systemic value as it would have when used by an adult. One of the general consequences of orthographic transcriptions is that we can forget that they represent the utterances of small children, and so make grammatical analyses of the transcriptions rather than what they stand for.

Non-segmental aspects

A rather more serious limitation of the orthography and its effect on our analysis of what the child says is its failure to provide for the representation of such features as intonation, pause and stress - what we might call 'non-segmental' aspects of speech. The limited set of punctuation marks available are only minimally helpful for indicating pause, and of no help for a systematic notation for intonation. For the purposes of the analyses of Sophie's language, we will augment our orthographic transcription with conventions indicating pause, stress, tone-unit boundaries and the direction of nuclear tone movement.[12] It must be emphasized that this is not a complete non-segmental analysis and would be quite inadequate for an analysis which had as its goal the investigation of the child's non-segmental development (see Crystal 1985). It will, however, suffice as a minimal non-segmental analysis relevant to questions we may wish to ask about various features of the child's grammatical development. We can illustrate this claim by considering examples in which pause, stress and pitch-movement marking can be important.

Pause

The pause distinctions used are as follows: . indicates a brief pause; - is used if the pause is long relative to a pulse of the speaker's rhythm, and - - , - - - are used for proportionately longer pauses. Using such distinctions can, for example, help to isolate potential comprehension problems, as the following example from a language-delayed child of 3;6 indicates. (In this conversation A indicates adult and C child, A is a speech therapist, and she and the child are talking about toy objects and people in a doll's house.)

A Hùgh/
   lòok/
   what's thís one/ - -
C bèd/ -
A 'good bôy/
   it's a bèd/
   'what shall we 'do with the gìrl/
   shall we 'sit her úp/ or 'lie her dòwn/
C dòwn/
A shall we 'make her sít/ or lìe/
C dòwn/ - - -
A Húgh/ -
C dòwn/ dòwn/
A yes 'what's thàt for/ - -
C gìrl/
A the gìrl/ -
C * yès/
A * Is she going to sít/ or lìe/
C lìe/
A hḿ/
C lìe/
A lìe/
C yès/ - -
A thère/.
   what a'bout gràndpa/ I mean dàddy/
   is 'he 'going to sìt/ or lìe/ - -
C sít/

A sìt/
C yēs/ - - -
A ôo/. I've bent his ˈlegs the ˈwrong wày/ (laughs)
what's he dòing/ - - -
he's sìtting/.

There are a number of questions asked of the child here, most of which he responds to successfully. When asked to identify some object as *what's this one* (l. 3), he can respond appropriately. When presented with alternatives, as in *is she going to sit or lie* (l. 18), he can understand that he is required to respond with one of the alternatives. When he is asked a question that must have a verb as a response - *what's he doing* (l. 31) - he fails to reply. His lack of response is indicated by the long pause following A's question. This differential responding to questions may be significant for either delayed or normal children in providing information about their level of comprehension of questions. The absence of information about pause in this transcription could lead us to believe that *he's sitting* in the last line of the text is the therapist's immediate response to her own question, and to miss the information about null response altogether.

Stress

As we have indicated above, the existence of unstressed forms, and their implications, goes unnoticed in an orthographic transcript. An adult utterance like *have you seen George* may indeed (though rarely) have its first two words pronounced [ˈhæv ˈjuː]. But a wide variety of pronunciations are possible, including [həvjə], [əvjə] and [vjə]. In any assessment of the child's syntactic ability in relation to *have* auxiliary and associated verb forms, it would be important to know which of these instances occurred, and how frequently, as we have already indicated. As a minimal first step towards this knowledge, we need to mark stressed monosyllables and primary stress in multisyllabic words. The incidence of stress is also important for evaluating the relationship between maternal and child language. Suppose we wish to examine *have* auxiliary use in the mother's language and in the child's: we would want not only to log the incidence of all *have* forms in the mother's speech, but also to divide these into full forms and reduced forms of various kinds. Generally in adult-to-adult connected speech, the full form is less frequent than its reduced counterparts. Accounts of 'motherese', however, stress the slower speed, in general, of much early maternal speech to children (see Ferguson 1977; Garnica 1977). It is assumed that this slow and hence more careful pronunciation will reduce the number of variants of any single lexeme that the child has to deal with, and so facilitate the learning of pronunciation and, also, in certain cases, syntactic function. This is a complex hypothesis which we shall return to later (see below, p. 36). As far as transcription is concerned, it should be clear that in certain specified areas, for instance that of auxiliaries, it would certainly be advantageous if we provided an accurate broad phonetic transcription of each auxiliary form, together with marking of stressed syllables; at the very least, we need to remember that by representing each variant pronunciation uniformly in the orthography, we may be concealing crucial information.

Tone

More generally, we will want to see at least the broad outlines of the development of the prosodic system and its relationship to syntax. We will therefore (following Crystal, Fletcher and Garman 1981) indicate, in addition to stress, tone group boundaries, and the location and direction of the nuclear tone. First, there are some contrastive uses of pitch movement in English and we will want to keep an eye on the development of these. Tag questions, for example, can vary in their meaning, depending on whether they use a falling or rising tone. Compare she's lèaving/ isńt she/ with a rising tone, which indicates that the speaker is requesting information (the 'asking', 'please confirm for me' type), with she's lèaving/ isǹt she/. Here, the falling tone (or 'telling' type) indicates not that the speaker requires confirmation, but that he accepts the truth of the proposition of the main clause. Sophie's first tags appear on the sample for 20.10.80 (nearly a year after the beginning of the project), and are to begin with all marked with falling tone. Unless we indicate at least nuclear pitch movement, we would not be able to follow, in the child's development, the differentiation of tags which are written as the same, but because of their intonation have distinct meanings. Second, it is quite possible for children to use aspects of the intonational system quite idiosyncratically, particularly at a time when they do not have a wide range of syntactic resources for the conveyance of various lexical or grammatical meanings. Halliday (1975) reports a consistent distinction between rising and falling tone in his child's utterances for a period. Halliday termed rising-tone utterances, which required some kind of response by the listener, 'pragmatic'. Falling-tone utterances, which did not require a response, were labelled 'mathetic'.[13] In Sophie's data, there are occasions, in the early days before she has developed any auxiliary system, on which she uses rising tones on utterances which are interpreted as questions. (In this example, S refers to Sophie, and F, to her mother, Fran. They are discussing Sophie's friends, Amy and Jack.)

F. ˈwhat are you ˈgoing to máke/
S. ˈsee Jàck/
ˈAmy see m̀e/
ˈsee m̀e/
ˈnot Jack/
F. ḿm/

S. 'only m̀e/
F. 'only yóu/
S. you 'take a biśsy/
F. 'cause I was hùngry/
S. 'me want a bìssy/

Here the mother responds to the rising tone on *you take a bissy*, by interpreting it as equivalent to a *why*-question. It is important to emphasize that we cannot conclude that rising tone 'means' question. Although it may be true that rising tones are less frequent than falling or level tones for Sophie, they do not always occur on utterances interpreted as questions; in addition, the reverse holds true - utterances with falling tones can be interpreted as questions. The adult interpretation of any utterance by the child is based on a complex interplay of syntax, lexis, intonation and context. We can underline this by considering Sophie's 'negatives' at the same age (2;4). In the sample for 14.11.79, Sophie has a variety of ways of negating or denying, as these extracts show:

(a) Use of *no* plus assertion:
S. me 'want daddy come dôwn.
F. he's wôrking sweetie.
S. nô.
nô.
'find her 'cheque bôok.

(b) *Nothing*
F. 'what have you 'got on your dréss?
S. nòthing.

(c) *Not* plus NP
F. 'aren't they 'going to the coúntry?
S. nò.
only òne.
not all thôse.

Her way of denying a proposition at this point is to use (a), *no* followed by a counter-assertion. The often reported clausal negation strategy of using *not* or *no* initially in clauses (for example, *not daddy work*) is not employed by Sophie. There are two instances in the sample, however, where Sophie is not responding to a prior assertion by her mother, but appears from the context to be negating:

(a) F. I 'think they're funny shòes actually/
'made to look like tòes/

S. why lòok/
hòrrid/
that hòrrid/
lòok.
'me like thàt/
F. nô/

(b) F. 'who went in the càr/
S. 'baby went in the càr/
'her slèep/
'her got blânky/
'her want a blànky/
'where's a blánky/

In (a), Sophie and her mother are looking at a toy catalogue together, and discussing a particular kind of doll, which Sophie makes it plain she does not like. The mother's final *no* of agreement in (a) only makes sense if she has interpreted Sophie's final utterance as negative, and indeed in the context of her own previous statements, Sophie's final utterance only fits if it is a negative. Similarly, in (b), *her got blanky* only makes sense in the monologue as a negative. The transcription of the two utterances makes clear, however, that they do not have similar tonics, and the attractive hypothesis of a consistent intonational marking, for a grammatical meaning for which the child does not yet have the syntactic resources, cannot be maintained. The intonation is only part of the reason for our interpretation of these utterances as negatives.

Context

The contextual information available to supplement a transcription of a language sample is almost limitless. The precise bounds set depend on the theoretical assumptions for practical requirements of the investigation. Some accounts of early linguistic development go so far as to use contextual information as part of their syntactic data base (see Bloom 1970). At the time when the child's production is limited to two or three lexical words, without inflections or grammatical words, ambiguous utterances (constructional homonyms) can result. As we have already noted, it is generally not possible (since we are talking about 2-year-olds) to secure judgements from the children on their own output, and so some researchers have advocated the use of context as a substitute. Suppose, for example, that on some occasions a child produces subject-verb-object sequences (*daddy see me*), generally has consistent adult-like word order, but then on another occasion produces *daddy coat*, and he happens to be pointing at his father's coat.

Suppose also that on another occasion, this time when the father was holding open the coat for the child to put his arm in, the child says *daddy coat*, again. It might be argued that *daddy coat* is a constructional homonym, which in the first case manifests the structural relations *possessor-possessed* (that is, it is essentially a noun phrase). The second instance of *daddy coat* would then be regarded as a subject-object sequence, reduced from the normal subject-verb-object because of performance limitations. Then contextual information would play the same role in assigning structural descriptions in this child's grammar as native-speaker intuitions in the adult grammar. It should be apparent that the approach is not all plain sailing. It will not be easy to justify an unequivocal interpretation of a particular context. Thus with our *daddy coat* example, it may be argued that, in the situation where the child is pointing at daddy's coat, the child's intention is to convey that daddy has forgotten his coat, or is going to put it on - that is, a 'subject-object' relation rather than a 'possessor-possessed'. The interpretation of the child's intention (and hence of the syntactic relations, which are represented in the utterance) may well vary from occasion to occasion and from person to person.[14]

Context is more fruitfully (and less problematically) employed to give information about language use, rather than language structure. The extent and nature of the information supplied here will depend on the goals of the investigation. If the focus of attention is the productive development of prepositions, then it will be important to know how accurately and in relation to what objects *in*, *on*, *under*, etc. are used. If we are mainly interested in time reference, then the focus changes. In examining past-time reference, for example, we will require that the contextual notes make clear what point along the time axis a particular tense or aspect choice in the child's utterances refers to. The categories selected for the analysis of temporal reference will depend on the question being asked. For example, in examining the place of *-en* overgeneralizations in Sophie's system, it was necessary to determine whether the inflection had the same range of uses as a past tense. Sophie was using, particularly between 2;6 and 3;0, irregular and regular pasts as well as the *-en* overgeneralizations. It would be quite possible for her to have used the *-en* marked verbs for one set of events (say immediately past events in her environment), and past tense for more remote events. To examine this, the set of categories listed at the foot of table 1.2 were applied to both *-en* and past-tense marked verbs. The time axis is divided into immediate past (IMM), where the event referred to in the verb occurred up to five minutes before the time of speaking; very recent past (VREC), six minutes to one hour before, or prior to the beginning of the sample; recent past (REC), prior to the sample, same day; on the previous day (PAST); up to one week previously (REM); more than one week prior to the beginning of the sample (VREM). If the event referred to by the verb was unspecified - if, for example, past tense was used in a question to the

TABLE 1.2 Temporal reference of past-referring forms: some examples from Sophie

Date (1980)	*Utterance*	*Past-time category*[a]
6.4	some milk dripped, dropped on the floor	IMM
6.4	probably me left that ahind a Zoes and Rory's	REC
6.4	you got the littlest	IMM
17.4	Annabel came play our house	REM
18.4	animal came in your room and my room	PAST
18.4	daddy sayed me that red jumper will fit me	PAST
13.5	me called it peanut butter	IMM
13.5	that cos me had it a lunch	REC
13.5	you already had pud	IMM
13.5	that Humpty lost one	VREM
29.5	found my letter	IMM
31.3	me maden that	IMM
31.3	now me tippen that over	IMM
31.3	then maken, something maken a funny noise	REC
17.4	(Annabel came play our house) and her getten cold feet	REM
8.5	Mary given that when my birthday	VREM
13.5	me haden strawberries at lunchtime	REC
29.5	he closen it	IMM
31.5	(M. Who gave you that puzzle) nobody given it to me	UNSPEC
	(M. how did you get it then?) me just buyen it	UNSPEC
17.6	in that shop where you getten my slides	PAST

[a] Category labels: IMM: up to five minutes prior to time of speaking; VREC: six minutes to one hour, or to beginning of sample; REC: prior to sample, same day; PAST: previous day; REM: up to one week; VREM: more than one week prior to time of sample; UNSPEC: unspecified past time – even time not identifiable from utterance or context.

child – the label UNSPEC was applied. It is apparent from table 1.2 that *-en* and past tense do have a similar range of application across these categories. For the period covered here, at least, the child seems to be treating *-en* as a past referring affix like past tense proper. (See pp. 121–7 below for a more extensive discussion of *-en* marked forms.)

EXPLANATION

We have indicated already that there is a more intimate connection between methodological procedures and explanation in child language study than is often acknowledged. Data selection, decisions about how to transcribe the data, and what to count as data can all have subtle or not so subtle effects on the way the data are explained. We would now like to turn to a more direct consideration of explanation and review the most influential theoretical approaches to children's language development. There is no sense in which this review can be an evaluation of competing hypotheses with a satisfactory outcome; it is, rather, a search for some potential independent variables. It is hard to disagree with the view expressed cogently by Campbell (1985: 149), in relation to language development research, that 'what is both desirable and possible at the present time is more facts, more flower picking natural history'. We need to interpret this not as an excuse to limit child language study to endless description - a sterile and uninteresting occupation - but as a plea to make explanations responsible to the rich and complex data with which children provide us. In the absence of a unifying theory, there is no shame in exploring the complexities of the data and investigating a variety of factors which may be relevant. Indeed, this is likely to be far more useful for eventual explanation than forcing an unsuitable theory onto a recalcitrant data base. We will begin by examining explanations that rely on specific acquisition mechanisms, then consider briefly what is meant by the cognition hypothesis, and finally consider motherese as an independent variable in language development. No definite conclusions are reached; it is our contention that none can be reached at this stage in the development of the field. It is, however, important to review current approaches as a background to the general discussion of data in chapter 2.

Specific language-learning mechanisms

The earliest explanation for children's language learning, in the modern era, came from Chomsky, and became known as the 'innateness hypothesis' (although Chomsky himself (1979: 13) denies using the term, and calls it misleading). It might be supposed that the idea of a rich biological endowment for language learning had outlived its initial usefulness to language acquisition research. But those whose main concern is the elaboration of linguistic theory continue to contemplate a specific innateness hypothesis to explain what is seen as the rather narrowly constrained forms of 'humanly accessible grammars' (for example, Chomsky 1975: 13 ff., 1979: 35 ff.; Hornstein and Lightfoot 1981; Lightfoot 1979: 16-17; Smith and Wilson 1979: 27-31). Since, the argument goes, grammars of human language are constructed according to well-defined principles, which it is difficult to imagine the child arriving at inductively, a plausible alternative is to hypothesize the existence of such principles as part of the child's innate endowment. For some time such intimate links between linguistic (particularly syntactic) theory and language acquisition were out of favour with child language researchers. They looked for explanations either in a framework which links language development to cognition (for example, Cromer 1974; Sinclair 1971), or to the characteristics of mother–child interaction (Snow and Ferguson 1977). Recently, however, there has been a revival of interest in language-specific learning mechanisms. First, a series of recent papers have taken up the cudgels again on behalf of a transformational generative approach to language – or at least syntax – learning (see Fay 1978; Goodluck 1985; Hamburger 1980; Hurford 1975). Secondly, other scholars have indicated that although they do not necessarily accept the details of the neo-transformational approach, they are not happy with explanations for language development which are rooted in cognition, and which see cognitive preconditions as both necessary and sufficient to explain the course of language development (for example, Curtiss 1981). We will consider possible cognitive bases later in this chapter. Here, we will concentrate on rule-learning as the basis for the child's learning of grammar, in view of the recent revival of interest in this topic.

Rule-learning

The search for evidence of grammatical rule-learning in children's language was the initial result of the influence of Chomskyan theory on the field in the late 1960s. The next decade saw a change of emphasis. In an influential paper, Campbell and Wales (1970) argued that children (like everyone else) speak sentences in context, and that linguistic competence involves not only the learning of the internal syntactic structure of sentences, but also the relations between these sentences and larger units, and the context in which they are spoken (the child has to learn to construct sentences which are *appropriate* in both these senses). This criticism, together with the realization that the child's linguistic environment was much more structured than Chomsky had claimed, led to a change of emphasis. There was a swing away from pure grammatical research towards cognitive bases, the nature of interaction and the characteristics of input. Important as these wider perspectives are, diminishing the importance of the child's construction of grammar was an overreaction. Children continue to make mistakes which seem to show that at least part of their language-learning involves the learning of rules. For this reason, and because, as we saw above, the relationship between Chomskyan theory and language acquisition is enjoying something of a revival, we should consider what part rule-learning may play in the language-learning process. To assess this, we will consider in detail two areas, one morphological and one syntactic.

Past tense

In trying to explain language use and change in children, errors that are made have assumed a disproportionate importance as evidence. It is true that errors are important – an occurrence of an utterance by the child that looks the same as an adult's tells us very little about its grammatical status, whereas errors made by the child, particularly systematic errors, may provide a window on the developing system. In this connection, overgeneralizations of regular past-tense English are perhaps the most commonly cited errors made by children as evidence for rule formation. Occurrences of *goed*, *hurted*, *singed*, *leaved*, etc. cannot be the result of imitations by the child, it is argued, and must reflect some active constructional strategy. This must involve at least the recognition of verb stems and past inflections together with the morphophonemic knowledge necessary to apply the appropriate inflection to the stem. There are two questions that immediately arise: what is the nature of the rule the child has formulated, and how general is this rule in accounting for that aspect of the child's language behaviour to which it is relevant?

We can illustrate the problem with a simple example by looking at the first *-ed* overgeneralization from Sophie. This appeared on 2.2.80 as *falled*. Up to this point (and from the beginning at 2;4 on 14.11.79), she had used a number of correct irregular past forms – *found*, *got*, *broke*, *had*, *left*, *gave* (see Hart 1982: chapter 4 for details). The data also yielded regular *-ed* forms: *called*, *lived*, *covered*, *wanted*, *wrapped*, *climbed*. Of the latter, by far the most common was *called*; out of 29 *-ed* forms recorded between 20.11.79 and 2.2.80, 23 are *called*. The error of course meets the morphophonemic constraints in English for past-tense suffixations, in that a voiced-stem final has *-d* suffixed to it. But to attribute this rather general rule to the child seems premature. The simplest explanation for the child's production of *falled* would be in terms of its sound-relationship to *called*. This is an almost unnaturally clear-cut example, but it serves to make the point that there are a variety of possible bases for the linguistic behaviour we record. One overgeneralization does not constitute evidence that the child has formulated a rule – made a generalization – in much the same way as a linguist would formulate the same rule. Nor by extension do several overgeneralizations constitute such evidence, unless all possible alternative explanations can be ruled out.

The second issue relates to the generality of rule-based explanations. It is often thought that overgeneralizations identify a stage through which the child passes during which these errors are the norm. So the child proceeds from a first stage, in which there are irregular past forms only, through a stage in which overgeneralizations predominate, to normal adult usage. The reality is somewhat more complex. As expected from other accounts (for example, Brown 1973: 271), Sophie's early past-tense forms were irregular – *got*, *made*, *took*, etc. Although she did use both regular and overgeneralized pasts between 2;6 and 3;6, her major morphological overgeneralization to refer to past time during this period centred on the *-en* suffix. Table 4.1 lists the *-en* forms found in the data over approximately the age-range 2.5–3.5.

TABLE 1.3 Incidence of past-referring inflections, Sophie, 2;5–3;5

	-en *over-generalized*	-en	*Past irregular*	-ed	-ed *over-generalized*	*Other past participles*
Period 1 (23 samples; 25.11–15.1)	0	21	180	29	1	34
Period 2 (40 samples; 17.1–3.6)	82	32	381	58	9	78
Period 3 (40 samples; 6;6–19.12)	27	15	426	82	16	21
Total	109	68	987[a]	169[b]	26	133[c]
Verb-types	36	10	30	38	19	6
Type–token ratio	0.33	0.15	0.03	0.22	0.73	0.05

[a] *Got* accounts for 40 per cent of this total.
[b] *Called* (as in *what that called*, or *that called x*) makes up 47 per cent of this total.
[c] *Done* and *gone* together make up 97 per cent of this total.

(See below, pp. 121ff. and 178ff., for more detailed discussions of this data.) Novel *-en* productions are occasionally reported for other children (see, for example, Zwicky 1970), although the phenomenon is much less common than the frequently cited extension of the *-ed* rule application. For the time during which *-en* overgeneralization lasted, it was used to refer to past time and it was not the only means the child had of referring to past time. Table 1.3 indicates that, in addition, regular, irregular and overgeneralized past forms coexist with the *-en* forms. Indeed, a not untypical sample (20.3.80) has Sophie using these forms, for referring to events or actions in the past:

irregular past: *got*, *said*, *fell*, *left*, *made*
regular past: *finished*
overgeneralized past: *doed*
regular past participle: *taken*
overgeneralized past participle: *touchen*, *putten*, *haden*, *getten*, *see-en*, *rocken*.

So, although the child constructed, for this period of development, a morphological rule that is productive, it is not exclusive, but coexists with partially productive rules that have the same function. There is little question that any normal child from early in the third year, will give evidence of morphological rule-learning, whatever language is involved (see Berman 1981; MacWhinney

1978). Our evidence for this will be the kinds of errors produced. It is important to realize, however, that such a rule does not explain all relevant language production. So that even within the narrow domain of morphology, an exhaustive account of the child's behaviour will have to recognize not only the rules, but the restrictions on these rules and alternative strategies available to the child.

Question formation

In syntactic rule-learning, question formation has attracted much attention, since the relationship between declarative and question in English exemplifies the structure-dependent rule *par excellence* (see Chomsky 1975: 13 ff.; Erreich, Valian and Winzemer 1980; Fay 1978; Hurford 1975). The argument again depends on the mistakes children make, either (a) inability to use the appropriate devices to signal questions or (b) overmarking of either the auxiliary or inflection involved in the question. Examples 1 and 2 illustrate type (a) errors and 3-5 type (b) errors:

1. You tell me a story
2. What daddy will say
3. Did you came home
4. What did you bought
5. What shall we shall have

If we add the information that mistakes like 1 and 2 generally come from younger children, and 3-5 from somewhat older children, we can anticipate a plausible account of question formation which involves rule-learning. First, the child has no auxiliary inversion; next, the rule is imperfectly learned; finally, the child can approximate the adult rule. The mistakes which constitute the evidence for the second stage show that the child is formulating transformations to relate the questions to their declarative source sentences. The transformation for subject-auxiliary inversion involves, however, two *basic operations*, auxiliary copying (of, say, the modal *shall* in 5) to the front of the sentence, and subsequently deletion of the original auxiliary. Children making mistakes like those in 5 have mastered copying, but are omitting to delete. This hypothesis is undeniably attractive, linking as it does linguistic theory and language acquisition, but there are problems with it.

First, the kind of mistake cited here (particularly the crucial mistakes in 3-5) is rare in the individual child: type 5 is particularly rare: it does not, for example, appear *at all* in the Sophie data, and is not reported as appearing in a sample of 25,000 *wh*-questions recorded by Labov and Labov (1978) from their daughter. If errors are rare and (as with overgeneralized pasts) are heavily outnumbered by correct instances, it seems perverse to attribute the errors to inappropriate rule-learning, particularly as there are alternative explanations available (see Kuczaj 1978 for an explanation of mistakes like those in examples 3 and 4 in terms of processing limitations rather than competing internalized rules).

More generally, if we look in detail at the learning of this syntactic operation by an individual child, we find a slow and gradual process - not a process of sudden changes, which categorial rule-learning would predict. Labov and Labov (1978) in their study of question forms over an 18-month period show just how gradual the learning is. Frequency of questions and its relation to percentage inversion is shown in figure 1.2. The analysis of this data appear to indicate that, first of all, inversion success is related to question category.[15] From 3;6 to 4;0, the child showed an inversion success rate for question forms in the order *how*, *where*, *what*, *why*; in the next six months, inversion was generally successful after *how*, *where*, *what*, but not after *why*, where it remained at 10 to 15 per cent. In addition, inversion tended to take place, during the period of variability, in some syntactic environments more than others. So, for instance, past tense consistently favours inversion (Labov and Labov 1978: 20), whereas the progressive disfavours it. The picture presented by Labov and Labov (provided it is replicated in other children) should ring the death knell for theories which see grammatical development exclusively as a process of categorial rule change. In keeping with Labov's work in sociolinguistics, he substitutes the notion of variable-rule acquisition to explain the course of development. It is not clear, however, that variable rules - essentially probabilistic statements, based on the incidence of linguistic categories in corpora - are anything more than descriptive restatements. This is *not* to underestimate the importance of work like that of Labov and Labov; descriptive studies of this quality are fundamental to any progress in this area, and variable-rule statements which reflect a realistic data base, whatever their theoretical status, are infinitely preferable to categorial rules based on a vanishingly small number of errors culled at random from different children at different times.

We have considered only two examples, but they should serve to show the complexity of the issue. Although children do eventually construct syntactic generalizations - rules - the path to them may be long. Both examples, however, show that, as part of the language-learning process, children do actively construct hypotheses about the language on the basis of the information available to them. This is perhaps more obvious in the morphological example than in the syntactic one, but there is some evidence of systematic behaviour based on question-word types even here, during the period when the Labovs' child is using inversion variably. What the examples do make clear is that any approach to the child's grammar-learning that assumes an early mastery of categorial rules is a considerable oversimplification. (See below pp. 104-9 for discussion of Sophie's learning of questions.)

The search for rules was originally motivated by the desire to find evidence, however indirect, for specific language-learning mechanisms. The question of

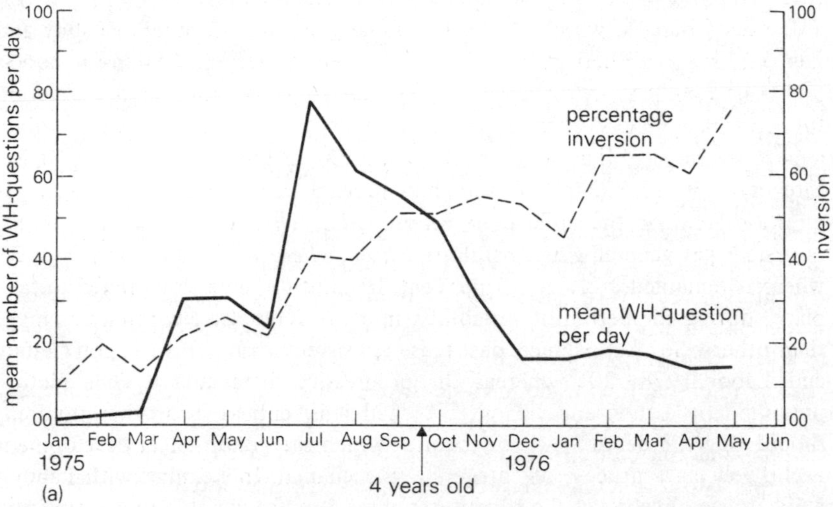

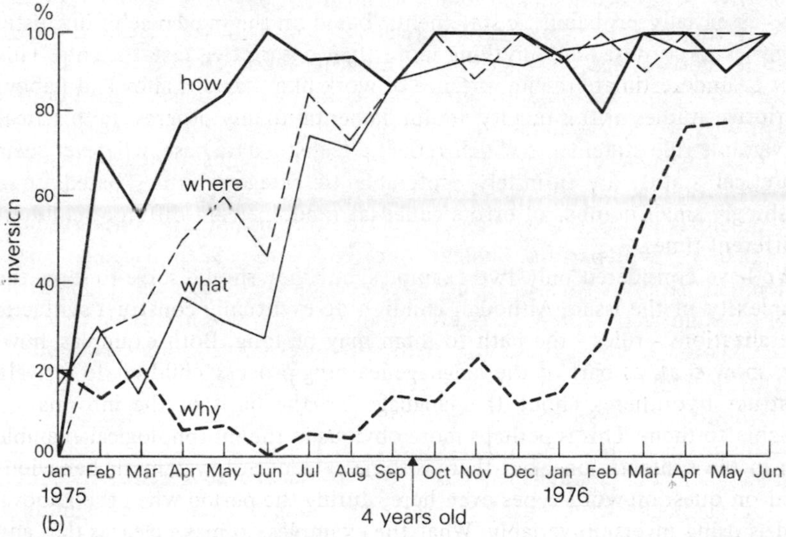

Figure 1.2 Percentage inversion of WH-questions by Jessie (a) overall and (b) by question category
(Labov and Labov 1978)

their relevance to language development remains open. We will now turn to consider, via specific examples, how scholars have tried to root aspects of language-learning in cognition.

Cognition

A major difficulty attending discussions of the link between language and cognition is the scope of the latter term. The problem can be illustrated by the definition given by Neisser in his influential textbook: 'the term *cognition* refers to processes by which the sensory input is transformed, elaborated, stored, recovered and used' (1967: 4). Child language researchers have tended to take a much more limited view, where 'cognition' refers to those mental capacities necessary (or presumed to be necessary) for linguistic representations. Thus the use of common nouns (for example, the application of *table* to a variety of instances of table) requires the identification by the child of a class of referents for the noun in question; the use of subject–verb sequences may depend on the prior appreciation of the separability of actors from actions; and the appropriate use of prepositions has to depend on locative concepts. More generally, Piaget's theory of cognitive development has been a major source of inspiration to those working on language-learning. Levelt (1975: 18), in his discussion of explanation in language development, points out that this link is made explicit relatively early in the psycholinguistic literature. Perhaps his most striking example is taken from Slobin (1971): 'Is it possible, to trace out a universal course of linguistic development on the basis of what we know about the universal course of cognitive development? (Can one take Piaget as a handbook of psycholinguistic development?)' As Levelt points out, this concern to link language to general cognitive development marks a return to an earlier tradition in developmental studies, rather than a new departure. Scholars like the Sterns (1928) placed language development firmly within a cognitive framework. Although this linkage has not been exclusively within a Piagetian framework, it was inevitable that this well-articulated theory should attract those concerned to establish cognitive bases for the child's linguistic structures.[16]

The linking of language and cognition has been most successful for the very young child, when his linguistic system is emerging. In an influential paper (Sinclair 1971), Sinclair, an associate of Piaget's, suggests why we may find direct links between early sensori-motor intelligence and the beginnings of language, but less obvious parallels between later intellectual operations and the acquisition of more complex linguistic structures. Two examples from relevant empirical work may illustrate the discrepancy.

Object permanence and naming

The first 18 months of the child's life constitute what Piaget refers to as the sensori-motor period. The major conceptual achievement of this time is the construction by the child of the idea of a world of objects that exist outside himself, independently of him and his actions. Evidence for the child's appreciation of the permanence of objects is his behaviour when the object is hidden from him. At an early stage in his development, he will not search for the object when it is hidden. Later, he will search for it, and these searches can become increasingly complex: the child will be able to follow the object through a series of locations, even though it might not be visible to him at any point. A number of scholars have suggested that naming or talking about objects at the one-word stage depends on the child having the notion of permanent objects. On the face of it, the assumption seems reasonable, certainly if it is *classes* of objects that are considered. We might expect, for example, that before the child had conceptual representations of objects, he might refer to them, but only in specific contexts; we might also expect such references not to persist in use. Once the child did have a representation of an object, then the term for it would persist, and would be extended to a number of different examples of the object. This point can be illustrated from the work of Bloom (1973: 79 ff.). In the early period of her daughter's language development, 'reference to objects – the use of substantive word forms – was not the dominant speech behaviour observed'. Although she used person names, and the names of very familiar objects, the object names were not applied outside familiar contexts. If new object words were used, they tended to disappear once the context changed. 'Thus "flower" was used by Allison during a week's stay in Florida; it did not occur again after our return home.' Allison's later devlopment of noun labels for classes of objects is related to Bloom to her development of object permanence.

Though entirely plausible, this account suffers from the absence of any independent measure of cognitive ability. As Levelt (1975: 19) points out, if we are to discuss the relationship between cognitive structures and language, we need to operate within a paradigm that provides evidence on both the linguistic and cognitive abilities. Corrigan (1978) provides data on the relationship between the child's sensori-motor development and the development of language by investigating the two domains separately. As part of an 18-month longitudinal study, she modified previously standardized scales of object permanence (Uzigiris and Hunt 1975; Bell 1970) and applied them to three children. She also videotaped the children's interactions with their mother, at home. The object-permanence scale describes a series of increasingly more complex searches which the child has to make for hidden objects. Items 1, 2, 20 and 21, from opposite ends of the scale, are reproduced in table 1.4. In the earlier task, the object is initially visible to the child. It is then hidden under a screen, and the child's task is to find it. By item 21, the child has to find an object which he does not see to begin with; the experimenter moves her hand from screen A to B to C, having left the object under A. The child looks under C, then systematically searches under B and A, finding the object under A. Corrigan's results indicate that object permanence is not related to all aspects of language development, and that 'where there is a relation, the

TABLE 1.4 Object-permanence scale tasks

Item	*Hiding*	*Behaviour while searching*	*Description*	*Stage*
(1)	A̲	A̲	Object is hidden under A; child finds it under A.	4
(2)	A; B̲	A; B̲	Object is hidden under B; child finds it after searching under A.	
(20)	H→A→B→C̲; C̲←B←A←H	C̲ C̲	Object is sequentially, invisibly displaced from A to B to C; child searches directly under C in either direction.	
(21)	H→A̲→B→C	A̲←B←C	Hand is sequentially, invisibly displaced from A to B to C, but object is left under A. Child looks under C, then systematically searches under B, then finds object under A.	Preoperational 1

Note: A, B, C are screens under which an object is hidden; H is hand; → indicates direction of hiding or search; _ indicates place where object is hidden.
Source: Corrigan 1978.

degree of correspondence varies depending on the language variable in question'. There was not a general correlation between object permanence and a measure of the length or complexity of a child's language. There was, however, a general correspondence between onset of search for an invisibly displaced object (task 15 on the scale, the beginning of sensori-motor stage 6) and the onset of single-word utterances. There was also a general correspondence between entry into the pre-operational period (as measured by success on the final item - 21 - on the scale) and an increase in the child's total vocabulary. But it is interesting to note Corrigan's comment here, that 'presumably, language growth at this time would not be due to object permanence *per se*, but to the increased symbolic capacity necessary to perform on both tasks'. This underlines a general point that may be made in relation to studies that indicate correlations between two aspects of behaviour: although we may suspect a causal relation, we cannot demonstrate its direction on the basis of the correlation alone. In evaluating the hypothesis that cognitive structures determine language development, studies such as Corrigan's are necessary, but not sufficient evidence.

Later studies (for example, McCune-Nicolich 1981) have taken issue with Corrigan's approach. Investigating the links between cognition and language, even when the language is at an early stage, presents difficult methodological problems. Nevertheless there is here an attempt to meet the requirement of an independent measure of cognitive ability, in relation to the linguistic variable of interest. We will now turn to an attempt at a cognitive explanation where no such independent measure is possible.

Cognition and the order of emergence of grammatical structures

As Sinclair observed, links between later conceptual schemata and specific linguistic structures will not be easy to find. Indeed, apart from occasional attempts to link Piagetian stages of cognitive development and stages of linguistic acquisition (for example, Ingram (1976: 11), in relation to stages of phonological development), studies of the relationship between conceptual abilities and linguistic skills have tended to be relatively inexplicit about the character of these abilities, while relying crucially on them to explain developmental data.[17] An example which illustrates this is Cromer's explanation of the late appearance of present perfect (exemplified in sentences like *he has finished*, *have you seen her*) in the Brown corpora (Cromer 1974). Cromer points out that the first meaningful use of the perfect occurred at 4;6 for one of the children, and that another child did not use the form at all during the time records were kept on her (up to the age of 5;5). As Cromer points out, this late and rare usage is not easy to understand in purely linguistic terms. Grammatically, the present perfect is represented by a discontinuous constituent, *have + past participle*; but then the progressive, which requires similar discontinuity (*be + ing*), appears in the child's output much earlier (at around the age of 3, for the Brown children). So it might be argued that it is difficult to explain the discrepancy in terms of *linguistic* complexity. In addition, present perfect forms were apparently available for the child to hear in parental speech. Cromer's explanation for the data he has uncovered is in terms of what he refers to as a 'late developing ability to consider the relevance of another time to the time of the utterance'. The function of the present perfect is to apply 'current relevance' to the action described in the verb to which it is attached. If we say *he has finished*, we are emphasizing the relevance of his state to the time of speaking. Now whether or not we accept this exact characterization of the present perfect's meaning (for more recent views see Huddleston 1984: 158 ff. and Smith 1981), we can agree that the difference in meaning between the past and the present perfect is a subtle one. Both past and present perfect can be used to refer to the same relatively recent event (compare *he broke his arm*, *he has broken his arm*), and the choice of verb-marking seems to involve a more than usually subjective element. Cromer's explanation for the late appearance of the form, then, rests on the child's conceptual ability to appreciate these rather fine meaning distinctions. Though not capable of providing direct evidence for conceptual abilities, such an argument is circumstantially appealing. There are other possible explanations, however, as later data from British English show. Although the data do not rule out a conceptual explanation for the order of development of temporal and aspectual markers, they do demonstrate that other explanations may be possible.

In a report on the development of English auxiliary forms in his Bristol sample, Wells (1979) provides a frequency distribution which is reproduced in part in table 1.5. The table provides information on (a) the total frequency of occurrence of a range of auxiliary forms from 60 children, recorded at three-month intervals between 1;3 and 3;6; (b) the proportion of the sample using each form by 3;6; and (c) the age by which the form in question had been used at least once by half the sample. From the table it is apparent that the present perfect is the second most frequent item, that all of the children use it, and that half of them use it at least once by the age of 2;3. The apparent discrepancy between the British and North American data is probably partly due to a difference of definition: whereas Cromer seems to restrict definition of the present perfect to *have + past participle*, Wells includes forms that do not include the auxiliary. However, a more detailed breakdown of Wells's data (Fletcher 1981) indicates that at least some British children are using full perfect forms at the age of 3;3. If this is the case, then it becomes implausible to explain the American children's late development on purely conceptual grounds. It seems likely that an important variable will be input: writers like Comrie (1976), Leech (1971) and Palmer (1974) all suggest that British English speakers use the perfect more frequently than American

TABLE 1.5 Distribution of auxiliary forms, 60 children aged 15–42 months

	Total frequency	*Proportion of sample using form*	*Age in months at criterion*
do	1418	100	27
have + -en	1314	100	27
can	1210	98	30
be + -ing	1149	97	30
will	841	100	30
be going to	512	92	33

Source: Wells 1979.

English speakers; the latter will tend to use the past tense in a number of situations where Britons would use the present perfect. So, for example, in reference to the recent indefinite past American speakers tend to use the past tense, whereas British speakers use the perfect. In the context in which we might hear a British speaker say *I've eaten my dinner*, Americans would prefer *I ate my dinner* (see Trudgill and Hannah 1982: 57). It seems reasonable to assume that the British child is likely to hear more perfect forms, and thus have more opportunity to work out the uses of such forms, and to contrast them with the use of related forms such as past. Any more definite assertions await detailed comparative data from British and American parental input. The possibility of an alternative explanation, or, rather, of the relevance of an additional variable, underlines the difficulties involved in arguing from developmental linguistic facts to conceptual abilities.

This seems a convenient point to turn to input and its role in language development. The examples we have considered here are only a small sample of an extensive literature on the cognitive bases of linguistic behaviour. They nevertheless demonstrate the difficulty involved in specifying the role of conceptual abilities in explaining particular features of acquisition; we cannot of course show in this way that cognition is *not* relevant for the child's language-learning, and indeed this would be a highly implausible view. In the present state of knowledge, it seems best to take the line that conceptual ability constitutes one of the variables relevant for acquisition, and that it interacts with input and perhaps specific language-learning mechanisms in ways that we do not yet well understand.[18]

Input language

The focus on language-learning mechanisms, or cognitive abilities, as potential explanations for language-learning held the spotlight firmly on the child's linguistic behaviour, and his language environment was largely ignored. Occasional papers (for example Bynon 1968; Ferguson 1964) drew attention to some specific features displayed in talk addressed by adults to small children, in several languages other than English. But it was only at the beginning of the 1970s that language input to children came to be investigated in any detail. One reason for the upsurge of interest was a reawakening of theoretical linguistic interest in discourse, and in the possibility of linguistic units larger than the sentence. This led to approaches to language-learning which emphasize that the child is a partner in a conversation, and which look at interchanges between the child and his partner (his mother, or a peer), for recurring conversational patterns and their development (see, for example, Dore 1979; McTear 1985). Another stimulus to research on input was the hypothesis that the language used to the child, particularly by the mother, was an ideal teaching language. Interest in this hypothesis was encouraged by descriptive work showing that 'motherese' – as maternal input came to be called – appeared to constitute a distinct variety of the language, with characteristics all of its own. The term 'motherese' is misleading: the varietal characteristics are not limited to mothers. Fathers also are quite capable of similarly adapting their speech to small children (Gleason 1975; Rondal 1980). The 'motherese' label is also culture-specific: whereas in Western (particularly middle-class) cultures the mother remains the primary interlocutor of the child under 3 years old, non-Western cultures provide alternative caretakers, from whom children are apparently just as adept at learning language. This has been documented in detail for Samoan by Ochs (1982).[19] However, a substantial amount of research has now been undertaken on the characterization of mother–child linguistic interaction, and the relationship between motherese and the course of the child's language-learning. Since collections and survey articles are readily available (for example, Snow 1985; Snow and Ferguson 1977; Waterson and Snow 1978), there would be little point in trying to summarize this material. We will instead concentrate on two separate (but linked) points – the extent to which reliable information is available on the characteristics of motherese, in English, and the possible effect of motherese on language development.

Clarification in motherese

Ferguson (1977), in a detailed review of 'baby-talk' registers (by which he means talk *to* babies), provides a useful three-way classification of the characteristics of these varieties. He refers to simplifying, expressive-identifying and clarifying processes as ways of relating forms found in baby-talk to adult speech forms. The term *simplifying* refers to reductions in complexity, either paradigmatically (for example, by reducing the range of inflections used or the number of phonemic contrasts available), or syntagmatically (for instance, by simplifying consonant clusters, or using a restricted range of sentence structures). *Expressive-identifying* processes 'add affect to utterances' – as in the use of diminutives – or mark out in some way the speech being used, perhaps to get and gain the child's attention. The most commonly noted feature of baby-talk in English under this heading is the high fundamental frequency of a mother's speech to her young child. *Clarifying* processes are those which are said to *add* redundancy to the message. Repetition and expansions by the mother would come under this heading. In phonology, the use of exaggerated pitch contours (see Garnica 1977), and the complex of processes that are the consequences of speaking more slowly are referred to as 'clarified'. Indeed, it is the results of this slow, careful articulation of speech that Hockett (1955: 220) referred to as a 'clarity' norm (as opposed to the 'frequency' norm of normal conversation);[20] the term has been adopted by Ferguson for the set of processes which are not simplifying, but appear to modify in the direction of greater redundancy.

Since the characteristics of the speech addressed by the mother to the child are claimed to be important not only for phonology, but also for lexical and syntactic representations, it is worth examining the evidence available for mothers using *lento* speech to children. Slow and careful articulation could certainly facilitate the child's language development by reducing the number of variant forms available. We have already mentioned the range of pronunciations possible for *have* in sentence-initial position (see above p.17). If mothers were to reduce variants of *have* (and *can*, *would*, etc.), it is possible that the child would arrive at generalizations concerning these forms more easily. The most clarified input from a mother would show stressed forms of *have*, for example, in initial position, and uncontracted forms in declaratives. There is no evidence in samples 1 and 2 (which would be the crucial ones) that Sophie's mother does anything of the sort. Initial auxiliaries (as in adult–adult conversation) tend not to be stressed, and there is no evidence that Sophie's mother favours uncontracted forms of *have* in declaratives. This is, however, only one mother and child pair. What other evidence is available concerning lento speech in English?

Although Ferguson (1977: 223) makes reference to linguist's descriptions of lento speech in other languages, there is little evidence available on English. Indeed, there is only one source which is regularly cited as a demonstration that mothers speaking to young children characteristically use slower speech – a monograph by Broen (1972). It is instructive to examine this work a little more closely. The measure used by Broen to assess speech rate is words per minute used by mothers to children. There were two groups of children involved (younger: 18–26 months; older: more than 45 months), and the mother spoke to them under two conditions, a free-play condition and a story-telling condition. Maternal speech rate to adults was checked by recording mothers talking to the experimenter. The results are reproduced in table 1.6. The first point to be made is that words per minute as a measure of speech rate[21] is likely to provide a spurious estimate of the differences between the two conditions, since the free-play condition is likely to contain more pauses than the story-telling condition. If we take the story-telling rate, then, as more representative, it seems unlikely to be significantly different

TABLE 1.6 Mean words per minute spoken by mothers to children and adults

	Free play	*Storytelling*	*Conversation*
Mothers to young children	69.2	115.1	–
Mothers to older children	86.2	127.5	–
Mothers to adults	–	–	132.4

Source: Broen 1972.

from the rate at which mothers speak to adults, even for the younger age-group. There seems to be little foundation here for a claim that mothers speak more slowly to their young children.

But what of more qualitative studies? After all, we are not interested in speech rate *per se*, but in the effect of slower speech on the phonetic characteristics of maternal speech, and the possible effect of this on the child's learning. Again, there is little to go on, but one recent study (Shockey and Bond 1980) suggests that we require basic descriptive work in this area. One expectation deriving from the claims about slower and hence clarified speech is that some of the assimilation characteristics of fast speech - for example, the substitution of a glottal stop for a word-final [t] in some accents of British English (for example, hæt→hæ) - would disappear. They found, however, that not only did mothers fail to eliminate the assimilatory features, but even appeared to increase them, in speech to children (see table 1.7).

TABLE 1.7 Frequency of glottal-stop substitutes for [t] word-finally

	Adult–child		*Adult–child*	
Mothers	*Number of times SD for change encountered*	*Changed (%)*	*Number of times SD for change encountered*	*Changed (%)*
J.D.	117	64	69	68
Y.P.	94	40	74	8
M.F.	81	51	30	20
J.F.	138	55	59	46
P.J.	159	52	76	51
J.B.	246	22	117	23
L.R.	95	20	211	12
D.M.	223	45	38	29

Source: Shockey and Bond 1980.

Similar results were found for three other common assimilations. These results suggest that our knowledge of the segmental characteristics of maternal speech to young children is rather shaky and that we cannot take it for granted that lento speech, and hence clarified segmental forms, are always available for children. We return to this issue in chapter 6.

Effects of motherese

The most interesting question for researchers has of course been the effect of motherese on the child's development. Leaving aside the problems of lento speech, there is little doubt that the motherese register differs from adult to adult speech in structural characteristics and interactional style (see particularly Howe 1981). That there are differences is of course in itself no guarantee that the specific features identified are causally linked to changes in children's language. And the notion that motherese is a register by which the mother teaches the child syntax, by constantly adjusting the complexity of her utterances so that they are one step ahead of the child's current level of organization, is to attribute a more central role to syntax, and a more conscious control of language by the mother, than seems reasonable. It is now generally agreed that mothers have as a primary aim the establishment and maintenance of communication with the child; the modifications which are undoubtedly present function to facilitate comprehension by the child and so to serve this primary aim. There is, however, no reason why the kinds of modifications made should not, as a by-product, have some relevance for the course of language development. We shall now consider evidence from studies which indicate that this may be the case, by showing correlations between maternal language and child language growth.

The first study, reported in Newport, Gleitman and Gleitman (1977) is in fact an eloquent and detailed defence of the position that 'many features of the child's language environment have no discernible effect on how his language grows' (p. 144).[22] They examined 15 mother–daughter pairs, recording two 2-hour conversations at six months apart. At the first recording, the children fell into three groups (12-15 months, 18-21 months and 24-27 months). Table 1.8 shows the measures that were applied to maternal speech down the vertical axis. These measures (from the first interview) were correlated with the child's growth scores on the five measures along the horizontal axis. The arguments made by Newport and colleagues for the relative unimportance of maternal speech style on acquisition rest partly on their evaluation of the relative importance of what they call 'universal aspects of language', as opposed to 'language-specific aspects of surface structure' (1977: 145-6). The universal features of the child's speech are measured by the propositional-content categories - verbs per utterance, and noun phrases per utterance. These content-word categories, which arguably carry the core of the 'message' of the utterance, could be said to be universal in that all languages have nouns and verbs, and messages in any language would be expressed in these terms. From table 1.8, it is clear that the measures of maternal speech selected are not related to children's propositional-content categories and so to what Newport et al. call 'universal design features' of human language. Now in terms of the measures selected for maternal speech, this would appear to be true. However, even if we ignore the possibility that alternative measures of maternal speech might show relationships to 'universal' language growth measures, how significant is this finding? It is possible to argue that the more important relations are between the maternal measures and language-specific features - for example, that between *yes–no questions* and *auxiliaries per verb-phrase* ($r = 0.88$, $p < 0.001$). The rhetoric of the paper plays this down, but surely the child is indifferent to whether a linguistic feature is 'universal' or 'language-specific', and such a correlation suggests that the more a mother uses auxiliaries in sentence-initial position, the more likely the

TABLE 1.8 Double partial correlations between maternal speech and child language growth

Measures of maternal speech	*Measures of child growth*				
	Grammatical functors		*Length*	*Propositional content*	
	Auxiliaries/ verb-phrase	*Inflections/ noun-phrase*	*Morphemes/ utterance (MLU)*	*Verbs/ utterance*	*Noun-phrases/ utterance*
Declarative	0.25	0.01	0.10	0.16	0.02
Yes–no question	0.88***	−0.05	0.50	0.35	0.16
Imperative	−0.55*	−0.52	−0.38	−0.29	0.19
Wh-question	−0.36	−0.07	−0.29	−0.02	−0.24
Interjection	0.53	0.22	0.49	−0.08	0.11
Deixis	−0.09	0.58*	0.13	−0.12	−0.08
Expansion	0.51	0.14	0.23	0.03	−0.16
Repetition	−0.58*	−0.51	−0.50	−0.05	−0.27
Mean length of utterance	0.34	0.10	0.14	0.38	0.22
S-nodes/utterance	0.21	−0.05	0.37	0.05	0.31

$p < 0.08$ * $p < 0.05$ *** $p < 0.001$

Source: Newport et al. 1977.

child is to be using them six months later. Whatever the basis for the mother's use of *yes–no questions* (and we suggest below that it is communicative), this finding seems to demonstrate the child's sensitivity to some features of the language environment, and indicates that the question of the effect of motherese on the child's course of development is worth pursuing. Newport and colleagues may well be right to assert that simple syntagmatic noun-verb structures are indifferent to differing maternal speech styles (for argument and evidence from cases of restricted input which support this view, see Sachs, Bard and Johnson 1981). That paradigmatic aspects like the auxiliary, which are so important for questions, negation and a wide range of temporal and modal meanings in English, are 'sensitive to delicate variations in mother's style' (Newport et al.: 135) is surely a matter worth more detailed investigation.

It is of interest that a quite separate study (Furrow, Nelson and Benedict 1979), on seven mother–child pairs, finds the same relationship between *yes–no questions* in maternal speech and auxiliary use in the child. Among other relationships, they found a correlation for these two measures of 0.85 ($p < 0.25$, one-tailed). On the basis of these and other findings, the apparently contradictory views that (a) children can learn language with very restricted input and (b) variations in maternal style are associated with variations in child language development are quite compatible once it is clear that in (a) we are talking about basic propositional content and in (b) systems such as auxiliaries and inflections. Holding view (b) is also consistent with the view that maternal language has as its primary aim something other than the teaching of syntax. Although neither Newport et al. nor Furrow et al. make it clear, it is likely that the majority of the auxiliaries that appear in the language of their children as they get older are *can* and/or *will*, either in sentence-initial position or in negatives. Sophie's language demonstrates this clearly, as we shall see later. But the term *yes–no question* as applied to items like *can me go now*, although syntactically accurate, is actually somewhat misleading. These forms are not questions, for the child, but requests and particularly requests for action (see also Fletcher 1979: 300 ff.). The same is true of the appearance of these items in the speech of Sophie's mother. She uses *can* and *will* in initial position to get the child to act as she wants her to. The early appearance of these auxiliaries in the child's language is thus a by-product of the syntactic form of requests and indirect commands in English. Nevertheless the phenomenon exists and would seem to bear witness, on the basis of these two studies, to the sensitivity of the young child to the input language – for whatever purpose the mother may have constructed it. (See chapter 6 for further discussion.)

We have now outlined the methodological preliminaries and exemplified some of the explanatory hypotheses relevant to child language study. With this chapter as background, it is now time to turn our attention to samples of conversation between mother and child.

2

Data and Analyses

INTRODUCTION AND BACKGROUND

The remainder of the book is largely taken up with conversations in which a child called Sophie took part; the conversations are spread over a one-and-a-half year period, beginning when Sophie was 2;4. The samples are transcribed for the most part orthographically, although there is, where necessary, some broad phonetic transcription, and (as outlined in chapter 1) a limited set of prosodic conventions. Accompanying each transcript is a set of summary measures, and, following this, a detailed commentary, which isolates interesting features of the transcript under a variety of headings. The purpose of this chapter is to discuss in general terms the likely course of Sophie's development up to the first sample, to justify the data summary procedures, and to outline and explain the headings for the commentary.

Sophie was a healthy baby whose development proceeded normally. Her mother records that she spoke her first word at about 14 months. By the time of the first sample, then, she had been using language for about 15 months. Why are we concentrating on later language development, and what will have happened during the period since the onset of language? The reasons for concentrating here on language development after the age of $2\frac{1}{2}$ are straightforward: despite the intensive research in language development in the last 20 years, there is much more published information on children under that age than in the crucial pre-school years. In his book which summarizes the decade of work on his longitudinal project, Brown only gets as far as his stage II, complete in the three children he studies by 21, 35 and 36 months respectively. Although individual studies may examine particular facets of language in 3- to 5-year-olds, it is difficult to gain any general impression of how the child's contributions to conversations change over the pre-school period, or how syntactic structures become more complex, or how grammatical systems develop. By charting change in a child over part of this period, we hope to shed some light on these questions. Illumination will come in part from the succession of samples at six-monthly intervals, but also from the fact that, after the first, it is possible to provide summaries of the salient features of Sophie's development between samples. The extracts that appear here are part of a much larger corpus of Sophie's conversations with her parents and sisters in her third, fourth and fifth years.

EARLY LANGUAGE DEVELOPMENT

We will emerge with a quite comprehensive picture of changes in Sophie's language from 2;5 onwards. What of her earlier development, in the 15 months prior to the first sample? We have no detailed data, but we can construct an outline from accounts of other children's early language. The initial phase of this is the slow construction of a vocabulary. The initial stage from the onset of recognizable words to the development of a lexicon of about 50 words, may take the child some time. Benedict (1979), in examining both comprehension and production vocabularies in a group of children aged 0;9 to 1;8, found that in production the average time taken by the group to develop from 10 to 50 words was 4.8 months. This gives a rate of 9.09 new words per month, or one new word every three days. Growth in the comprehension of new words was much quicker: the average time taken to get from 10 to 50 words was 2.69 months, a rate of 22.23 words per month, or about two words every three days. We might assume on this basis, then, that Sophie may have had a productive vocabulary of about 50 words at the age of 1;7.

The number of words that are available to the child is only a part of the information on this stage of acquisition that we are interested in. Particularly if we are looking to the emergence of early constructions in the child's language, we will want to ask if there are identifiable categories of lexical items in the child's output, and, if so, whether these correspond in any way to categories like noun and verb, on which her syntactic constructions will eventually have to build (cf. Garman 1979). In Benedict's study, a system of semantic classification for lexical items was applied (similar to that used by Nelson 1973). The major categories were:

A. Nominals: these included proper names like *Daddy*, names for objects, and pronouns.

B. Action words: defined as 'words that elicit specific actions from the child, or that accompany actions of the child', these include both items that are verbs in the adult language, such as *get*, *give*, *find*, together with 'action inhibitors' like *no*.

C. Modifiers: these are words that refer to properties or qualities of objects or events (*pretty*, *there*, *mine*).

D. Personal-social: this category includes assertions like *yes*, *want*, or 'social expressive' words like *his*, or *bye-bye*.

In Benedict's sample, representatives of all these categories were available from the start, although the largest classes were general nominals and action words. This finding emphasizes the variety of early word-types in production: social expressive words, for example, built into routines like seeing a parent off to work or an elder sister to school, may be a noticeable feature of the child's early repertoire. Items like *yes* and *no*, which have crucial functions in conversation, but are not relevant for the organization of syntactic structure, may make an early appearance. In addition, deictics like *that* and *there* may be common in early productive vocabularies.

A second finding by Benedict was that, at the 50-word level in production, the general nominals (which include both common nouns and pronouns) are around 2.5 times as numerous as action words. There is other evidence that nominals develop more quickly than verbs (Gentner 1982). Since by definition clauses require verbs, this may have meant that Sophie's early constructions were not clauses as we know them in the adult grammar; sequences like *mummy there*, *that pretty* and *that ball* may have been much more frequent initially than *me want juice*, *daddy go* and so on. By the first sample, of course, she has a fairly wide range of verbs available, and plainly has a much more extensive vocabulary than 50 words. If Sophie continued to acquire words at a constant rate, then, using Benedict's estimate, we would expect a productive vocabulary of 150 words. But we have no basis for assuming a constant rate of development; indeed, what evidence there is points the other way. Smith (1926), in presenting vocabulary growth as a function of age, estimates a vocabulary of 22 words for the child at 1;6, of 272 for the 2-year-old, and 446 for the child of 2;6. This represents an increment of 250 for the six months up to 2;0, but one of only 174 for the next six months. The age of this study does not indicate its reliability – rather, the scarcity of soundly based vocabulary-growth studies. But it does at least indicate that growth in this area, as in others, may not be uniform. If we simply take the number of lexemes in Sophie's first (full) sample, we find a figure of 125, split in the proportions 2:1:2 among general nominals, verbs, and others. It seems from this that Benedict's more recent study is a better basis than Smith's for vocabulary projections, not only in terms of overall size, but in the distribution of items through categories. It is also worth noting how a relatively small productive vocabulary can serve as the basis for extended conversations. This in itself should indicate caution about assumptions of productivity of syntactic types which appear to be represented in the child's data.

It is apparent from the range of lexical items appearing in the *Other* category in sample 1 that Sophie has made considerable progress since 14 months in the range of lexical items available to her. We will refer to some of these in more detail later. Here we should simply note that the list contains adjectives (*red*, *orange*, *horrid*), the conjunction *and*, possessives (*your*, *my*), prepositions (*in*, *on*), determiners (*the*, *any*) and question words (*where*, *why*, *who*).

DATA SUMMARIES

Some general comments are perhaps necessary initially on the summary measures adopted. Linguists in particular are used to summarizing data in as neat and elegant a fashion as possible, and may find in the measures adopted here what they would see as redundancy and overlap. What is the system, they will ask, which underlies the various taxonomies selected to treat these data? There are two problems in answering this question, both of which we have already referred to. The first concerns the nature of the data. Any sample of the child's language, from a particular point in time, is a single stage in a long process - it could be compared to a still from a film. As such it will contain relics from the past, features of the present and indications of the future. The linguist's instinct, quite rightly so far as the adult grammar is concerned, is to look for generalizations. He can assume, for any set of data, that a good deal of what he sees is rule-governed, and he can set about finding the best way to formulate the rules. In the young child's corpus, however, the expectation of productivity does not necessarily hold (see, for example, Matthews 1975: 336): stereotypes which are highly lexically specific abound, and a search for rules cross-sectionally is not always helpful. The second problem is that it is not possible to distinguish productive pattern from stereotype by checking the child's intuitions about his language. As we mentioned earlier, they are not normally available from pre-school children. The recognition of these difficulties argues for data summaries which allow us to inspect clause patterns and their realizations, in an attempt to identify relatively productive and non-productive sentence types at particular points in time, and changes in productivity over time. It is only in this way that we may discern a system or its basis. The summaries adopted here are thus pre-theoretic statements (in so far as this is possible), and are seen as necessary preliminaries to systematic statement.

MLU(m): a measure of length

It has been usual in child language studies to apply some overall measure of length to utterances, using as a unit of measurement either word or morpheme. Although such measures have been subjected to some well-merited criticism from a linguistic point of view (for example, Crystal 1974), they continue to be used as a basis for initial comparison and evaluation of language samples. The mean length of utterance in morphemes (MLUm) was used by Brown as the basis of his assignment of language samples to stages, and since then has been the one measure common to practically all researchers. It should therefore facilitate gross comparisons between Sophie's utterances and those of other English-speaking children, and also provide a rough index of her own development. The procedures adopted for measuring MLU(m) are based on Brown (1973: 54), with adaptations from Miller (1981: 24), and are as follows:

(a) Base the MLU(m) count on 100 consecutive utterances by the child, starting with the 51st of the transcript.

(b) Use only fully transcribed utterances, not those which contain blanks or unintelligible stretches.

(c) Include exact utterance repetitions, but count false start once only. So if the child said

find – find his drink/

only one occurrence of *find* would be counted in this utterance.

(d) Do not count items like *mm*, where they occur utterance-internally as fillers, but do count them if they constitute the child's part of a conversational turn, for example,

Mother	do you want a drink
Child	mm
Mother	well lets go and get one from the kitchen

(e) There will inevitably be problems in deciding in certain cases, particularly compounds or derivations, how many morphemes are involved. In general, err on the side of conservatism. Proper names such as *Santa Claus*, *Mr Fussell*, compounds such as *greenhouse*, *cheque book*, and reduplicated items such as *night-night*, *quack-quack* should all be counted as one morpheme.

(f) A similar problem will arise with inflections. In general, all irregular pasts should be counted as single morphemes, as should words apparently containing diminutives, such as *doggie*, *mummy*, *horsie*. (These will not be the only problem cases that arise; other examples are dealt with in the texts.)

(g) All auxiliaries, full and contracted, count as single morphemes, as do all regular tense, aspect, plural and progressive markers. Synthetic verb forms (particularly copulas, for example, *is*, *was*, *were*) count as a single morpheme.

Vocabulary

Quite apart from the measures referred to above, the study of vocabulary has been of considerable interest to researchers concerned with the child's semantic development, or at least with semantic aspects of lexical development. Of major concern has been the inference of the child's intensions for words, and changes in intension, from the child's extensional behaviour.

Since the main focus of our analysis is syntactic, we will only refer to this type of study where necessary, because of some feature of the child's lexical use in a sample. As a simple measure of vocabulary size we will provide a lexeme count for each sample, and in addition an overall type-token ratio. Other more detailed aspects of vocabulary range and use will be addressed in the commentaries.

Type-token ratio

The type-token ratio is computed for overall vocabulary in the samples examined. Such ratios were originally used by Templin (1957) as a measure of vocabulary diversity in spontaneous language samples. They have recently been rehabilitated by Miller (1981). Templin studied 480 children between the ages of 3;0 and 8;0, and found that the average TTR was about 0.50 constantly across all age-groups, and for both sexes, and all socio-economic groups (see Miller 1981: 41 for a summary). This is a useful yardstick against which to assess any sample we collect: if the TTR falls well above or below 0.50, we can conclude that the lexical diversity is not normal. Why this should be, of course, we will not know without investigating further. As a measure, TTR is inevitably crude: but a low TTR is a flag for possible restrictions on the range of use of vocabulary by the child in his syntactic structures. The approach used for computing TTR is as follows:

1. Use a 100-utterance sample, preferably the same one used for assessing MLU(m).
2. Contractions of auxiliaries, modals and copula are counted as one word, as are negative contractions.
3. Each part of a complex verb phrase is counted as a separate word; so *have been playing* is counted as one instance of *HAVE*, plus one instance of *BE*, plus one instance of *PLAY*.
4. Homonyms, where readily identifiable, are counted as separate types. There may thus be two *DO* types - a *DO* auxiliary, and a *DO* main verb - and similarly for *HAVE*.
5. Compounds are treated as single words.
6. (a) Count the total number of words used (tokens).
   (b) Count the total number of different words used (types).
   (c) Divide (b) by (a) to obtain TTR.

GRAMMATICAL ANALYSES

LARSP

The second data summary is a syntactic profile (of a 50-utterance sample), adapted from the LARSP procedure used for clinical assessment and described in Crystal, Fletcher and Garman (2nd edn, 1981). As illustrated in the data summaries in subsequent chapters (see, for example, p. 69), this is, simply put, a taxonomy of clause and phrase types in English based on Quirk et al. (1972). Full details of the procedure are available in Crystal et al. (1981); a full list of examples for each structural type in the adapted profile appears in table 2.1 (p. 52). To summarize, each utterance by the child is analysed, where possible, at clause, phrase and word level; the incidence of each clausal and phrasal type is then logged on the profile chart. So, for example, the utterance by Sophie from sample 1, *you put bissy on there*, would be analysed as follows:

	you	*put*	*bissy*	*on there*	
Clause	S	V	O	A	Stage IV clause
Phrase	Pron	–	–	Pr Adv	Stage III phrase; Stage II phrase
Word	–	–	–	–	

The application of the analysis to a corpus of utterances provides a 'profile' of the syntactic structures being used by the child, and profiles obtained from different samples at different times can be compared. Although clearly of considerable practical utility, by virtue of the analytical detail it provides, such an approach has its drawbacks. By concentrating on the incidence of syntactic *types*, the profile can obscure differences in token realizations between different children, or samples from the same child at different times. Consider two hypothetical children, A and B, who produce these utterances:

Child A	*Child B*
me want a drink	me got teddy
me help mummy	me got drink
me push your chair	me got juice
me tell Kate	me got more
you drunk my tea	me put drink
daddy find his pipe	me put cup

The summary of clause-type incidence would be the same for these children: SVO = 6. It is, however, clear that this aspect of the syntactic profile is concealing important differences between the children. First, A is using a wider range of main verbs than B – six different verbs, to B's two. Then, A is using alternative subjects – *me*, *you*, *daddy*, as opposed to *me*, for B. A is also making use of a wider range of nouns as objects of verbs, although the difference here is not so marked. And finally, all A's utterances are grammatical, whereas the last two B uses are not. The problem with these is that PUT requires both an object *and* an adverbial – something that B does not seem to realize. To pick up information about lexical differentiation, the realizations of clause elements and the child's subcategorization of verbs, we will use a supplementary grammatical analysis, the verb valency profile.

Verb valency

This profile addresses the questions of the subcategorization of verbs (the syntactic company they keep) and the realizations of clause elements, as well as the range of main verbs available to the child in a 50-utterance sample. Some justification is required for taking this approach to child language samples. In the linguistic literature, a valency analysis is associated with dependency grammars (see, for example, Allerton 1982; Herbst, Heath and Dederding 1980: 32 ff. or Matthews 1981: 97 ff.). Such an analysis recognizes the dependence of nominals (usually subjects and objects) and other clause elements (usually adverbials) on the verb. So, for example, in English PUT requires a subject (in common with all verbs in English), an object *and* an adverbial. We can say *she put the biscuit on there*, but not **she put the biscuit*. The first part of the analysis simply indicates the number of *arguments* a verb takes, in relatively traditional terms like subject, direct object, indirect object, adverbial. The application of the analysis to child data recognizes that, to some extent, clause structure depends on verb choice. Verbs like *see* and *tickle* are divalent (cf. Allerton 1982: 145 for examples of the use of this and similar terms). This means that they require at least two arguments in addition to the verb (for example, *John saw Mary*, *Bill drank his tea*). Verbs like *give* and *put*, however, are trivalent - they require a subject, plus two arguments following the verb: *Joyce gave a brooch to Nora*, *Sophie put a ship in a bottle*. Clause structures associated with these verbs will have at least four elements in them, in LARSP terms, if they are to be grammatical. The distinction between SVO (*John saw Mary*) and SVOA (*Sophie put a ship in a bottle*) is therefore, in examples like these, dependent on the specific verb realizing the V element. It might plausibly be supposed that children learn the kinds of arguments associated with particular verbs, rather than clause structures as such. To the extent that we find, via the valency analysis, that the difference between, say, SVO and SVOA in the child sample is attributable to the choice of specific verbs like *see* and *put*, rather than to the use of truly optional adverbial elements, the assumption will be supported.

An additional benefit of the valency approach as a way of fleshing out the grammatical profile is a second stage of the analysis, which 'describes the syntactic quality of the [arguments] in purely formal (or morphological) terms' (Herbst et al. 1980: 31). The verb valency analysis thus lists not only the arguments for each verb occurring, but the realization of each argument in more grammatical detail. So, for example, the analysis of *me put bissy on there* would be:

PUT	S -	O_d	A	I
	Pron -	Nc	Pr Adv	II

(S = subject; O_d = direct object; Nc = common noun; Pr Adv = preposition + adverbial)

The advantage of the two-stage analysis is that, once it is applied to the whole corpus, we can see at a glance important realizational features: for example, in sample 1, that the vast majority of subjects are personal pronouns, or that most noun phrases do not have determiners. Seen in this way, the valency analysis is a supplement to the LARSP analysis in highlighting distributional restrictions with which the child may be operating.

It is possible to implement a third stage of description, in which the individual head nouns of arguments are identified. In this way, their specific lexical realizations can be linked to the verbs with which they occur, and any restrictions noted. There are two kinds of information of interest here. In the first place, for any specific sample, stereotypes can be readily identified. Analysis in terms of grammatical categories tends to obscure the use by the child of learned routines, or non-productive patterns. These would emerge from a valency analysis extended to a third stage, as sequences of arguments with highly specific lexical realization always linked to the same verb. Secondly, it is arguable that we can learn a good deal about the meanings of individual verbs for the child by examining the lexical nouns with which they co-occur. In the data summaries we will not systematically extend the valency analysis to this third (lexical) stage, because of the amount of detail involved. We will, however, make reference to such an analysis in the commentaries from time to time.

COMMENTARIES

Pronunciation

The transcripts are orthographically transcribed, so the purpose of the section on pronunciation in the commentaries will be to draw attention to the distance between such transcriptions and the sounds the child makes. We will pay attention in particular to systematic errors in pronunciation, and where possible relate these to the literature on children's phonology.

Grammar

The initial basis for the discussion of the child's grammar will be the summary statements discussed above (particularly the profile and the valency analysis). In addition, we will discuss the developing role of (a) deictic elements such as personal pronouns, articles, demonstratives and place adverbs, (b) personal pronouns, (c) articles and (d) verb-forms (inflections and auxiliaries). These areas have been of increasing interest to researchers in recent years as the emphasis in child language studies has moved from a purely structural one to a concern for the functional relevance of linguistic units within a communicative perspective.

Deixis

The term *deixis* comes from a (classical) Greek word meaning 'pointing', or 'indicating', and has become a cover-term in linguistics for a heterogeneous group of (usually) grammatical items which 'relate utterances to the spatio-temporal coordinates of the act of utterance' (Lyons 1977: 636). That is, there are various aspects of utterances that are fully explicable only by a consideration of their spatial or temporal contexts. So, for instance, looked at purely from a grammatical point of view, *this* and *that* are demonstrative pronouns or determiners; together with *these* and *those*, they form a closed class, with four contrasting units. The appropriate choice of one of them in an utterance, however, depends on the assessment by the speaker of information other than the appropriate structural position for the items. He has to decide whether what he is referring to is singular or plural, and also whether relative to himself the object is near (proximal) or far away (distal). Thus in *do you want this one or that one*, the contrast expressed should be between something near the speaker and something further away. Natural language is rarely as simple as this, however, and there are qualifications to the simple picture, and extensions to the spatial conditions under which particular deictics are used. In the example above, *this* and *that* are contrasted. It is perhaps rare that such explicit contrasts appear in language to children. One of the purposes of the commentary under this heading will be to examine the mother's language for the kinds of deictics used, and their contexts, as well as commenting on the child's use. In addition to *this/that*, we will try to examine systematically uses of *here/there* by Fran and Sophie. The restriction to these four items will be relaxed if comments on other aspects of spatial deixis are appropriate or relevant.

Personal pronouns

Under this heading we will deal with the set of personal pronouns used for speaker/hearer and third-person reference (*I/me*, *you*, *he/she*, etc.), the possessive determiners (*my/your/his*, etc. followed by a noun), and the possessive pronominals (*mine/yours/his*, etc.). See table 5.6, p. 175, for a complete list.

Articles

This is perhaps the simplest system we consider, formally speaking, but its functional role is complex, and is probably not fully mastered by the child until the early school years (see Karmiloff-Smith 1979). We will concentrate on Sophie's use of *a* and *the* under this heading in subsequent chapters.

Verb-forms

There are three general areas to be covered here - tense, modality and aspect. Of these, it is the temporal referring forms (particularly past tense and progressive) that have drawn most attention from researchers. The use of modals has been neglected, by comparison - a surprising omission, given the extensive use by children of *can* and *will* in early protocols, and the importance of the meanings carried by other modals. In the commentaries we will pay attention to all three areas. Under the heading of tense, we will consider forms the child uses to refer to the past, present and the future. Under aspect, we will take note of grammaticalized aspectual forms such as the progressive (*be + ing*) and, if relevant, lexical aspect markers in English such as *keep* in *he keeps hitting me*, for habitual actions, and *finish* in *he's finished singing*, for completed actions. Modality will cover both the set of verbs which can grammatically be defined as modals - *can*, *may*, *will*, *shall*, *must*, *ought to* - as well as other verbs with similar meanings, like *have to*, *have got to*. In addition, we will consider, where relevant, the relationship between temporal referring forms and adverbials.

TABLE 2.1 Examples of LARSP profile categories

Stage I	Minor Social		*yes*, *no*, *maybe*, *mhm*, etc.
	Stereotypes		*the more the merrier*, *here y'go*, etc.
	Major		
	(under Command)	'V'	*run*
	(under Question)	'Q'	*who*, *what*, etc.
	(under Statement)	'V'	*run*, *running*, *ran*, *broken*, etc.
		'N'	*ball*
		Other	*red*, *there*, *mine*, etc.
Stage II	(under Command)	VX	*go there*, *hit him*, *no eat*, *let go*
			V A V O Neg V *let* V
	(under Question)	QX	*what there*, *where him*
			Q A Q ?
	(under Statement)	SV	*he left*, *the red plane is landing*
		VC	*is happy*, *looks small*, *costs a lot*, *became a doctor*
		VO	*hit John*, *looked up the number*
		SC	*he tall*, *that man very sad*
		SO	*Daddy teeth*, *Peter ball*
		AX	*ran fast*, *Mummy in garden*, *happy now*, *no there*, *there soon*
		NegX	*no run*, *no there*, *no Daddy*
Stage III	(under Command)	VXY	*go there now*, *hit him hard*, etc.
			V A A V O A

TABLE 2.1 – continued

		let XY	*let me ride* *let* S V
		do XY	*do stop that* *do* V O
	(under Question)	QXY	*where Daddy gone, why leave now* Q S V Q V A
		VS	*has Daddy gone, will you go there* V- S -V V- S -V A *tomorrow* A
	(under Statement)	SVC	*Daddy is happy, John is a dentist, this bike weighs a ton*
		SVO	*John slammed the front door*
		VCA	*became a doctor last year*
		VOA	*saw the man in the garden*
		SVA	*John ran in the park*
		VO_dO_i	*gave Nora a present* V Oi Od *gave a present to Nora* V Od Oi
		NegXY	*not Daddy go, not go there* Neg S V Neg V A
Stage IV	(under Command)	+ S	*you eat your breakfast* S V O
	(under Question)	QVS	*where has Daddy gone* Q V- S -V *why did you leave at six* Q V- S -V A
		QXYZ	*where Daddy gone now* Q S V A
	(under Statement)	SVCA	*Daddy is happy now*
		SVOA	*John slammed the door yet again*
		AAXY	*he left yesterday in a huff* *now I'm going to wait in the pub*
		SVO_dO_i	*George gave Nora a present* *George gave a present to Nora*
Stage V	(under Exclamatory)	how	*how* nice to see you again
		what	*what* a close game that was
	(under Question)	tag	*she's a nice girl, isn't she* S V C *he might come, mightn't he* S V
	(under Statement)	Coord 1	
			John kicked the dog and *ran up the road* S V O *and* V A

TABLE 2.1 – continued

Coord 1+

John kicked the dog but *missed the cat* and *ran up the road*

S V O c V O and V A

Subord 1. 1+ = Clause: A 1, 1+:

John kicked the dog when he came to amuse the children

S V O A A

s S V s V O

Clause: S

what I said was the truth

S V C

s S V

Clause: C

the situation is as I have described

S V C

s S V

Clause: O

I think she is highly unusual

S V O

S V C

John realizes that he'll be blamed for this

S V O

s S V A

Comparative

John is happier than Bill is

S V C

s S V

Phrase structures

These are analysed and profiled as illustrated below, regardless of whether they occur in Statement or other types of Clause structure.

Stage II	DN	the	
		a	man
		some	water
		this	apples
		those	
		her	
	AdjN	red	
		big	man
		one	hat
		many	boxes
		gold	station
		soldier	
		two	
	NN	Daddy's hat	
	PrN	in box	

TABLE 2.1 – continued

	VV	want (to)	go
		go	shopping
		keep	running
	VPart	keep up	
		come on	
		put off	
	IntX	very hard	
		really big	
		all clean	
		just now	
Stage III	DAdjN	some refreshing water	
	AdjAdjN	cool clear beer	
	PrDN	in the house	
	NAdjN	Johnny's big train	
	Cop	(forms of *be* verb in SVC patterns)	
	Aux	have	Verbed/Verben
		be	Verbing
		can/will/may/must/shall/should/etc. Verb	
	Pron	I, me/you/he, him/she, her/it/we, us/they, them	
Stage IV	NPrNP = NP Pr NP	lots of chocolate	
		top of the house	
		the boy in the car	
	PrDAdjN	in the big box	
	cX	and me	
	XcX	boys and girls	
		running and jumping	
		up and down	
		the man and the young girl	
	NegV	didn't go	
		might not sink	
	NegX	not yet	
		not here	
		not that man	
	2 Aux	should be going	
		might have waited	
Stage V	Postmodifying clause 1		

the man who is standing in the corner

S

s V A

the man standing in the corner

S

V A

Postmodifying clause 1+

the man who is standing there wearing a red hat

S

s V A V O

TABLE 2.1 - continued

Postmodifying phrase 1 (= Stage IV NP Pr NP); 1+
the man in the corner with the red hat

					S				
	D	N	Pr	D	N	Pr	D	Adj	N

Word level	-ing	John's com*ing*
	pl	the *men* saw the boy*s*
	-ed	she *sat* down and cri*ed*
	-en	he's eat*en* all that I've cook*ed*
	3s	when he want*s*, he can come in
	gen	John'*s* hat
	n't	he is*n't*
	'cop	John'*s* tall
	'aux	John'*s* running
	-est	bigg*est*
	-er	bigg*er*
	-ly	slow*ly*

3

Sophie at 2 years 4 months

BACKGROUND TO THE SAMPLE

Sophie, the child who participates most in the conversations in this book, is the third daughter of a middle-class family living in the south of England. Her parents both use the non-localized British accent referred to as Received Pronunciation (see Wells (1982: 117 ff.) for phonetic details of its characteristics). Their dialect is Standard British English with no noticeable grammatical or lexical peculiarities. Sophie was a healthy baby whose development proceeded normally. Her mother records that she spoke her first word at about 14 months, and language development at the point at which we meet her (when she is, to be precise, 2;4.28) had not attracted concern. As will be apparent from the sample, Sophie had already learned a considerable amount by the time we first recorded her.

In the first recording, the mother (Fran) and Sophie are alone, for the period of the recording, in a downstairs room of the house. The child's father is working upstairs. Her two elder sisters (referred to as Zeldy and Hessy) are at school. The mother and child engage in various activities in the course of the session: (a) from about l. 29 on, among other things, they play 'snakes and ladders' together; (b) from l. 165, they look together at a toy catalogue (which partly explains the motley assortment of items referred to between l. 165 and approximately l. 250); (c) from about l. 270, they play with a set of coloured plastic octagons which slot together, and some 'play people'. So, for example, in the extensive sequence about house-building from l. 285 on, it is the coloured octagons that are used as building-blocks for the 'house'. The other people who appear in the transcript are (in order of appearance): Jack (l. 10), a boy of 1;11 at the time of the recording, who is a familiar, though largely non-verbal, playmate of Sophie's; Amy (l. 11), a 9-month-old baby, who is the daughter of a family friend; Paul (l. 26) is the writer; Mary (l. 39) is another of Sophie's regular playmates, and is 2;1; Muffy (a pet-name for Matthew) is a boy of 3;6, whom she sees from time to time (l. 279); and Kate (l. 288) is another adult, who spends some time in the house.

Transcript conventions

(a) In general, each tone-group by child or mother is placed on a separate line, except where there is some grammatical construction across the tone-groups. A tone-group boundary is marked with /.

(b) Within tone-groups, stressed syllables are marked by ˈ preceding them, and the accented syllable is marked with a tonic, indicating the direction of the tone: ˋ = a fall, ˊ = a rise, ˆ = rise-fall and ˇ = fall-rise.

(c) Pause within utterances is marked by -, - - or - - - for short pause, longer pause and very long pause (relative to speaker rhythmicity). Where there are extra long pauses between utterances, the length of the pause in seconds or minutes is noted.

(d) Non-intelligible sequences may be marked within utterances by, for example, (4 syll.), indicating the number of syllables perceived.

(e) Overlapping utterances are indicated by * preceding the portions of utterance from the two speakers which are begun at the same time.

SAMPLE 1 SOPHIE AT 2;4.28

F. ˈwhat's what lóvey/
S. ˈme want thàt/
F. what ìs it/
S. [sìːn]
F. Plâsticine/
S. m̀m
[unintelligible sequence due to external noise]
F. ˈwhat's it fòr/
S. (1 syll.)
F. ˈwhat are you ˈgoing to máke/
S. ˈsee Jàck/
ˈAmy see mè/
ˈsee m̀e/
ˈnot Jàck/
F. ḿm/
S. not Jàck/
ˈonly m̀e/
F. ˈonly yòu/

S. (4 syll.)
'you take a bíssy/ (= biscuit)
F. 'cos I was hùngry/
S. 'me want a bîssy/
F. 'there you aré/
'you have a 'bissy tòo/

[8-second pause]

S. ȏh/
'what thàt/ (catches sight of microphone)
F. its just - - Pàul's/
Pàul's thing/

[6-second pause]

S. (3 syll.)
'you play 'snakes and ladders mè/
F. yes 'I'll play 'snakes and làdders/
'where ìs it/
S. 'over thère/
F. 'will you gét it/
S. and thàt/ -
and thàt/
F. yès/
S. 'you carry 'that [ə] mè/

[8-second pause]

F. 'there you aré/
S. 'Mary còme/
'Mary come mè/
F. nò
'Mary isn't 'going to 'come todày/
S. yès
F. 'are you 'going to play thát side/or the òther side/
S. 'nother sìde/
'daddy come 'down tòo/
F. 'who's coming 'down tóo/
S. dàddy
F. dáddy/
nò/
'where's dáddy/
S. me 'want - - 'daddy come dôwn/
F. wòrking 'sweetie/
S. nò/
nò/
'find her 'cheque bôok/

F. 'finding her chéque book/
S. m̀m/
F. òh/
[5-second pause]
F. how 'many d'you wánt/
S. fìve/
F. 'well maybe fòur/ yès/
S. bìg ones/
'only bìg ones/
F. 'whose túrn is it/
S. mìne
F. 'there you àre/
[10-second pause – dice-shaking]
F. shall we 'take one oút/
'put it thére/
S. nò/
F. nó/
S. nò/
F. òh/
do you 'want a 'turn nów/
[5-second pause – Sophie shakes dice]
F. 'aren't you 'going to 'throw them oút/
[5-second pause]
S. (4 syll.)
F. 'there you arè/
S. (1 syll.)
'that your tùrn/
F. mỳ turn 'is it/
S. m̀m/
(3 syll.)
(3 syll.)
F. 'put thère/
[5-second pause]
S. 'that's a mèss/
mèss/
F. mèss/ iś it/
S. m̀m/
'on thàt/
F. òh/
'what hàppened/
S. 'bissy on thère/
'only bìssies/
[5-second pause]
S. '[uː] put 'bissy on thère/

95 F. I 'didn't put 'biscuit on thère/
'wasn't it yóu/
S. nò/ (3 syll.)
'me want 'play snakes and làdders/
'me push you ìn/
100 'please me 'push you ìn/
F. oh alright
S. pùsh you/
(5 syll.)
F. 'what have you 'got on your dréss/
105 S. nōthing/
F. it's all wêt/
[5-second pause]
I 'can't go 'in any fur̀ther/
my knèes hit it/
[5-second pause]
S. 'me want drìnk/
110 F. we'll 'have one in a mìnute/ yés/
S. nô/
'me want your tèa/
F. well it's too hôt/
'you tàste it/
115 S. hòt/
'want put 'milk in thêre/
F. 'did you 'have a drìnk/ upstáirs/
S. nô/
F. nó/
120 S. m̄m̄/
ỳes/
you – you 'get my 'drink for m̀e/
'get my drínk/
F. where 'is your drìnk/
125 S. upstàirs/
upstàirs/
F. 'where did you pùt it/
S. upstàirs/ (fortissimo)
F. oh àlright/ I'll 'get your drìnk/
[5-second pause]
130 F. 'is it 'on the táble/
S. m̀m
[15-second pause]
S. lóok/ wàter (said while mother still out of room)
F. 'here you àre/
okáy/

[5-second pause]
135 S. 'you take your bìssies/
F. I've èaten them/ – –
S. me 'want more bìssies/
F. 'no you've 'had one of m̀ine/
S. 'me want nother bìssie/
140 F. 'well you'll 'have one làter/
S. nō/
'Mary come m̀e/
'only little bìt/
F. not todày/ cos it's Wèdnesday/
145 S. whý
'Jack còme/
F. nò/
'they came yêsterday/
S. (5 syll.)
150 F. 'where did you pùt it/
S. 'over thère/
nô/
F. would you 'like to 'tidy up the dólls house/
S. where (1 syll.) gó/
155 'where's the doll hôuse/
F. hère/ 'on the flòor/
shall we 'put this awáy/
S. nò/
nò/
160 I plày that/
'I want 'play [ə] 'snakes and làdders/
F. you 'want to 'go on 'playing the 'snakes and làdders/ dó you/
S. lōok/
'me – 'me play thât/
[15-second pause, with some unintelligible sequences interspersed]
165 S. 'me want to 'read thàt/
F. okày/
'let's read thàt/
S. 'read thàt
[5-second pause]
S. (2 syll.)
170 'wrong sìde/
F. I 'think you've 'got it upside dòwn/
S. lòok/
'look her tòe/
F. ùgh/
175 hôrrible/

I 'think they're 'funny shòes actually/
'made to 'look like tòes/
S. whȳ/
lòok/
F. m̄m/
S. 'horrid (3 syll.)
lòok/
'me like thàt/
F. nô/
S. 'me want 'find the - - pàge/
F. 'what do you 'think of thòse/ - -
S. Snòopy/
F. yês/
S. (1 syll.)
'I got some thòse/
F. yes you hàve/
S. yès
and pìnk
and some pìnk
F. háve you/
S. yès/
F. (2 syll.)
S. 'me got - - 'Jack got 'some of thòse/
F. hás he/
S. yès/ - - -
not mè/
F. nò/
S. nò/
'I got any hòover/
'look Zelda pīano/
F. m̂m/
S. lally lally (sings)
F. (laughs)
S. 'me want 'that pìano/
F. 'you've got a rêal piano/
S. why̆/
F. it's upstâirs/
S. why̆/
why̆/
F. 'what do you 'mean whý/
S. whý/ (fortissimo)
F. it's upstàirs/
'you've got a rèal piano/
'you've got Zèldy's piano/

S. why̌/
'you get 'nother one Zèldy/
F. anóther one/
S. Zèldy/
'you get - 'one [ə] Zèldy/
F. 'what sort shall I 'get for Zèldy then/
S. 'you - 'you give 'me one [ə] Zèldy/
'you [k]. buy 'me one agàin/
F. anôther pi̧ano/
'what a bíg piano/
S. yès
like Zèldy's
* (1 syll.)
F. * like Zéldy's/
we 'can't have twò big 'pianos/
'cost a 'lot of mọ̀ney/
S. 'Hessy want a pìano/
F. hás she/
S. yēs/
F. what 'else has Hèssy got/
S. 'Hessy - want 'those sort of ône/
F. ôh
[5-second pause]
S. 'me want - - -
lôok/
bālls/
you 'like those bálls/
F. yês
S. bàll/
kìck/
kìck/
'daddy kìck/
F. 'that's rìght/
you 'have to kìck it/ dòn't you/
S. m̄m/
[əm] - [əm] - 'kick hàrd/
'only kick hàrd/
(3 syll.)
(2 syll.)
'you get 'those (1 syll.) óff/
'our play thât/
on flòor/
'our play 'that on flòor/
nôw/

'our play [nə] thàt/
'on flòor/
'our play 'that on flôor/ - - -
no thât/
nôw/
F. àlright/ - - -
S. múmmy/
'come on 'floor m̀e/
F. yēs/
S. 'you tip 'those oùt/
F. ḿm/
àlright/
[8-second pause]
S. (6 syll.)
'that one bròke/
F. òh/
'when did thàt 'happen/
S. 'Muffy step on thât/
F. whó stepped on it/
S. Mùffy/
F. Mùffy stepped on it/
S. yès/
[5-second pause/
S. (5 syll.)
'me - 'me want make 'house [ɪʔ] yòu/
F. yès/
S. hoúse/
for Káte/
'me want 'house for Kàte/
'me want make 'house for Kàte/
you - you hèlp/
'you make 'house for Káte/
F. àlright/
'which one shall we put òn/ - -
S. òrange/
F. álright/
S. and - and [ə] rèd one/
F. álright/
'where shall we pùt them/
S. (4 syll.)
nò
'orange (1 syll.) thêre/
F. 'orange in thére/
S. 'orange thère/

'orange thère/
[unintelligible sequence for 8 seconds]
S. 'that my ówn one/
F. mhḿ/
S. 'me put 'nother bit mòre/
'me put 'nother bit 'more my hôuse/
'me put 'nother bit 'more my hôuse/
[4-second pause]
S. my hòuse/
brôke/
'why those two 'nother -- things brôke/
ôw/
(5 syll.)
[8-second pause]
S. 'children in * thère/
F. * that's lòvely/
S. 'children in thère/
'where's the chìldrens/
F. the children (2 syll.)
thère they are/
S. (1 syll.) 'all those chìldren/
'me playing 'all those chìldren/
me want those (4 syll.)
(8 syll.)
in the câr/
(2 syll.) drìve/
(3 syll.)
[8-second pause]
F. thàt's right/
a bit smâll though/ ìsn't it/
it 'doesn't really fit ìn/
'I think we'd 'better make a bìgger place/ don't yoú/
S. nō/
F. nó/
S. lòok/
(3 syll.)
F. ōh/
S. lòok/
* slèep/
F. * going to sléep/
be 'better going to 'sleep on the bêd I 'think/
S. 'you make -- the bèd/
(2 syll.)
F. mˇhm/---

345 S. 'men in the càr/
'men in the càr/ - -
'men in the càr/
'who in the càr/
F. 'who went in the càr/
350 S. bàby went in the car/
'her slèep/
F. òh/
S. 'her - 'her got blànkie/
'her want a blànkie/
355 'where's [ə] blánkie/
F. 'I don't 'think we've 'got a blànket/
'here would thís do/
S. (1 syll.)
F. if we 'fold it up smáll/
360 S. yès/
[unintelligible sequence for 10 seconds]
[10-second pause]
F. is 'that smáll enough/
S. yès/ - - -
'her can't sêe/
F. oh dèar/
365 then 'don't put it 'up so hîgh/
thère you are/
S. 'all that fall ôff/
F. shall we 'tuck it ín/
S. (1 syll.)
370 yès/
F. 'like thàt/
S. mm̄/
F. * thère/
S. * go slèep/
375 F. yès/
S. (1 syll.) 'go sleep nòw/
'make nother one - thìng/
F. 'well I don't 'think - - we've 'got the - -
hêy/
380 'look what Ì've found/
'thing for the lìght/
S. 'where's nòther bit/
(2 syll.) down thère/
F. díd you/
385 S. yès/
'me took one bòx/

F. I 'can't find the other 'legs to thàt sweetie/ - - -
'we'll have to 'get some mòre/ wón't we/
S. (2 syll.)
390 F. here's a 'nurse for the hòspital/
[8-second pause]
S. (4 syll.)
F. ḿm/
S. bàby/
bàby/ - - -
395 bàby/
'her bàby/
'in a bìg bed/
F. m̀m/
S. 'baby in big bèd/

DATA SUMMARIES: SAMPLE 1

(a) MLU(m) = 2.53 (beginning at 51st utterance)
(b) TTR = 0.34 (using same set of utterances)

(c) LARSP (beginning at 51st utterance)

Stage I (0.9–1.5)	*Minor*		*Responses*		*Vocatives*	*Other*	*Problems*	
	Major	*Comm.*	*Quest.*	*Statement*				
		'V' 4	'Q' 7	'V'	'N' 2	Other 3	Problems	
	Conn.	Clause				Phrase		Word
Stage II (1.6–2.0)		V *X* 2	Q *X*	SV 1	A *X*	DN 13	VV 4	
				SO	VO 1	Adj N 1	V part	-ing
				SC	VC	NN 1	Int *X*	
				Neg *X*	Other	PrN	Other 6	pl 2
		X + S:NP	*X* + V:VP	*X* + C:NP	*X* + O:NP 2	*X* + A:AP		-ed
Stage III (2.0–2.5)		V *X Y*	Q *X Y*	SVC	VCA	D Adj N	Cop 1	
		let X Y		SVO 15	VOA 1	Adj Adj N	Aux$^{M}_{O}$	-en
			VS(*X*)	SVA 1	VO$_d$O$_i$	Pr DN		3s
		do X Y		Neg *X Y*	Other 1	Pron$^{P\,19}_{O\,5}$	Other 2	gen
		XY + S:NP	*XY* + V:VP 4	*XY* + C:NP	*XY* + O:NP 10	*XY* + A:AP 1		
Stage IV (2.6–3.0)		+ S	QVS	SVOA 2	AA *X Y*	Np Pr NP	Neg V	n't
			Q *X Y* +	SVCA	Other	Pr D Adj N	Neg *X* 1	
		V *X Y* +	VS(*X* +)	SVO$_d$O$_i$ 1		c *X* 2	2 Aux	'cop 1
			tag	SVOC		*X*c *X*	Other	'aux
Stage V (3.0–3.5)	*and*	Coord.	Coord.	Coord. 1	1 +	Postmod. clause 1	1 +	
	c	Other	Other	Subord. A 1	1 +			-est
	s			S C	O			-er
	Other			Comparative		Postmod. phrase	1 +	-ly

Verb valency analysis

(Figures in square brackets indicate the number of times a particular structural configuration, associated with a specific verb, is represented in the data.)

Total verb types: 19   *Total verb tokens:* 50

	Type	*Tokens*	*Frames and realizations*				
1.	BUY	1	S	-	O_i	O_d	A
			Pronp		Pronp	Prono	adv
2.	BREAK	2	S	-			
			D N				
3.	COME	3	S	-	A		
			Nprop		Pronp		
			S	-			
			Nprop				
				-	A	A	
					Prep N	Pronp	
4.	FIND	1	S want	-	O		
			pronp		D N		
5.	GET	3	S	-	O	A	
			pronp		D N	Prep N	
				-	O		
					D N		
			S	-	O	A	
			pronp		D N	Nprop	
6.	GIVE	1	S	-	O_d	O_i	
			pronp		D N	Prep Nprop	
7.	GOT	3	S	-	O		
			pronp		D N		
			S	-	O		
			Nprop		D prep N		
			S	-	O		
			pronp		D N		
8.	HELP	1	S	-			
			pronp				
9.	KICK	3	S	-			
			Nprop				
				-	A		
					adv		
			A	-	A		
			adv		adv		

10.	LIKE	2	S	–	O		
			pronp		prono		
			S	–	O		
			pronp		D N		
11.	LOOK	2		–	O		
					D N		
				–	O		
					N N		
12.	MAKE	3	S want	–	O		
			pronp		N_c		
			S want	–	O	A	
			pronp			Prep Nprop	
13.	PLAY	7	S	–	O		[3]
			pronp		prono		
			S want	–	O		
			pronp		Nprop		
			S	–	O	A	[2]
			pronp		prono	PreP N_c	
			S	–	A		
			pronp		I D N		
14.	PUT	4	want	–	O	A	
					N_c	Prep Adv	
			S	–	O		
			pronp		3 element phrase		
			S	–	O	A	
			pronp		3 el.phr.	D N	
15.	READ	2	S want to	–	O		
			pronp		prono		
				–	O		
					prono		
16.	STEP	1	S	–	A		
			Nprop		Prep prono		
17.	TAKE	1	S	–	O		
			pronp		D N		
18.	TIP	1	S	–	O	A	
			pronp		pronp	adv	
19.	WANT	7	S	–	O		[4]
			pronp		D N		
			S	–	O	A	
			pronp		Nc	Prep Nprop	
			S	–	O		
			Nprop		D N		
			S	–	O		
			Nprop		4 el. phr.		

COMMENTARY

Pronunciation

As we have noted, orthographic transcripts generally produce a misleading impression of very young children's pronunciation, as we inevitably read in adult values for both segmental and non-segmental features, unless alternatives are indicated. An example of the normalizing involved in transcription is the utterance by Sophie at l. 29, represented as *you play snakes and ladders me*; this has a broad phonetic transcription:

[ˈʋːʃeɪˈʃeɪkənlædəzmìː]

You is normally pronounced [ʋː] by Sophie in this sample. Although *play*, where it occurs elsewhere (for example, l. 160) has an initial [pl] cluster, in l. 29 the error appears to be an anticipatory one for the [ʃ] that substitutes for adult [sn] (in *snake*). Other features of this utterance to note are the generally accurate vowels. Despite this, the consonantal errors would render the utterance unintelligible to the uninitiated listener. Although this is an extreme example, it is a useful one to reinforce the by now familiar point that the transcription we use is a highly idealized representation of the child's speech. The purpose of this section is to remedy this impression so far as is necessary by making some general points, and then drawing attention to items of detail and their specific location in the text.

Consonant clusters

Simplification of consonant clusters to singletons (as attested in a number of studies of young children's speech – for example, Smith (1973)) does occur, as in the [ʃ] realization for target /sn/ above. But the majority of Sophie's attempts at clusters, though not wholly successful, do generally represent both the segmental targets. Of the 28 targets in sample 1, 26 can be represented as clusters in Sophie's utterances. The majority (15) are consonant and liquid clusters (pl, bl, fl and sl); 14 of these are distributed across just four words – *play*, *blankie*, *floor* and *sleep*. These items are all accurately pronounced. Other items are more variable: the /dr/ of *drink* varies, as between [dʋɪŋk] and [dʒɪŋk]; *drive* is pronounced correctly. The first of these is intriguing, as in the same sample we have *Jack* pronounced as [dæk]. As *Jack* is elsewhere pronounced as [dʒæk], we can assume that /dʒ/, /dr/ is an area of articulatory instability for Sophie.

There are two linked issues of general interest for phonological development that these examples raise: variability and the relevance of the child's perception to pronunciation error. Ferguson and Farwell (1975), in a careful descriptive study, first indicated the potential range of both inter- and intra-word variation in children at the one-word stage. Olmsted (1971) demonstrated that this variation, in relation to adult targets, was common in children up to 4 years of age at least. In the examples above from Sophie, we see evidence of this tendency in the variants of /dr/ and /dʒ/. The overlapping of these variants is particularly interesting. In discussing what Smith (1973) referred to as the 'puzzle' phenomenon (in which the medial /z/ of *puzzle* is realized by the child as [d], whereas the medial /d/ of *puddle* appears as [g]), Macken (1980) suggests that at least some of the child's pronunciation errors may be perceptual in origin. There are two factors which are relevant to her argument: (a) a period of instability in the child's system, with gradual change and (b) a plausible acoustic explanation. Sophie's realizations (of [d] for /dʒ/ but [dʒ] for /dr/) resemble Smith's 'puzzle' case, although there is in fact a more general overlapping for her (since initial /dz/ is also [dz] in this sample). There is also a potential acoustic explanation for the variability, in the similarity between /dr/ and /dʒ/: both are described by Gimson (1970) as affricates, /dʒ/ as palato-alveolar and /dr/ as post-alveolar. The affricates have the same point of articulation for the stop phase, and the fricative releases for both tend to be voiceless. The articulation similarities could well lead to acoustic confusion for the child. There can of course be no direct evidence on the child's perceptual difficulties, if any, from production data, which can only be suggestive. A more direct and systematic approach is required, such as that suggested by Locke (1980). The existence of variation in the child's phonetic realizations, and the potential involvement of perceptual factors in the child's pronunciation errors suggest that characterizing the child's phonological development will not be a straightforward matter.

The only instance in this sample of the well-attested simplification by the child of a stop + consonant cluster to the stop is in *piano*, which appears twice as ['pænə]. Smith (1973: 169) notes the extremely late appearance of stop + glide clusters in his data (for his child this did not occur until close to 4 years of age) and it will be interesting to see how this works out in Sophie's speech.

Singletons

Consonants. We have already noted the simplification of /dʒ/ to [d] in some instances. We might expect from other data available that affricates would cause problems, and that they would tend to be substituted for by stops. The only voiceless affricate to appear in this data is the initial /tʃ/ of *cheque book*, which is correctly pronounced. In general, stops have their correct realizations, as do fricatives except for /ð/: this is often substituted for by [n], as in [næt] (*that*), [nɛə] (*there*). Other realizations are [l] ([lɛə] for *there*), [d] ([dæt] for *that*), and in one case [ð] in *the*. Although a stop substitute ([d] for /ð/) is common in young children's speech, [n] is more unusual. Other points of note in this sample are the realization of all occurrences of *on* as [mɒn], and the omission of initial [j] in *you*.

Vowels. In the main, vowels are accurately pronounced, and their realization is hence predictable from the orthographic transcription. But there are occasional errors: *mess* (l. 85), is pronounced [mæs]; *come* (l. 40) is pronounced [kɒm]. These are, however, isolated instances.

Grammar

The MLU value of 2.53 places Sophie early in Brown's stage II, the stage in which 'grammatical morphemes' are expected to develop. These, for Brown, include the progressive and past-tense inflections, articles and some prepositions. There is little here to suggest more than a beginning of this process: one *-ing* form, two (possible) irregular past-tense forms, one or two articles, and very restricted prepositional use. We will look at this in more detail later. So far as MLU and its relationship with age is concerned, the Miller and Chapman data (1981) put Sophie roughly in line with her (US) peers: their data from spontaneous conversations between 123 children aged 17 months to 5 years, and their mothers, predict a mean MLU of 2.54 for a child of 2;6. This is close to Sophie's observed MLU.

Sophie's type–token ratio (TTR) (for the same set of utterances used for MLU) is 0.34, based on 97 lexemes and 282 tokens. This TTR suggests that younger children's samples are likely to be less lexically differentiated than indicated by Templin's figures for children who are over 3 years of age (cf. Sophie's TTR in later samples). The restriction on lexical types is partly accounted for by the extensive use of pronouns in this sample (see below, p. 79), and partly by the absence of auxiliaries and the restricted range of prepositions.

The LARSP profile

The LARSP profile and verb-valency analyses are based on 50 clauses which occur for the most part within the 100 utterances used for the MLU and TTR analyses. However, since there were only 45 clauses in this set, five extra clauses were added (from l. 308 on). It must be emphasized that by 'clause' here is meant an utterance which contains a finite verb; thus 'immature clauses' of the type 'orange there' (l. 305) were not included. Since the LARSP analysis was designed to take account of children's early proto-constructions, the profiles here are to this extent distorted by the omission of such utterances. Since Sophie is already able to construct clauses with verbs, however, this does not appear to be a serious drawback. It also has the advantage of permitting direct comparison and contrast with the valency analysis.

Clause types

The most common clause type is SVO (*me play that*, *me want that piano*, *I got any hoover*) followed by SVOA (*our play that on floor*, *you get my drink for me*, *you tip those out*). Since these are extremely common English clause types, this is not surprising.

Some comment is perhaps necessary at this point on the analyses presupposed by these type labels. For SVO, the examples cited above are straightforward. The label was also applied to utterances like *me want find the page*, where *want find* is taken as a verb phrase with *find* as head. This sits uneasily with more common generative analyses in which *find the page* would be taken as the complement of *want*, in a structure like [[me want it] [me find the page]]. Although there may well be justification for a complex sentence analysis of such verbs in the adult language (the issue is much debated, however - see Matthews (1981: 192 ff.)), there is little in the child's utterances at this point to support it. First, *want* is the only such verb – there are no other 'complement verbs', nor indeed any clearer examples of complex sentences. Second, *want* is almost always in pre-main verb position, and is at this point separated from the verb (as in a structure like *me want daddy come down*). The analysis of *you tip those out* as SVOA might also be questioned by those familiar with other analyses which would take *tip out* as a verb + particle sequence, in this case obligatorily separate because the object of the verb is a preposition. Thus we can have in the adult language sentences like *tip the rubbish out* or *tip out the rubbish*, but only *tip it out* and not **tip out it*. The problem at this point in the child's development is that there is no evidence for the mobility of the 'particle': *out* and other similar items that can be particles or adverbs occur utterance-finally in all cases. From the data available, SVOA with a A realized as an adverb is a more appropriate analysis.

The SVO incidence figure would be even higher, except that the decision was made to analyse utterances like *Mary came me* as SVA. The form is SVO – the absence of a preposition in this and other cases means that what should be SVA is assimilated to the dominant SVO pattern in the data. The application of the SVA label is, at this point, merely a way of keeping apart true and spurious SVO structures.

There is an added complication here, however, which provides further illustration (if any were needed) of the risks attendant on profile analysis couched (for very good reasons) in adult terms. The three SVA structures, so-called, in this sample are *Mary come me*, *Muffy step on that*, and *me playing all those children*. Of these, the second is formally defensible as an SVA structure. The other two, it might be argued, should be considered as distinct. Both omit prepositions; but whereas *Mary come me* could plausibly be considered the precursor of an SVA structure, the *playing* construction could be thought of as SVO, since *play with* can be plausibly argued to be a unit (phrasal) verb in English. Whether constructions like play + with + NP are verb + adverbial or verb + object is probably not resolvable; this is an instance of what Matthews (1981: 17 ff.) calls 'indeterminacy' in English syntax. We would justify our choice of type label here by noting that, whatever the difficulties with the adult analysis may be, the child, at this point in her development, treats the elements following *come* and *play* as the same, in one sense, by omitting them both.

Statement clause types, then, are concentrated on SVO and SVOA structures. There are few formally marked questions in the data - in particular, no yes/no questions - because of the absence of auxiliaries from the child's repertoire. There are of course statement-like structures, which are interpreted by the mother as questions, for example (ll. 19-20)

S. 'you take a biśsy/
F. 'cos I was hùngry/

Here, as we have already noted (p. 19), a combination of intonational and contextual cues leads the mother to interpret this utterance as a question. Sophie uses three wh-questions in this sample: *where's the doll house*, *why those two nother things broke*, and *where's the childrens*. On the profile chart, two of them have been entered as QX, despite the apparent contracted copula on *where's*. There is, however, no evidence of copulas appearing elsewhere in the sample. In addition, the inappropriateness of *where's* (instead of *where are*) in the *where's the childrens* utterance (l. 319) makes it fairly clear that the child has no control over the *'s* as a grammatical entity; rather, she is simply reproducing what she hears in the speech around her as a common pronunciation of initial *where*.

The other clause type allowed for on the chart is *Command*. Four structures have been placed under this heading: *look her toe*, *get my drink*, *come on floor me* and *look Zelda piano*, largely on contextual grounds. The tendency of children at this stage of development to omit subjects, and also any main verb markings, means that formally there are likely to be a number of structures which look like imperatives, but whose function is ambiguous. As it happens, there are few in this sample: *look Zelda piano* is one of them. It could mean something like 'look, it's a piano like Zelda's', as well as the interpretation implicit in our clause-type label 'look at Zelda's piano'. We have taken the latter interpretation largely because the prosodic structure of the utterance is that of other verb + object constructions in the data. The other ambiguous sequence in this sample is one that we have placed under *Statement*, *read that* at l. 168. Here, although the sequence could be said to be an imperative construction, the context makes clear that it is plausible to interpret Sophie as the subject of the verb.

We have already referred to the absence of any complex (that is, multi-clause) sentences in the data. This is made clear on the profile by the absence of any clauses at stage V, which has provision for coordination and subordination to be marked. The child's constructional capacity seems to be limited to relatively simple declarative clause structures with restricted phrasal realizations. An omission by the child that we have not yet noted is that these structures are all affirmative - no overt negative markers appear in the sample. We have already noted, however (see p. 19), that, just as there are declarative structures that are interpreted as questions by Sophie's mother, other declaratives are interpreted as negatives. One of them, *I got any hoover* (l. 204), although it does not have an overt *not* or *n't*, does have the determiner appropriate to a negative sentence (cf. *I haven't got any hoover*). There are other occasions, however, when there is no clause-internal clue to the negative intent of the utterance, and we have to rely on the maternal interpretation. One of these is at ll. 183–4, where Sophie says, with reference to a picture that they are both looking at, *me like that*, and the mother says *no*. We cannot be absolutely certain of Sophie's negative intent here, but in the light of her apparent reference to the picture as 'horrid', two lines earlier, the mother's interpretation seems reasonable. A similar case occurs outside the profile clause set, at l. 353: *her got blankie* was interpreted by the mother, when reviewing the transcript, as a negative, and this again seems plausible in the context: in the next line Sophie indicates that the baby wants a blanket, and then asks where one is. There was no alternative referent available in the context who already had a blanket. This omission of negative markers is unusual - no other reports of it appear in the literature. The usual progression (cf. Klima and Bellugi 1966) is held to be from clause-external negative elements (*not mummy go*) to clause-internal elements (*mummy not go*), prior to the appearance of auxiliaries, when contracted forms (*can't*, *won't*) become common.

Phrase types

If we now consider individual clause elements and ask how many are 'expanded' - that is, how many of them have realizations which themselves could be regarded as phrase level constructions - we find relatively few. It is possible in the language for any clause element to be expanded, but the only significant expansion in this sample appears to be of O elements in three-element clauses (XY + O: NP = 13), for example, *look* [*her toe*], *me want* [*nother bissie*], *you like* [*those balls*], *I got* [*any hoover*]. The expansion of adverbials is precluded generally because of the absence of prepositions, and the only verb expansions (XY + V: VP) reflect our decision to treat *want* as a quasi-auxiliary. The variety of the phrase structures themselves is limited, to DN in noun phrases (as illustrated above), and in adverbial phrases to PrN (*on floor*, *for Kate*), Pr + Pronoun (*with you*), or Pr + adverb (*in there*). The latter two structures are entered under *Other* at stage II phrase. There are occasionally longer noun-phrase structures, like *two nother things*, or *those sort of one*, but the errors Sophie makes only serve to underline the fact that she is out of her constructional depth with phrases more than two elements long. Apart from the phrases we have noted, the most frequent realization of S (particularly) and O elements are pronouns; subjects are almost always personal pronouns, and objects may be, but also can be *that* (*me like that*). This is in keeping with reports in the research literature such as Limber (1976).

Valency analysis

The 50 clauses in the sample analysed are distributed across just 19 verbs, a verb type–token ratio of 0.38, a figure very close to the TTR of 0.34 for the whole sample. The most common main verbs used are WANT and PLAY, both with seven tokens, followed by PUT with four. We have chosen to treat GET and GOT as distinct verbs, because the meaning of tokens of GOT is not related to the meaning of tokens of GET in the same way as, for example, *found* is to *find*. The utterances containing *got* all have present reference, and refer to current possession (*I got some those*, *Jack got some those*). When *get* occurs (as in *you get my drink for me*) it means 'fetch', or 'bring into my possession'. Although there may well be an argument for seeing 'getting' as prior to the state of possession signified by 'got', this relationship is different to other present–past relationships in English between forms of the same lexeme, and we have therefore chosen to treat the two forms as members of distinct lexemes, unless evidence to the contrary appears. Such evidence would be, for example, the child following an utterance like 'get it for me' with 'you got it for me', once the item was in her possession. Such evidence is of course available from adults, and the relationship between *get* and *got* that much more complex.

A note is also necessary concerning BREAK. The only representatives of this verb are two forms *broke*; given the contexts in which they appear, there must be some doubt as to whether these are indeed main verbs or simply a kind of adjective: *that one broke* (l. 276) and *why those two nother things broke* (l. 313). In both cases, Sophie is referring to plastic octagons she is playing with which have pieces broken off, and in both cases the time reference could be past or stative present. There is really no way to decide. The only (rather weak) argument in favour of the analytic route taken is that there are no other SC (subject + complement) structures in the data with adjectives realizing the complement, whereas there are other SV structures.

Arguments

Perhaps the most notable feature of the data is that the great majority of the verbs used have the arguments that would be expected from the adult grammar. A verb like COME, for example, which can occur with or without an adverbial, is treated so by the child. The verb BUY appears with its appropriate indirect object and direct object, as does GIVE. In general, obligatory arguments appear; the one exception is the occurrence of PUT at l. 308, where *me put nother bit more* lacks an adverbial. This omission is, however, immediately rectified (l. 309) and the correction emphasized (l. 310). If this is (and has been) generally true of the child's utterances, then it puts a somewhat different perspective on a syntactic profile couched in terms of successively longer clause structures. An utterance like *you tip those out* is SVOA not because the child has managed to increase the length of her clauses by adding adverbials to what were previously SVO structures, but because TIP is a verb that requires A (assuming of course that it is appropriate to label *out* thus). The child similarly has very little option about SVO structures where the verb is transitive; WANT is a frequently used verb in this sample which falls into that category. Of course there are optional adverbials which are used (optional in the sense that the verb does not require them, although the sense or context might): for example, *you buy me one again*, *our play that on floor*, where the latter would also have SVOA structure. It should be clear, however, that a label like SVOA does not distinguish optional from obligatory constituents, and so to that extent obscures one lexical dimension to syntactic development which it may be useful for the analyst to recognize.

Realization

A quick glance at the realization analysis makes it clear how limited the realizations of subject in the data are. Of the 39 declarative clauses represented in the analysis which have subjects, 31 have personal pronoun subjects, and seven have proper names. Only one (*that one broke*) has a noun phrase subject. This tendency for young children to restrict themselves to agent subjects, usually realized as pronouns or proper names, has been noted before (Limber 1976). It is something that we will continue to see in later samples. Information of this kind is a useful supplement to the interpretation of syntax profiles like LARSP. Although it would be incorrect to assume that the child has the capacity to use and interpret only human agent subjects (cf., for example, l. 367, *all that fall off*), at this point it is for the most part only agents that she chooses to talk about.

Object realizations show more variety both in structural realization (they can be pronouns or noun phrases) and in the lexical diversity of the noun phrases. Of the 34 objects in the sample, 25 are noun phrases, generally of the form determiner + noun (though note that 'determiner' here is a broad category subsuming possessives (*her*, *my*), demonstratives (*that*, *those*), the idiosyncratic blend *nother* (as in *nother one*) and articles (*the*, *a*). Of the 25 noun phrases, 18 have head nouns (*toe*, *page*, *hoover*, *piano*), whereas the rest have pronoun heads (*my one*, *some those*) or heads with vague reference (*bit*, *sort*). In the lexical noun phrases, there does not appear to be any restriction on the nouns that a particular verb can take as object, although the sample is limited, and the verbs themselves (*get*, *look*, *got*, *like*, *find* etc.) of a type that allow a very wide range of objects. What is perhaps most striking about the realizations of subjects and objects overall is that lexical heads are in such a minority. Of 73 subject or object elements, 47 are realized by pronouns or phrases with pronoun heads.

There are eight prepositional phrases, appropriately realizing As, in the 50-clause sample, and six occasions on which a preposition is omitted, leaving either a noun phrase or a pronoun. It does not seem to be the case that the prepositions omitted, so far as one can tell, are distinct from those that appear elsewhere. Sophie uses *on floor* (l. 261); at l. 309, it seems to be *on* that she omits in *me put nother bit more my house*. She is at this point building a 'house' with plastic 'bricks'. It could be argued that *on* is not the only possible preposition in this context - we might use *for*, for instance, or perhaps *in*. The absence of a preposition may reflect similar uncertainty on Sophie's part. When she is faced with the expression of a prepositional phrase, she may be greatly helped by common collocations in input, particularly when no alternatives are available: *on floor* falls into this category - she is much less likely to have heard *in the floor*, *with the floor*, *for the floor* than *on the floor*. The influence of common phrases in input may also be seen in Sophie's use of *in there*, and *in the car*. Uncertainty as to the appropriate preposition for a locative relation, particularly where the location is expressed as a lexical noun, may be the source of some of her difficulties. Not all of the prepositional phrases she uses (or doesn't use) are locative, however, and the 'uncertainty' explanation will not apply in all cases. For example, *with* is commonly omitted (for example, l. 270, *come on floor me*, where it has a comitative meaning). When it does occur (once, at l. 285), it is pronounced as [ɪ?]. Since no alternative to *with* is plausible at l. 270, we might suppose that pronunciation difficulties are also interfering with the expression of some prepositions. There is, in general, no doubt that, for whatever reasons, the range and application of the preposition category is severely restricted at this point in the child's acquisition.

Deixis

We mentioned earlier that explicit contrasts between *this* and *that* in input to children may be rare. This view may find support from the fact that when a contrast does appear in the sample, at l. 44, it is between *that* and *the other* as modifiers in *are you going to play that side/or the other side*, rather than between *this* and *that*. As we look through the complete sample, we find examples of both *this* and *that* used as pronouns by Sophie's mother, but not contrastively:

l. 157 shall we put this away
l. 167 let's read that

l. 278 when did that happen
l. 317 that's lovely
l. 329 that's right
l. 357 here would this do
l. 361 is that small enough
l. 371 like that
l. 387 I can't find the other legs to that sweetie

From these examples it would appear that *that* (as pronp) is more common in input than *this*. If we look in a little more detail at the context in which *this* (in l. 357) and *that* (in l. 361) are uttered, we can see that the purely spatial proximal-distal contrast is not necessarily the basis for the contrast in the mother's language. In these instances, *this* and *that* have the same referent, namely a tissue that the mother offers as a 'blanket' for the child's doll. In l. 357, *this* refers to something the mother thinks of and produces, from a tissue box, as a solution to the 'blanket' problem. The reason for this seems to be not so much its spatial proximity to her, but its introduction as a solution. When Fran uses *that* in l. 361, she is talking about the result of her folding the tissue, and is in fact asking whether it is now an appropriate size to serve as a blanket. There seems no spatial distal meaning involved. Indeed, it would have been perfectly acceptable to use *this* in place of *that* in l. 361. These two examples (l. 44 and ll. 357–61) should at least make us cautious about the assumption that the spatial contrastive meanings for *this* and *that* are the basic ones, and are likely to be transparently available to children in conversation.

In the 50-utterance subsample, Sophie's use of demonstratives perhaps reflects the frequencies in her mother's speech. She only uses *that*, and the majority of occurrences are pronominal (eight pronominal uses to one determiner use, in *that piano*). In the full sample we see the same picture. There are no occurrences of *this*, and hence no suggestion that Sophie at this stage has any control over a deictic contrast. *That* is used by her as an all-purpose object pronoun. Similarly, there is no evidence of any *here*/*there* contrast, even though *there* appears, appropriately, usually following a preposition (*on there*, *in there*, *over there*). Sophie has determined its locative function and controls one of its syntactic positions, but does not appear to know its relationship with *here*.

Personal pronouns

A restricted set of personal pronouns emerges from the sample: *I*, *me*, *you* and *our*. Of the two subject pronouns used by Sophie, *me* is the more common, appearing about four times as often as *I*. She also uses *me* in object position, and as the object of a preposition. She is, on the evidence of this sample, in control of the *I* (*me*)/*you* distinction, in using *I*/*me* for speaker, and *you* for addressee. Like most children, she does not appear to find it a problem that the referent of these terms shifts with conversational role (cf. Clark 1978: 100).

When children begin to use personal pronouns, they do not always cope with this distinction immediately. Some apparently entertain the hypothesis that the referents of *I/me* and *you* are fixed, with *I/me* always meaning adult, and *you* meaning child. So, for example, Clark (1978: 101) cites an example of a child of 1;11 saying to his mother *you want to put the frog in the mug*, *you want mummy red toothbrush*, when the context made clear that he was referring to himself. See also Chiat (1981). We should perhaps also note (cf. Tanz 1980: 55, citing a paper by McNeill) that the child in her use of *I/me/you* in this sample is speaking only with her mother and has no opportunity to demonstrate her ability with speaker/hearer shift with other hearers.

The only other personal pronoun in the subsample is *our*, which is used in subject position for *we*. She has understood that plural reference is required when she is referring to her mother and herself (in *our play that*), and that a first-person item is required, but has wrongly made her selection from the possessive set. Her possessives are *my* (and *mine*), *her* and *your*, all appropriately used for person and number. *Her*, however, is used to refer to her father (in *finding her cheque book*). This is presumably a result of the greater frequency with which she will have heard feminine forms, given that she has two sisters. What is more remarkable than these minor errors is that, by 2;5, she has uncovered as much as she has of the factors controlling the pronominal system.

There is, however, one major omission we should note at this point – third-person pronominal reference. There are not too many opportunities in the sample for Sophie to refer to a third person, but when she does, she uses proper names (Amy, Jack, Mary, Kate, etc.). Now at the first introduction into a conversation of person referents, this is entirely appropriate. However, on at least two occasions when her mother has already introduced a proper name, Sophie in her response uses the same name, instead of an anaphorically referring pronoun:

l. 225	F.	What sort shall I get for Zeldy then
	S.	You give my one [ə] Zeldy
l. 239	F.	What else has Hessy got
	S.	Hessy – want those sort of one.

These examples suggest that the absence of third-person pronouns is not a sampling artefact, but represents a limitation in her system at this point.

Articles

We will concentrate under this heading on *the* and *a*. These are rudimentary in Sophie's language at 2;5. Assessing just what she can do is made more difficult by the pronunciation problem she has with [ə]. She does insert a schwa before sounds where an indefinite determiner would be appropriate: (l. 19) *you take a bissy*. She also omits any realization at places where *the* or *a* are equally possible: (l. 94) [*u*ː] *put bissy on there*. And occasionally she produces - correctly - *the*, as in (l. 185) *me want find the page*. In the 50-utterance subsample, *the* is used correctly twice, and *a* once. Sophie omits *the* twice (both times from *on* floor), and omits *a* four times (three of these are from *make house*). There is little evidence here that she controls the factors that govern the insertion of these articles; we shall consider them in more detail in relation to the next sample.

Verb-forms

The most striking feature of the sample is, perhaps, the absence of forms signalling modal, aspectual and tense meanings. There are no forms of *be*, *have*, *do* and only one modal, *can't* in the entire sample. We have discussed above the possibility that *broke* may be an irregular past tense, and we note the appearance of *went*, as an immediate imitation of the mother, at l. 350. In addition, at l. 323, there is one *-ing* suffix: *me playing all those children*. But this is very little to set beside the rich set of verb modifications available to the mature English speaker. Clearly, at 2;5, Sophie's verb-forms are minimal, and this sample will provide a useful baseline against which to assess her later development.

4

Sophie at 3 years

BACKGROUND

The second sample was taken four days after Sophie's third birthday. In contrast to the first sample, Sophie is not, for the first part of the session at least, alone with her mother. Her next oldest sister, Hester, is present. Hester dominates the conversation with her mother in the early part of the sample, and continues to play a role throughout, even though she has moved to another part of the house. The session opens with Fran and Sophie doing jigsaw puzzles and this continues as a motif, with interruptions and occasional excursions on to other topics, up to about l. 455. The first puzzle is of a large 'mother Hubbard' shoe house, inhabited by mice, while the second is a 'Mr Men' puzzle. Further details of participants, and notes on events, appear at appropriate locations in the transcript. The sample is 579 lines in total, rather longer than Sample 1. A longer excerpt was considered necessary because of the nature of the conversation in the early part of the sample, particularly as it represents Sophie. The fact that she and her mother are playing jigsaws leads to a particular style, in the first 200 or so lines, which underrepresents her linguistic abilities. It is for this reason that the MLU sample begins at l. 244 (Sophie's 51st utterance) rather than at the 51st utterance in the sample, as previously.

SAMPLE 2: SOPHIE AT 3;0.4

S. lôok/
F. well dône/
S. lôok/
F. is that ríght/
I can't sèe lovey/
S. thàt/

F. nò/
that 'can't be right cán it/
nò/
càn't be right/
cos he's sideways/
S. lôok
'can't get it òff now/
F. it 'must go thère/
[3-second pause]
S. * hāve to
F. 'which corner goes thére d'you 'think/ - -
S. thìs corner/
F. 'that's not a còrner/
iś it/
no 'that's just an èdge/
'that's a córner/
and 'that's a córner/ - - -
S. then 'this better gō
F. well nò/
it 'has to go at the èdge/
it 'goes like thàt/
there 'isn't anything to fìx it to/
no it dòesn't go 'there/
'what about thàt one/ - - -
nǒ/
'I think 'that goes thêre/
'no sweetie a còrner/ - -
gōes/
it's the two èdges/
'that's a stràight bit/
and thàt's/ - - -
[10-second pause; F. & S. are playing with the jigsaw; the conversation is resumed by Hester, S.'s elder sister]
H. 'just give m'face a clèan-out/
S. lôok/
F. is thát right/
H. 'this is a sort of 'make-up bàg/
F. m̂m/
H. what - mummy lòok/
shall I 'show you 'how many cràyons I've 'got/
lòok/
oh 'they're not ìn that one/
F. well dône/
S. thère/
'why's he 'looking out of thére/

F. no idèa/
he 'seems to be 'shut in a shóe/ doèsn't he/
'does he 'live in a shóe/ d'you thínk/
H. yès/
cos - - cos he 'can't get oùt/
'cos there's no dòor/
he's cùtting it/
F. ôh
he's 'cutting the dòor/
F. oh Ì see/
H. * 'now he can get òut/
F. * 'cutting a 'door out of the shòe/ - -
'very 'very 'funny pùzzle/
H. I knòw/
I think it's
F. he's pàinting the 'shoe/
H. I 'think it's the mìce/
I 'think it's the - [əm] - how many
they're 'too many 'children but in mìce/
yòu know/
F. oh the old 'woman who had 'so many 'children she
'didn't know what to dò/
H. yèah/
but I 'mean in mìce/
F. yès/
H. mummy lòok/
sée/
I've 'even got a 'white in hère/
S. * thàt/
H. * whíte/
'n gréy/
S. 'come ôn/
F. 'come on yoùrself/
H. and I've 'even got a 'red and yèllow/
F. 'where does 'that bit gò/
H. can't 'really * fit any more în/
F. * that's ìt/
[3-second pause]
H. I 'wish I could go out'side with these shòes/
F. look 'don't ask about these 'shoes any mòre/
H. Sòphie will/ - -
* Sòphie will/
F. * 'Sophie's are 'much tougher than yòurs/
and she 'hasn't even gòt any others/
'they're funny * hêels those/

S. * lòok mummy/
[7-second pause]
S. mummy lòok/
F. well dône/
S. [kə] - [kæ] - 'can our 'do this - this rèd one/ (can = [kæn])
F. yès/
if you wànt/
[3-second pause]
S. múmmy/
F. 'where's the 'rest of the blòck/
S. 'me will 'put it ìn/ (whispers)
nò/
can me 'put it in like thàt/ (can me = [kəmɩ])
F. I 'don't know that I cân/
H. 'why are these 'tougher than mìne then/
F. cos they àre/ (to H.)
'they're the only ònes/
now swèetie/ - - -
I 'don't think I càn darling/ (to S., continues from l. 104)
'I'll do thàt
S. and 'put it hère/
[25-second pause, during which S. and F. continue with the jigsaw, and H. leaves]
F. 'there we áre/
S. dìd it/
F. yès/
S. do thìs one 'now/ (change of jigsaw to 'Mr Men')
F. the Mìster Men one/
rìght/ - - -
on the flóor/
[6-second pause]
S. 'that is Mister Small's ońes/
F. iś it/
iś it/
S. m̀m/
and h̄e (5 syll.)
F. who ìs that one/
S. don't knòw/
Mister Hàppy/
F. iś it/
S. Mister Hàppy/
yèah/
'always Mister Háppy/
why - why 'do me have to 'put one slíde in/
F. 'keep your 'hair out of your fàce/

'otherwise it's all òver you/
hère/
there's some more còunters/ (these are left over from an earlier game of 'Snakes and Ladders')
will you 'pass me that 'green còunter/ (will you = [wjə])
S. whìch green counter/
F. thàt/
S. whìch green counter/
F. thàt/
S. whìch green counter/
F. Sŏphie/
S. pìnk counter/
F. yes àlright/. - - -
S. whìch pink counter/
F. the grèen one/
S. whìch pink counter/
F. the grèen one/
S. which pìnk one/
[5-second pause] (F. picks up counter and slips it through the side of the 'Snakes and Ladders' box)
'why did you 'post it thròugh mummy/ - - -
F. póst it/
S. put it thĕre/
F. it doesn't 'go in the bòx/ doés it/
oh yes it dòes/
let's 'turn all the pieces òver/ sháll we/
S. mm/
'me did gòod/
'me did 'some of thòse mummy/
F. díd you/
S. 'when you been 'tidying ùp/
just been leave(d) there mummy [liːvdɛə]
hēy/
whàt/
'that not 'go in thère/
F. dóes it/
nò/
S. whý
F. dàrling/
there's a 'bit of rèd there 'sweetheart/
S. ôh/
F. ôh/
S. [duːz] it '[hæ?] to go thìs side/
[duː] thìs go/

['du:] it go thìs side/
F. nò/
S. nò/
[8-second pause]
F. oh dârling/
'don't be sìlly/
S. pârling/
pàrling/
pàrling/
F. 'there's a 'bit of light grèen/
'where does thàt go/
oh it 'goes down hêre/
yēs/ (in response to a call from H. elsewhere in the house)
I can't hèar/ (in response to another call)
H. I've 'got a runny tûmmy/ (from another part of the house)
F. 'what's she sáy/
S. she's 'got a runny tùmmy/
F. òh/
'just a sèc/ (to S. - F. leaves room)
'you carry òn/
[break for 70 seconds, during which S. sings to herself on the theme 'runny tummy', and continues with the jigsaw]
S. where àre you 'mummy/
F. upstàirs/ (returns)
S. 'why did her 'have a runny tùmmy/
F. Ì don't know/
còme on/
'let's go and 'do your pùzzle/
H. (inaudible) (from upstairs)
F. we'll 'do it again in a mìnute/ (to H.)
[5-second pause]
F. wàit a minute/
there's a bit hère lovey/
S. it doesn't 'go that wày/
go thìs way/
F. ôh/
sòrry/
nòw/
'where does 'this gó/
F. 'this goes - - - * hêre/
H. * (unintelligible) (from upstairs)
F. oh shùt up 'Hester/ (to H.)
S. lòok/

it 'does go thère/
F. who's thàt one/
S. Mister Hàppy/
F. nô/
'that's Mr Nòsey/ isń't it/
S. nò/
'that is Mr Hàppy/
his - - - fèet/
F. who's thìs one/
S. don't kn̄ow/
F. a wórm/
Mr Wórm/
S. yès/
F. 'is there a Mister Wórm/
S. yès/
F. 'I've never 'heard of a Mister Wórm/
that goes thĕre/
who's thàt one/
what's thàt/
S. Mister [bàːm]/
F. Mister [wāːm]/
'that goes thĕre/
'gosh it's a bìg puzzle/ isǹ't it/
S. mm̄/
a hùge - puzzle/
lòok/
pister Pèpper/
mīster
'what is 'that mister cálled/
'what - is he cálled/
F. Mister Hàppy/
S. ǹo/
what thìs one called/
F. I don't kǹow/
Mr Hàppy
S. nò/
cos lôok/
'that is Mr Hàppy/
F. nò/
he's the 'one with the long àrms/
I don't know 'what he's càlled/
S. thàt is - Mister Happy/ and thàt is Mister Happy/
F. 'two Mister 'Happys are thére/
S. m̀m/

F. nòw/
'that goes thére/
S. 'two Mister Hàppy/
'what is 'that one cálled/
F. Mister Grèedy/
S. 'what is 'that one cálled/
F. Mister Smàll/
S. 'why is it 'called Mister Smáll/
F. 'cos he's smâll/
I suppôse/
S. is hé Mister Happy/
F. I 'think the big 'yellow one is 'Mister Happy isń't it/
S. and 'that one 'that cos lòok/ – – –
lòok/ and lòok/ and lòok/ and lòok/
there – thère's his face/ and – he's 'Mister George Hàppy/
F. Mr Small Háppy/ – –
I've 'never heard of thàt/
'where does thàt go now/
[5-second pause]
S. me 'don't want hêlp/
F. you don't wànt any 'help/
S. mm̄/
F. 'want to 'play it yoúrself/
S. lòok/
lòok/
you – yòu do it 'all by your'self/
F. 'what are yôu going to 'do/
S. and me dòn't/
F. are 'you going to wátch/
S. 'me going to 'watch you 'doing your rìding lesson/
(the reference to the riding lesson for F. is fantasy; S.'s sisters are at this time having lessons)
F. my rídìng/
'what are you tálking about Sophie/
S. ['huːz] that jacket món/ (for [huːz] see below, p. 109)
['huːz] that jacket just thère/
F. it's yòurs/
S. ôh/
[5-second pause]
Mister Grèedy/ (fortissimo)
Mister Grèedy/
F. yès/

S. Mister Grèedy/
Mister Grèedy/
F. that's rìght/
'where's a bit mòre/
hère we are/
S. shall me 'sit mon my légs/
'mon my bóttom/
F. mhm̌
S. 'why did - - -
'why did - -
Mummy 'why - -
'why did - - - 'Hester be fast aslèep mummy (H. had slept earlier in the afternoon)
F. 'she was tîred/
S. and 'why did her 'have - two swèets mummy/
F. 'cause you 'each had twò/
thàt's why/
she 'had the 'same as yòu/
ooh dèar/
nòw what/
S. 'daddy dìdn't 'give me twò in the end/
F. yes he dìd/
S. he dìdn't/
F. he dìd/
S. lòok/
he 'given one to - 'two to Hèster/ and 'two to ûs/
F. yês/
that's ríght/
S. 'why did he gìve/
F. 'cos there were sìx sweets/
that's twò each/
'what goes down thère/ - - -
nǒ/
S. Mr Bister Bìster/
Mr Pister Pister (sings)
F. have you 'got any more 'bits of this swéetie/
are there 'any more in the bóx/ - - -
S. lòok/
'me don't 'know where bòx is now/
F. 'under the tâble/
[5-second pause]
S. nǒ/
nò mummy/
F. nó/

S. (1 syll.)
F. 'I'm a bit pùzzled by 'this/
S. is 'this a bóx/
'this a bóx/
F. yês/
I suppòse so/
S. that a tôp/
F. 'where do you
ah hère they are/
thèn what/
S. look me gòing/
F. other síde/
oh hère we are/
(4 syll.)
there we áre/
nòw/
'what do we 'need nòw/
S. 'nother one of thèse/
F. we 'want a green èdge/
thát/
and thát/
(3 syll.)
'there we àre/
S. 'look our 'found that other bít/ (missing puzzle piece)
F. yes I 'found it in 'Hester and Griselda's ròom/
'wasn't that lûcky/
it was the 'bit that was míssing/ wàsn't it/
S. mm/
F. 'here's the òther one/
S. 'why did it been thére/
F. I 'have an idèa/ that when 'Hester had flù/
she dìd that puzzle/ dìdn't she/
I gàve it to her/ - - - (during the Easter holidays)
so 'that was 'where it wàs/
[4-second pause]
I don't think 'that's quite rìght/
S. 'why did you 'give her - - 'to her when her been flú/
F. to 'cheer her ûp/
'give her something to dò/
S. 'what did 'her have wròng with her/
F. flù/
S. 'why - 'why do - me[dɪ] -
'why didn't 'me get flu éver/
F. I don't knòw/
you dìdn't get it/ dìd you/ thàt time/

S. why̌/
ˈwhy didn't ˈme get flú/
F. ˈcause you're so hèalthy/
S. ˈwhy are me so health – héalthy/
F. you're ˈsuch a fātty/ - - -
ˈwhere does thàt go/
S. ˈwhere [də] thìs bit/
F. I haven't foùnd that bit ˈyet/
ˈwhat would it have òn it/
S. me fòund it/
F. is ˈthat the right óne/
(unintelligible sequence)
they're ˈhaving a bit of a fìght out there/ àren't they/ - - -
(G. & H. offstage)
wouldn't you sáy/
S. thère/
Mister Smàll/
Mister Smàllie/
Mister Smàll/
ˈwhy's he called Mister Smáll/
F. cos he's smàll/
S. ˈwhy's he so smáll/
F. I expect he ˈdidn't eat his brèakfast/
S. ˈwhy is he so bìg/ (points to Mr Greedy)
F. I don't knòw/
S. ˈwhy is he so bìg/
F. he's so grèedy/
what's thát/
S. lôok/
F. (unintelligible sequence)
I ˈthink you're right/
yès/
S. lòok/
ˈthat bit ˈgot a bit of grèen/
F. yes you're rìght/
and ˈthat goes thére/
S. ˈme – got a bit of grèen mummy/
F. yèp/ - - -
that goès/
S. nò/
mê want to ˈdo it/
F. it ˈgoes the other way ròund lovey/ - - -
S. yès/
F. yès/ - - -
would ˈyou like to fínish it ˈnow/ - - -

S. 'why do me hàve to/ ---
F. 'that goes thére/
S. 'what goes in this hòle/ ---
F. nŏ/
S. thìs way/
F. ǹo/
I think 'that bit goes hère/
no 'that - 'that's a bit ---
is that ríght/ ---
[6-second pause]
nò lovey/
it's upside dôwn/ ---
S. thís way/
F. mhm̆/
it's upside dòwn/
[10-second pause]
S. can 'our do it agáin/
F. oh nò/
S. yès/
F. well 'you'll have to 'take it to pìeces/
S. lòok/
[5-second pause]
F. 'don't throw them aroùnd/
cause if we lóse them/ 'you won't be able to 'get any mòre/
S. lòok
shall 'me shall 'me do this flòppy thing/
so flòppy/
F. flóppy/
S. 'you say slòppy/ when 'me do this/
F. slóppy/ or flòppy/
S. slòppy/
F. slòppy/
S. me 'did it nòw/
[5-second pause]
hère's a bit/
F. would you 'like an ápple/
S. yès/
H. I 'need to 'go to the lòo again/ [H. comes into the room again]
F. oh dèar/
S. are those smáll apples/ or bìg apples/
H. 'I need to 'go to the lòo/
F. come òn then/ (to H.)
I'll 'give you some medicine/

S. 'who you giving médicine to/
F. Hèster
S. whý
F. be'cause of her tùmmy/
S. give m̀y one to – 'her/
F. nò/
it 'won't help tùmmies/
S. 'which one 'do it help – tùmmies/
'me got a tùmmy ache/
F. háve you/
S. yès/ – – –
'are those sḿall apples/ or bìg apples/
F. quite sm̀all/
S. òh/
F. 'one for yóu/ 'one for m̀e/
S. yès/
two smàll apples/
[10-second pause]
'one is bíg/ and 'one is sm̀all/
here's yòur – one/
F. 'that one's 'got a bìte out of it/
d'you mínd/
S. nò/ – – –
'me bitten thìs one/
'me have thìs one/
[10-second pause] (S. eats the apple)
it hàrd/
F. is it hárd/
S. m̀m/
F. góod though/
S. m̀m/
F. 'is it the sort of 'apple you have at schóol/
S. yès/
F. 'who cuts 'up the 'apples at schòol/ (the slicing and sharing out of apples is an important ritual at S.'s nursery school)
S. don't kǹow/
[ɪ] those – – [ɪ] those 'don't – join ìn/ [eɪ] '[mæt]
go into [ə] 'kitchen, with the tèachers/
F. they 'don't join iň/
S. nò/
F. ôh/
whó doesn't join in/
S. [əm] – – [əm] – – Lucas/ (Lucas is a classmate of S.'s)

F. do 'you join iń/
S. m̀m/
but 'sometime me - me 'don't - me - - - 'go to the tèacher/
mē
[20-second pause; Sophie eats her apple, and hums a tune]
S. me 'always 'go with Màggie/ (Maggie = teacher)
F. whó do/
S. m̀e/
just 'go with Màggie/ - - -
'me don't mìnd go/
'me don't (2 syll.)
F. com̂ing/ (F. leaves room in response to a request from upstairs)
[4-minute break]
S. where arè you 'mummy/
F. whát/
S. where arè you 'mummy/
where arè you/
F. 'where's Grisèlda gone to/
S. don't knòw/
múmmy/
'why did you 'put that in my rŏom/
F. whát/
S. thàt/ - -
drèss/
'that blue drèss/
F. well I 'think it's yôurs now/ iśn't it/
I 'think it's 'too small for Hèster/
nŏw/
(unintelligible sequence)
S. yeāh
'that hèr/
mum 'is this mỳ (2 syll.)/
'is this mińe/
is this mińe/
F. whát/
S. this/
F. I don't knòw/
'I've never sèen it before/
'where does it còme from/
S. don't knòw/
me fòund it/
F. whére/
S. once - 'once our came 'back from sòmewhere/ - -
'once our came 'back from sòmewhere/ and me

545 'found it thère mummy/
F. whére did 'we come 'back from/
S. don't knòw/ - -
just foùnd it/
F. òh/
550 S. 'why are you just dùsting it/
F. I'm drỳing it/
S. ôh/
F. because it 'gets rather full of s̀pit/ (recorder)
[10-second pause]
S. 'can me 'take this to Lóndon/
555 F. whát/ - - -
S. me - 'me helping 'put all the 'clothes on the * (2 syll.)/
F. * àlright/ (to G. & H. off)
S. 'me help - all the 'clothes give 'em to Jó mummy/
F. 'what did you sáy dear/
560 S. 'help to 'give 'em to Jô/ (Jo = family helper)
F. díd you/
'that was 'kind of yóu/
S. clòthes/
but 'me didn't 'do it any mòre/
565 'helped - Zelda with her [tàː] thing/ ([taː] = guitar)
F. ôh/
S. thíng/
'what - 'what are these 'pictures doing hére/
F. càreful of them darling/
570 gàngan painted them/ - - (gangan = grandmother)
they're prètty/ àren't they/ - - -
S. 'me like [ə] little one bèst/
F. dó you/ - -
S. 'why have it got flówers on/
575 F. 'cos she pàinted the 'flowers darling/
thàt's why/
S. 'which one do you like fírst/
[ə] bíg one/ or [ə] lìttle one/
F. 'I like that whìte one/

DATA SUMMARIES: SAMPLE 2

(a) MLU(m) = 3.82 (beginning at Sophie's 51st utterance)
(b) TTR = 0.31 (using same set of utterances)

(c) LARSP (beginning at Sophie's 51st utterance)

Stage I (0.9–1.6)	Minor	Responses			Vocatives	Other	Problems	
	Major	*Comm.*	*Quest.*	*Statement*				
		'V'	'Q'	'V'	'N'	Other	Problems	
	Conn.	Clause				Phrase		Word
Stage II (1.6–2.0)		V X	Q X	SV	A X	DN 12	VV 1	
				SO	VO	Adj N 5	V part	-ing 3
				SC	VC	NN	Int X 3	
				Neg X	Other	PrN 4	Other 2	pl
		X + S:NP	X + V:VP	X + C:NP		X + O:NP	X + A:AP	-ed 8
Stage III (2.0–2.6)		V X Y 1	Q X Y 2	SVC 1	VCA	D Adj N 3	Cop 13	-en 2
				SVO 8	VOA	Adj Adj N	$Aux^{M\ 3}_{O\ 15}$	
		let X Y	VS(X) 5	SVA 5	VO_dO_i	Pr DN 3		3s 1
		do X Y		Neg X Y	Other	$Pron^{P\ 42}_{O\ 9}$	Other	gen
		XY + S:NP 7	XY + V:VP 6	XY + C:NP		XY + O:NP 8	XY + A:AP 2	n't 6
Stage IV (2.6–3.0)		+ S	QVS 14	SVOA 2	AA X Y 1	Np Pr NP	Neg V 6	
			Q X Y + 1	SVCA	Other 3	Pr D Adj N	Neg X	
		V X Y +	VS(X+) 2	SVO_dO_i		c X	2 Aux	'cop 6
			tag	SVOC		Xc X 3	Other 2	'aux 1
Stage V (3.0–3.6)	*and* 2	Coord.	Coord.	Coord. 1 1	1 +	Postmod. clause	1 1 +	
	c 1	Other	Other 1	Subord. A1 1	1 +			-est
	s 2			S C	O2			-er
	Other			Comparative		Postmod. phrase	1 +	-ly

Verb valency analysis

Total verb types: 19 *Total verb tokens:* 50

	Type	*Tokens*	*Frames and realizations*				
1.	BITE	1	S	-	O		
			Pronp		DN		
2.	COME	1	A	S	-	A	A
			adv	Pronp		adv	Pr adv
3.	DO	6	S	-	O	A	
			Pronp		Prono	III Phr.	Other
			S	-	O	A	[2]
			Pronp		Pronp	adv	
			O	S	-	A	
			what	DN		adv	
			S	-	O		
			Pronp		D Adj N		
					Pronp		
4.	DUST	1	A	S	A	-	O
			why	Pronp	adv		Pronp
5.	FIND	5	S	-	O		
			Pronp		D Adj N		[2]
			S	-	O		
			Pronp		Pronp		
			S	-	O	A	
			Pronp		Pronp	adv	
			A	-	O		
			adv		Pronp		
6.	GET	3	A	S	-	O	A
			why	Pronp		N	adv
			A	S	-	O	
			why	Pronp		N	
7.	GIVE	6	S	-	O_i	O_d	A
			Pronp		Pronp	N	PrDN
			S	-	$O_i O_d$	*and*	$O_i O_d$
			Pronp		N Pr N		N Pr N
			A	S	-	O_d	A
			why				*Clause*
			O_i	S	-	O_d	O_i
			who			PN	Pr
				-	O_d	O_i	
					DN	PrN	
				-	O_d	O_i	
					Pronp	PrN	

	Type	*Tokens*	*Frames and realizations*					
8.	GO	9	S	–	A			
			what		PrDN			
			A	S		–	A	
			adv	Pronp			PrDN	
			S		A	–	A	
			Pronp		adv		PrN	
			A	–	A			
			adv		PrN			
			S	–	A			
			Pronp		adv			
			A		S	–		
			where		Prono			
			S	–	A			
			Pronp		DN			
				–	A			
					DN			
			S	–	A			
			Pronp		DN			
9.	GOT	5	S	–	O			
			Pronp		D Adj N			[2]
			S	–	O			
			Pronp		NP Pr NP			
			DN					
			A	S		–	O	A
			why	Pronp			N	adv
10.	HAVE	2	A	S		–	O	
			why	Pronp			D Adj N	
							Adj N	
			O	S		–	C	A
			what				adj	adv
			S	–	O			
			Pronp		DN			
11.	HELP	1		–	O		A	
					N		Pr D Adj N	
12.	KNOW	1	S	–	O			
			Pronp		*Clause*			
13.	LIKE	2	O		S		–	A
			which one		Pronp			adv
			S	–	O		A	
			Pronp		Adj N		adv	
14.	MIND	1	S	–	V			
			Pronp		inf			

Type		*Tokens*	*Frames and realizations*			
15.	PUT	1	A why	S – Pronp	O Prono	A Pr DN
16.	SIT	1	S Pronp	– A Pr DN		
17.	TAKE	1	S Pronp	– O Prono	A PrN	
18.	WANT	1	S Pronp	– O N		
19.	WATCH	1	S Pronp	– O *Clause*		

COMMENTARY

Pronunciation

Most singleton consonants are now correctly pronounced, with the exception of [ð], which is sometimes omitted, sometimes appears as [d] and sometimes as [n], as well as occasionally being pronounced correctly. Affricates continue to constitute a problem, with [dʒ] realized as [d], initially, for example, *join* (1. 496), and as [ʒ] finally, in *huge* (1.237). Sophie's difficulties with consonant clusters appear to have been largely ironed out by this point, except for C + j initially (see above, p. 73). So, for example, in this sample the [hj] at the beginning of *huge* is pronounced [h]. There are other mistakes which either seem to represent fossilized word pronunciations – where the errors are specific to particular lexical items, or could be interpreted as motoric difficulty, consequent upon longer utterances. In the first category, we still find *on* as [mɒn], *that* as [næt], and *there* as [nɛə]. In the second, we find her pronouncing *kitchen* (in 1. 499) as virtually a monosyllable [kɪtʃ], with just the hint of a schwa vowel for the second syllable. This word occurs towards the end of a long utterance which shows other mispronunciations. Generally the errors noticeable in this sample are not the systematic substitutions of target sounds, but more random errors which are either phonological idioms (lexical items which have a phonetic specification for the child that does not fit with her current phonological system), or else reflect the immediate constraints of on-line production processing on her speech. In this latter category, we should also refer to some noticeable dysfluency which appears in some of her utterances. By this term we mean either the repetition of syllables, part words or phrases within an utterance, revisions within an utterance (false starts) or significant pause within an utterance. Some of those occurred in sample 1: repetition, for instance, occurs at 1. 122: *you – you get my drink for me*; a revision can be seen at l. 198: *me got--Jack got some of those*; and the kind of pause referred to is exemplified at l. 52: *me want--daddy come home*. In sample 1 revisions are much less numerous than word repetition (which always occurs utterance-initially - see ll. 285, 291, 326), and utterance-internal pause (see ll. 185, 313). In sample 2, the clause-internal pauses are least frequent; the only relatively lengthy one appears at l. 220, *his---feet*. The sentence-initial repetitions are still here, although the wider range of items repeated reflects the syntactic advances Sophie has made since the second sample: see, for instance, l. 96: [kə] - [kæ] - *can our do this - this red one* (note also the internal repetition here), and l. 133: *why-why do me have to put one slide in*. (See also ll. 271, 281, 303/6, 446, 496, 568.) The number of revisions has increased, and it is tempting to interpret this as a processing problem due to an increase in the syntactic complexity of her utterances. The best example comes at l. 303, where Sophie is attempting to formulate a *why*-question. The initial phrase *why did* at l. 303 is followed by a repetition of the phrase, and a revision (*mummy why*). Sophie then reverts to her original *why did*, which is followed by a long pause before she presents the subject NP, *Hester* (see also ll. 377 ff., for a similar example, and ll. 319, 372, for other kinds of revision). We will return to the link between dysfluency and syntactic complexity below. These examples, from both samples, should serve to make the point, however, that dysfluent utterances are to be expected, in normal children (although the degree of dysfluency may vary dramatically from child to child - see Crystal (1981: 114 ff.)) and Yairi (1981), and that the location of at least one category of them is not random, with respect to syntactic structure.

Grammar

The MLU value of 3.82 for a 100 utterance sample from Sophie's 51st utterance puts her into Brown's stage IV. The value for this sample compares with a value of 3.62 morphemes for the whole sample, and split-half values of 3.42 and 3.82. The value for the first half of the sample is actually outside Brown's lower band of 3.50 for stage IV, suggesting that the nature of the sample obtained is going to play a role in determining a child's linguistic abilities, if these are going to be assessed purely on the basis of conversational data. (For some further discussion of this issue see Fletcher, Peters and Hixson 1982.) The range of morpheme values for Sophie's utterances is 1-11; coincidentally 11 is the target value for the upper bound for stage IV in Brown's data (Brown 1973: 56). Although there are only one or two utterances in the sample which reach this value, they are not isolated items at one extreme of the distribution. There are a few items which are 10 morphemes in length, and a number which are 9. The major constructional process for which Brown names stage IV is embedding or complex sentence formation in Sophie's utterances. Whether we want to call this embedding or not is a question we will postpone for the moment. There is no doubt, however, that the sample 2 increment, on the rather crude measure of length that we have adopted, is accompanied by changes in syntactic complexity.

The type–token ratio for the MLU sample is 0.31, derived from a value for lexemes of 108, and a value for tokens of 347. (This compares with a TTR for the whole sample which is lower – 0.25, based on 171 lexemes and 693 tokens.) Once again, the value falls well below Templin's mean value of 0.50 (see above p. 47), but is beginning to look consistent for Sophie. Pronouns are still used extensively in the sample, particularly personal pronouns, but there is now one entirely new category, that of auxiliary, and a wider range of prepositions.

The LARSP profile

There are three major changes in the LARSP for sample 2: the appearance of auxiliaries, the linked development of interrogative forms, and the occurrence of the first complex sentences. We will deal generally with auxiliaries under *verb-forms* later in the commentary. Here, we will consider interrogatives and complex sentences in turn.

Interrogatives

Half of the clauses in our sample are interrogatives.[1] On the face of it, most of them have appropriate auxiliary inversion. Of the three that do not have inversion, it might be argued that only one is incorrect. They are:

1. what this one called
2. what goes in this hole
3. who you giving medicine to

The first sentence does omit the auxiliary, which is an error; the second has the wh-element as subject, and so does not require an auxiliary; the third, given the input the child hears, where the [ə] that represents *are* may be difficult to hear or simply not present in adult speech, is a pardonable omission. It seems, then, that for both yes/no and wh-questions, the child may be argued to have mastered, following the acquisition of auxiliary verbs, the syntactic rule of inversion that marks interrogative structures in English.[2] Since this is an interesting and important issue, which harks back to our discussion in the first chapter, it is worth looking at in a little more detail. In particular, we might want to examine development in wh-questions particularly (since those form the majority of interrogatives in our sample), but also yes/no structures, in samples which fall in between the two we have chosen to examine in detail. To return to a point made in our discussion of sampling, it may be that the abruptness of the change we see in Sophie's behaviour between our two samples is simply a result of the seven-month gap between them. What is the picture if we look at interrogative structures at roughly monthly intervals *between* samples 1 and 2? The figures for the proportion of wh-questions inverted for six intervening samples at roughly monthly intervals are as follows:

December	0.40
January	0.63
February	0.43
March	0.75
April	0.90
May	0.90

From December on, there are large numbers of inverted yes/no questions in the samples, for the most part with *can*-initial. Although it is straightforward to compare a non-inverted and an inverted wh-question (cf. *what dress me must wear* and *what are that* from 17.4.80), identifying comparable pairs for *yes/no* questions is much more difficult, since a 'non-inverted' yes/no question is structurally indistinguishable from a declarative.

For the wh-questions, the figures seem to suggest that over the period between sample 1 and sample 2, Sophie gradually improved her success rate with inversion, to the point where, at her third birthday, she was close to adult performance. If we compare her performance with the published data of Labov and Labov (1978), we find that the *gradual* improvement in percentage inversion over time fits with data from their subject, Jessie, but that Sophie is about six months ahead of Jessie in her success rate.

Simply considering the overall inversion success rate can be misleading, however. In our earlier discussion of Labov and Labov (see above p. 28), we mentioned their finding that Jessie's inversion ability appeared to vary with question-type. For instance, when Jessie's inversion success rate is at about 0.40, these are the apparent values for four different types of question:[3]

How	0.92
Where	0.82
What	0.75
Why	0.04

The remarkable discrepancy here is performance on *why*-questions, which is paralleled by Sophie at the point where she has the same overall success rate as Jessie. The figures are as follows:

How	0.75
Where	0.70
What	0.80
Why	0.00

Again, despite some differences between the two children in the *how/where/what* types, both are alike in their poor performance on *why*. What could explain the difference between this question-type and the others?

Although we do not have access to Labov's data, a more detailed examination of the basis for these figures reveals that the difference is to a considerable degree an artefact of the analytical procedure adopted. Following Labov, interrogatives used by Sophie in the December sample (on which the figures immediately above are based) were counted as inverted if they contained a contracted copula. So these utterances are entered as successful inversions:

where's mummy
where's a mummy

in addition to utterances such as

how do you get that hat off
how do you open that
how do you get that out

To interpret *where's mummy* as transformationally derived seems unnecessarily complex (a conclusion at which Labov and Labov also eventually arrive (1978: 31)). If we exclude all wh-words that have auxiliaries contracted on to them from the inversion count, we have a set of figures that no longer isolates *why* questions:

How	0.75
Where	0.00
What	0.00
Why	0.00

If we further note that *all* successful *how*-questions are of the form, how do you ([həʊdʒʊː]) + VP (see examples above) – that is, they consist of a formulaic initial phrase, plus a variable predicate – we are in a position to discount inversion, at this point, as a syntactic rule in Sophie's repertoire.[4]

This pattern continues, so that in the February sample we can again explain away apparent inversion as the result of analysing pre-subject copulas and the *do* in *how do you* ... as inverted forms. In this sample, *why*-questions continue to fail to show any auxiliary (for example, *why you throw Jossy's sponge away*. That there are severe limitations on the use of *do* by the child is also apparent from *where*-question examples like *where that go*, *where you found that*, which require forms of *do*, but do not at this point get them. A new form which has appeared since the December sample is exemplified in *what are me sing*, *what are me singing*, where the *are* is represented by a short schwa vowel, [ə]. The lack of dependency between this and the main verb again suggests a strategy on the child's part of auxiliary insertion, rather than inversion. If we discount the *what are* sequences as well as the *how do*, then the proportion of inverted questions of any type falls to zero.

We should at this point mention for the first time the yes/no interrogatives. There are a large number of these – in the sample for 15.2.80, for example, roughly half of all interrogatives are of the *yes/no* type;[5] of these, almost all are *can*-initial:

can me cut in this side
can you put that in my hair
one day can our go park
can you help me do the piano, etc.

The only other *yes/no* type questions to appear are *have/has* initial:

have you got some paper
has you got some scissors

Such forms are successors to *is*-initial questions in earlier samples:

is you got some little letters

However, whereas the *has/have* type are used only with *got*, the earlier *is*-initials did appear occasionally with other verbs:

is me going a bed (January sample)

At this point *have/has* only appear initially, and not in pre-verbal position in declaratives with *got*.

To sum up the between-sample development of interrogatives as far as we have taken it, we find:

1. only a limited range of auxiliaries are available to the child;
2. different auxiliaries from this set are used with the *yes/no* type and the wh-interrogative type;
3. there is considerable context-specificity in the use of some auxiliaries: for example, *do* only occurs with *how*, and *has/have* with *got*;
4. there is considerable distributional asymmetry between pre-subject and pre-verbal position: the only auxiliary from pre-subject position to appear pre-verbally is *can*, and with very limited frequency; none of the other forms which we have discussed appear pre-verbally. On the other hand, there are a number of forms used pre-verbally, from the January sample on, which do not appear in pre-subject position (for example, *don't*, *didn't*, *should*, *could*).

All these points taken together suggest that, at least up to April, there is little evidence for considering the source of pre-subject auxiliaries to be inversion.

The very fact that the argument above eliminates the possibility of the *gradual* spread of inversion through wh-questions does, however, allow us to consider anew the possibility of across-the-board rule change in May/June. For if we examine sample 2, we find that practically all the questions now have pre-subject auxiliaries.[6] The change is perhaps most apparent in *why*-questions, where we have the following examples:

why did you post it through mummy
and why did her have two sweets
why did you put that in my room
why are you just dusting it
why do me have to

Other question types are also correct:

where are you mummy
what is that one called

This pattern has been apparent since the May sample. Does this mean that we can discuss Sophie's acquisition of the subject–auxiliary inversion rule, at the age of 2;11, even if, by comparison with the adult rule, it is a restricted one (in terms of the range of auxiliaries falling within its scope)? Evidence from the errors that exist in sample 2 alongside 'correct' instances, suggest that there are more plausible explanations.

The correct examples above in the *why*-questions seem to be appropriate cases of '*do*-support', in terms of position, tense (so far as we can tell) and where relevant subject-verb agreement. There is, however, crucial evidence against this view in the form of errors such as these:[7]

why did Hester be fast asleep
why did it been there

These are instances which, to be correct, would require a copula following the wh-word (*why was Hester fast asleep*, *why was it there*). These errors suggest, rather, that Sophie has a general strategy for asking *why*-questions which involves inserting the appropriate form of *do* between *why* and the subject (or alternatively prefacing a declarative sequence with *why* + the appropriate form of *do* – *did* for past and *do* for present). This works well in many instances, such as the 'correct' examples listed earlier: *why did* + *you post it through* results in an unexceptionable structure. *Why did* + *Hester be fast asleep*, however, though (if we are right) arrived at in exactly the same way, is an ungrammatical sequence (by adult standards). Once again, the errors a child makes are crucially revealing about the construction processes being used. In this case, *why*-questions which appear to have had subject–auxiliary inversion operated on them can be plausibly accounted for by formation rules which do not require the movement of constituents.[8]

What of other types of interrogatives, though? The argument cannot be made so clearly, as there is not a comparable contrast between 'correct' and 'incorrect' instances. There are, however, examples like *why have it got flowers on*, where the lack of dependency between subject and verb might allow one to argue for a similar construction to the *why*-do examples, of *why have* + *it got flowers on*. Even where the auxiliary–subject dependency is appropriate, in *why are you just dusting it*, there is no reason why the construction should not result from the prefixing of *you dusting it* with *why are*. The fact that declaratives with progressive inflections on the verb do not contain *be* auxiliaries, at this juncture, is some support for this assumption.[9]

One other interesting error, which underlines neatly the earlier points we made about the care with which transcriptions need to be treated and also confirms that there are gaps in Sophie's analysis of auxiliaries and copulas in interrogatives, comes in the two utterances at l. 288 and l. 289. In both of these, Sophie's [huːz] at the beginning of each utterance has been left as a phonetic transcription. This could have been represented in the orthography as either *who's* or *whose*. It is possible to argue that at l. 288 (because of the preposition) the word would reasonably be transcribed as *who's*, whereas at l. 289 it might be (again, because of the sense) *whose*. But that would be to miss the point, which is that the homonymy of *who's* and *whose* in input is contributing to the difficulty Sophie has at this time in analysing the auxiliary/copula system.

Complex sentences

It is clear, comparing samples 1 and 2, that the presence of auxiliaries in sample 2 utterances is one of the factors contributing to the second sample's increased average length of utterances. A further factor is the appearance in sample 2 of what look like complex sentences. Following Bowerman (1979), we will consider as complex those sentences which have two (surface) clauses. The major distinction under this heading is that between coordination and embedding, or subordination. In the first type of complex sentence, two independent clauses are coordinated[10] by (most often) *and*, *but*, *or*. In embedded sentences, one clause serves as a constituent in another clause. So, for example, an embedded clause may fill an object slot in a matrix clause, e.g. John expected *Bill to leave*; or an adverbial slot, e.g. Bill put the money *where Mary had said*. Clauses can also be embedded in subject or indirect object position, although these are much less common in the kind of data we are considering. There is a further kind of embedding in which the subordinate clause does not fill a clause constituent slot, but rather modifies an NP, which is a constituent of the matrix: We saw the girl *that knows Mary*. The italicized clause here modifies *girl*, the object of the matrix clause, and is referred to as a relative clause.

These devices of coordination and embedding are important features of the language. They are potentially *recursive* operations: they can be used more than once to build sentences of greater and greater complexity, for example:

> the man who was mentioned finished his drink and walked to the car
> that was being watched.

Here each clause of the coordination has a relative clause embedded in it. Learning how to use coordination and embedding will be an important part of the child's progress towards mastery of the language. On the LARSP chart, complex sentences which occur in a sample are located at stage V: *coord* and *subord* (with various subcategories) cover coordinations and those embeddings where the embedded clause is a clause constituent of the matrix; relative clauses are entered under the heading 'Postmod. clause'. A glance at the LARSP chart for sample 1 reveals no entries at stage V; in sample 2, however, there are entries for both coordination and subordination (though not for relative clauses). We should now look at these (and their antecedents in intermediate samples) to determine their characteristics and, so far as possible, constructional status. If these sentences represent the beginnings of recursion for the child, this is a major advance in language-learning. As we have tried to argue with the interrogatives, however, advances may be made that are either idiosyncratic to the individual child or by routes other than those available to adults.

The number of putative complex setences is small, and we can begin by simply listing those that occur first in the LARSP sample. The paucity of examples is not unexpected. In Paul (1981) it is estimated that the proportion of complex sentences for a child at Sophie's language level will be between 1 per cent and 10 per cent.[11]

Coordination
that is Mr Happy and that is Mr Happy
one is big and one is small
Subordination
me going to watch you doing your riding lesson
me don't know where box is now
why did you give to her when her been flu

Elsewhere in the sample we find:

Coordination
once our came back from somewhere/and me found it there mummy

These represent a rather small proportion of the sample, but nevertheless do resemble complex-sentence constructions found in adult language. The coordinations are error-free; the subordinations have errors in them of pronominal choice, determiner omission, inappropriate verb form etc., but these are intra-clause (and arguably paradigmatic) problems which do not appear to affect the embeddings – if indeed this is the appropriate term to use.

The coordinated sentences in this sample represent the simplest kind of coordination, meeting exactly the definition above, of two independent clauses linked by *and*. Like all such short definitions, this is heavily oversimplified for the language as a whole, even though it suffices for the Sophie data in this sample. It excludes phrasal coordination, as in *he given one to Hester and two to us*, and clausal coordinations with ellipses in the second clause, i.e. omitted items that can only be understood by reference to the first. Such sentences (e.g. *Sophie will go to the cupboard and get a toy*, with a missing subject in the second clause) do not occur at this point in Sophie's development. They are, however, part of the adult speaker's competence, so we expect them to emerge eventually.[12]

Of course the structural possibilities for reduction or gapping in coordinations are dependent on contextual constraints. On the reasonable assumption that *Mr Happy* is used in *That is Mr Happy and that is Mr Happy*, to refer to two different pieces in the puzzle Sophie is playing with, no reduction is possible, though a more mature version of the second clause would have been *and so is that*. In her other coordination it would have been allowable for her to 'gap' the second clause and produce *one is big and one small*. So far as it is possible to tell from other studies, however, Sophie's coordinations are consistent with other children of her language level (as measured by MLU). Paul (ibid.) indicates that children with an MLU between 3.51 and 4.00 are most likely to use coordinations of the two independent clause type, with no reduction in the second clause. Lust and Mervis (1980), in their study of the development of coordination in natural speech, also report independent clause coordination for children at Sophie's developmental level, with no reduction even where it is contextually allowed, e.g. *they get a ball and they catch*.

For subordination also, although Sophie presents us with little data to go on, the structures are consistent with other studies. Limber (1973: 172) reports that the early subordinations occur as complements to a limited set of verbs - for example, *think*, *know*, *remember* - and that the earliest subordinators to appear are *where*, *when*. These can appear around 2;6, he reports. Similar findings are reported by Paul (1981). The children with an MLU range of 3.5-4.00, in her sample, are highly likely to produce sentences containing 'full propositional complements' (for example, Sophie's *me watch you doing your riding lesson*, *me don't know where box is now*). These tend to be linked to specific verbs, however.

Both coordination and subordination are thus strictly limited in sample 2. Coordination at this point shows none of the reduction or gapping refinements that are available to the adult. And in comparison with possible subordination types, the examples on show here are highly restricted. If we examine other samples around the same time, and look back over recent samples, it is clear that sample 2 is representative of Sophie's abilities. It is true that we can find an apparently coordinated clause as far back as 19 February, but the wrong conjunction used - or, at least, it is not clear what Sophie is intending to say: *you sit on that chair so you drink your coffee*. An early 'subordination' is *me can't where my room is*, glossed by her mother as *you can't remember*. In the same sample, however, we find also *me said all the black ones here*. But in the samples that precede sample 2, complex sentences of either general type are rare and, when they do appear, are not dissimilar to the examples listed for sample 2.

Phrase types

Apart from the appearances of auxiliary + verb phrases, which we shall discuss below under the heading of *verb-forms*, phrases are notable in this sample for greater length than in sample 1, and for representing a wider range of noun and prepositional phrases. In particular, phrases in the LARSP sample contain adjectives, or at least items which have an adjectival function in noun phrases. The items used fall into three groups: (a) common collocations, which are perhaps over-analysed by being assigned an *Adj* label: *riding* in *riding lesson*, *tummy* in *tummy ache*; (b) numerals and ordinals: *two* in *two sweets*, *other* in *other bit*; (c) 'lexical' adjectives: *big*, *huge*, *small*, *floppy*, *sloppy*, *runny*. Outside the LARSP sample we find a similar picture, except that examples under (c) have to be extended to include colour terms – *pink*, *red*, *green*. The most important function of the adjectives included under (c) for Sophie is to identify a referent. There is nothing in this sample to contradict the claim made by Nelson (1976). In a study of spontaneous speech samples, in which the oldest children are aged 2;6, she finds that children use 'descriptive properties of size and colour' most commonly for identifying referents.[13]

Although there is evidence in this sample of increased use by Sophie of noun pre-modification for referent identification (by specifying more precisely the extension of the head noun of a noun phrase), there is little evidence yet of any phrasal post-modification. For identifying what she is talking about, in the rather restricted contexts in which discussion is taking place, the rather limited NP structures she has available appear to serve her satisfactorily.

Valency analysis

The 50-utterance sample that provides the valency analysis was intended to begin at Sophie's 51st utterance, that is, the same place as the MLU analysis and the LARSP analysis. However, because this valency analysis requires lexical verbs, the sample turned out not to be coextensive with the LARSP utterance set. (To overlap at all with the LARSP set, we had to begin at l. 176). Once again, the 50 verb tokens in the sample represent 19 verb types. At least for this six-month period, then, greater verb-type differentiation is not a relevant developmental parameter. Only nine verbs in this second sample were represented in the valency analysis for the first, although this seems more likely to be the result of a sampling accident than any dramatic change in the number of verbs available.

Arguments

A simple count of the number of arguments per verb (token) between sample 1 and sample 2 provides figures of 1.58 for the former, as against 2.48. So in general there are more arguments per verb. To identify more precisely where the differences lie, it may be illuminating first to consider those verb types that are common to both samples. There are nine verbs that appear in both valency analyses: COME, FIND, GET, GIVE, GOT, HELP, LIKE, PUT, TAKE, WANT. A comparison of the frames in which they fall shows that it is the inclusion of adverbial elements which distinguishes the sets of arguments in the two samples (excluding PUT, where obligatory adverbials were already present in sample 1). Extending beyond the verbs common to the two samples, we find that 25 frames include adverbials (including WH-forms) in sample 2, as against 15 in sample 1. What kinds of adverbials are represented? Although the majority are locative as previously (either deictics like *here*, *there*, single adverbial particles like *in*, *on*, or prepositional phrases like *on my legs*, *to the teacher*), there are also temporal adverbials (either single items like *now*, *again*, or a clause - *when her been flu*); manner adverbials (for example, *good*, *best*); and one occurrence in *me helped Zelda with her ta thing*, of an adverbial as an argument complementing the verb (see Quirk et al. 1972: 331). This last example is a useful one for considering the role that these adverbials are playing for Sophie in her extended verb frames.[14] The phrase *with her ta thing* (i.e. with her guitar) is not grammatically obligatory, but it is informative for the hearer in a way that *me helped Zelda* is not. The range of adverbials that now appear, particularly where they are realized as prepositional phrases, provides a specification of time of action, or person, place or object relevant to the activity, more systematically (or at least more frequently) than was the case in sample 1. (See below, p. 168, for a more detailed discussion of the use of adverbials.)

Realization

It is perhaps surprising, first of all, to see again how limited the range of subject realization is in this data. Once again, the vast majority are personal pronouns, with the occasional other pronominal form or proper name. (In general, this is also the pattern of Sophie's mother's subject realizations.) These do include, in addition, however, a number of existential *there* forms, for example, l. 169: *there's a bit of red there sweetheart*, and occasional noun phrases, l. 255: *two Mister Happys are there*.) Of the 41 S elements in the valency sample, 39 are realized by personal pronouns, three by other proforms (*this*, *what*), one by a proper name (*Daddy*), and there are three NPs - *that bit*, *which one* and *these pictures*. The distribution of subject realizations is thus very similar to the first sample, except for the noun phrases, which may mark the beginning of a greater diversity of subject structures.

As before, objects show more diversity in structural realization. Of the 29 objects, eleven are pronominals and five consist of a single lexical noun or adjective. The remainder are phrases or clauses. The noun phrases have a variety of lexical heads, and some of them contain adjectivals in addition to determiners. The now more frequent adverbial elements also show a range of realizations, with approximately 50 per cent of these elements represented by phrases or clauses. With the now common appearance of auxiliaries with verbs (not shown in the valency analysis, but clear from the LARSP analysis), it is clear that a major difference between sample 1 and sample 2 is the elaboration of phrase structure in the realizations of clause elements. For pragmatic reasons this is less marked in subject position, but the effect of this advance in the child's abilities is noticeable in the other clause elements.

Deixis

There is in this sample what looks like evidence of a deictic contrast between *this/that*, at ll. 203/4:

S. it doesn't 'go that wày/
go thìs way/

Sophie uses *this* contrastively, with tonic placement, to accompany her action in changing the orientation of a puzzle piece her mother had put down. Although in sample 1 the available data indicated that *that* was used deictically, there was no evidence of a contrast between *this* and *that* in terms of their spatial functions. Even in the sample 2 example, however, although there is a contrast, it is not entirely clear that the basis for it is spatial. The experimental work in this area (see Wales 1985 for an excellent review) has assumed a proximal-to-speaker (*this*) versus not-proximal-to-speaker (*that*) basis for the difference in meaning between the two forms. It could be that Sophie here contrasts *this* as a speaker-oriented form (*my* version of the puzzle placement) versus a non-speaker-oriented form (*your* attempt at it – *that*), but it seems unlikely, from the sense of the exchange and from what we know of the context, that there is at this point a clearly spatial contrast. Experimental work has of necessity concentrated on the proximal/distal contrast, in order to have a viable basis for interpreting children's behavioural responses to verbal stimuli containing deictic forms. The experimental situation has to be clear-cut and controlled. So in the simplest situation,[15] the child and the experimenter sit at one side of a table which has two identical toys on, one close to and one further away. The experimenter says to the child, for example, 'make this dog jump', without any accompanying gesture. In the study reported in Wales (1985), this task and variations on it were presented to children of 4, 5, 6 and 7 years of age. What is most striking about the results from the experiment is that 20 per cent of all subjects across this age-range showed no evidence of understanding the contrast, and another 56 per cent showed only partial understanding. Only approximately 24 per cent had control of the deictic contrast. In general, older children did better than younger ones. How do we explain the discrepancy, between 3-year-old Sophie's contrastive use of *this* and *that*, and the much later acquisition that seems to be suggested by the experimental studies?

There are several possibilities. First, the discrepancy may only be apparent. The example, which appears to demonstrate the contrast, links *this* and *that* with *way*. In the context of doing jigsaw puzzles, it is possible that Sophie has learned just these collocations (*this way*, *that way*) as contrastive phrases which are used in this context, but not elsewhere, and are understood only in terms of the manipulation of puzzle pieces. In support of this idea we find *this way*, with tonic on *this*, used again at l. 427. But we also find *this corner*, used in a similar puzzle context, at l. 15, in response to the question *which corner goes there d'you think*. That Sophie's use of the contrast is not lexically restricted is finally demonstrated at ll. 247 ff., where she and Fran discuss the identification of puzzle pieces:

S. what thìs one 'called/
S. I don't knòw/
Mr Hàppy/
S. nò/
côs look/
'that is Mr Hàppy/

Another possibility to explain the developmental gap between spontaneous use of a *this/that* contrast, and evidence of comprehension of the contrast, may arise from the fact that, whereas in the experimental situation gestures are avoided, for obvious reasons, use of deictics by the mother are usually accompanied by gesture. We have no record of gestures in relation to conversations between Fran and Sophie, but Wales (1985) reports the results of an analysis of videotapes of mother-child interactions, in which the co-occurrence of deictic terms and gestures was noted. Nearly 80 per cent of the deictic terms were accompanied by gesture - though it should be emphasized that this term covers not only pointing to a reference object, but also 'handling' it - holding it, picking it up, putting it down.[16] Since this is the case, we might surmise that the *this/that* contrast is only possible for 3-year-olds in spontaneous speech with gestural support; until the child learns to disassociate the verbal stimuli from the contextual support provided by the mother's pointing or handling, he will perform poorly in an experimental situation where such support is necessarily excluded.

There is a further possibility, however: that the idea that the proximal/distal contrast is basic to distinguishing *this/that* in conversations with young children is incorrect. Since we do not have a videotaped record of the conversations from which our samples are drawn, we cannot argue this on the basis of firm evidence. In the examples we have so far considered, however, it is not clear that there is always a perceptible proximal/distal (or close-to-speaker/close-to-addressee) distinction for the use of the terms. As already suggested, in *this way* Sophie is merely contrasting her orientation of the puzzle piece with her mother's. It is quite conceivable that no shift in location of the puzzle piece relative to the positions of Sophie and her mother takes place at all. Again, in the extract following l. 247, there is no necessary reason for the first-mentioned Mr Happy to be near Sophie (and referred to by *this*), while the second one (referred to by *that*) is near Fran. The reverse could be the case. There seems no reason in either of these instances for a spatial interpretation of the contrastive *this*/*that* use. It would be quite in order with the data available to interpret the contrastiveness of the items in discourse terms, while still of course maintaining that *this* and *that* as used by Sophie are deictic outside of the discourse. *This* or *that* used contrastively would then simply mean 'this other one' by comparison with the item previously mentioned. Given the possible spatial orientations of referents to which *this* and *that* can be applied in mother–child conversations, in addition to the non-static locations of the two (or more) participants, this seems a more satisfying explanation of the developmental discrepancy between experimental *this*/*that* comprehension and its spontaneous use. Whether in fact *this*/*that* deixis is as spatially variable as we have suggested depends on detailed videotape analysis of mother–child conversation.

Personal pronouns

Me (mainly in subject position) and *you* are still, in sample 2, the most commonly used personal pronouns. Since the sample consists for the most part of a conversation between Sophie and her mother, this is not surprising. The list of pronouns used, however, has now grown to include third-person singular pronouns *he*, *she*, *her* and *it*, and plural pronouns *us*, *they* and *them*. The order in which pronouns have appeared in the Sophie data thus corresponds to the findings of other naturalistic studies (see Chiat 1985 for a review). The first- and second-person pronouns are earlier than the others (with the first-person form sometimes ahead of the second). Chiat, however, found that the emergence of the remainder of the pronoun set was not predictable, either in terms of order of emergence or speed of development: *he*, *she*, *we* and *they* are not ordered with respect to one another in a clear-cut fashion, and in some children second- and third-person pronouns appear at almost the same time, whereas in others there may be a gap of up to six months. All the studies on naturalistic data agree, however, that the pronouns are an early acquisition. By about the age of 3, a number of pronouns are widely used in children's speech.

In relation to Sophie's use of these items, it is the third-person forms, new in sample 2, that require our attention. She now appears to be able to refer to non-participants in a conversation using pronominal forms, whereas in sample 1, as we noted, she took advantage of other possibilities allowed by the language for non-speaker, non-addressee reference, by using proper names. As Chiat (1985) points out, reference by the participants in a conversation to each other must (except in very unusual circumstances) be pronominal. For non-participants, any noun phrase is structurally possible, although whether the NP selected is a full NP (*the man you saw at the weekend*) or a proper name or a pronoun depends on the linguistic and extralinguistic context. The most frequently used third-person pronoun in sample 2 is *it*.

It is used in both S and O positions, but more usually in O. As we have seen, most of the pronouns in S position are either first or second person. Tokens of *it* are used in three distinct ways. First, Sophie uses *it* non-specifically to refer to a completed action, for example, l. 112 ff.:

F. there we are
S. did it

where Sophie is talking about her completion of part of the jigsaw. Secondly, *it* is used exophorically to refer to an object not previously mentioned in the discourse, but present in the extralinguistic context (l. 150):

S. why did you post it through mummy

Here Sophie has noticed her mother putting a puzzle piece through a slit in the side of a box, and uses *it* to refer to the piece. The third use of *it* that we can identify is what appears to be an anaphoric usage at ll. 100 ff.:

F. where's the rest of the block
S. me will put it in
no
can me put it in like that

The two tokens of *it* both refer back to the block Fran mentions; this could be argued to be intralinguistic reference. As Karmiloff-Smith (1980) has pointed out, such reference is still supported by the presence, extralinguistically, of the object referred to, and so cannot be interpreted unequivocally as anaphoric reference.[17]

Although case errors (*me* for *I*, *her* for *she*) are still common in this sample, neither number nor gender errors are made. There are no instances of singular pronouns for plural referents, or vice versa. Among the third-person singular pronouns, *he*, *her* and *it* are appropriately applied to males, females and objects. The persistence of the case errors is well illustrated at ll. 188 ff., where for once Sophie uses *she*, the appropriate pronoun, in subject position, when a model is provided by her mother:

F. what's she say
S. she's got a runny tummy

A couple of minutes later, however, when Sophie refers to Hester again, she reverts to *her* in subject position (l. 197):

S. why did her have a runny tummy

As Tanz (1974) points out, the direction of error for case-marking in pronouns is almost always the same, objective for nominative. Why should this be so? Tanz explains the general finding by invoking an operating principle first proposed by Slobin (1973), the child's avoidance of exceptions (cf. also Kaper 1976). In English, the objective form of the pronouns marked for case occurs in a much wider range of contexts than the nominative form. The nominative form appears only in subject position, whereas the objective appears as indirect and direct object, following prepositions, as complement of *be*, and when a pronoun occurs in isolation as a response to a question. The widespread distribution of *me*, for example, compared to *I*, would then lead the child operating the 'avoid exceptions' principle to take *me* as basic and *I* as the exception. The problem with the explanation so far as Sophie is concerned is of course that it seems to work for *me* and *her*, but not for *he*. Sophie does not use *him* at all, but uses *he* on half a dozen occasions. Most of the occurrences come in the sequence from l. 388 on, where *he* is used four times in subject position. It is possible of course that the case-marking problem is being solved one item at a time, and that the masculine third-person pronoun is the first to be mastered. The issue may become clearer when we consider the period between now and sample 3.[18]

The other third-person pronouns, particularly *her*, show both pseudo-anaphoric and anaphoric usage. The sequence at ll. 188 ff., quoted above, could be argued to be similar to the use of *it* at ll. 100 ff. Both Sophie and her mother use *she* to refer to Hester; Sophie's *she* could be said to be anaphoric to Fran's use of *she*, but both are exophoric to Hester in another part of the house. At ll. 306 ff., however, it is difficult to see Sophie's *her* in *why did her have two sweets mummy* as anything other than anaphoric to the first mention of Hester in l. 306. This anaphoric use of pronouns is certainly limited, but it does seem to represent an advance on the first sample.

Articles

The first comment to be made on the articles *the* and *a* is that they are infrequent compared to other determiners (*this*, *that*, *my* etc.). There are five instances of *a*, all appropriate (for example, *me got a tummy ache*, *a huge puzzle*, *that a top*), four clear instances of *the*, which are also correct, and one case of omission of *the* (l. 332), *me don't know where box is now*. There are also three instances of [ə] being used in positions which require *the*:

l. 572 me like [ə] little one best
l. 578 [ə] big one or [ə] little one

All this seems to add up to a rather rudimentary knowledge of the article system. Although the indefinite article is used for non-specific reference in this sample, it is not entirely clear that the definite article is being used for specific reference other than in the 'larger situation' usage described by

Hawkins (1978) (see also Scott-Goldman 1983: 196 ff.). The term indicates that the referent to which *the* is attached is made specific in terms of knowledge shared between speaker and hearer. This knowledge can be shared by virtue of membership of the same family or some more extensive group. Both Sophie and Fran know the school she attends and the people in it, so the choice of *the* with teacher is appropriate. However, there is no evidence that the use of *the* in *the teacher* is a matter of choice for Sophie, rather than a repetition of a frequently heard collocation. Similarly, in *the clothes*, the choice of article here is much more likely to be a result of the frequency with which she has heard the two items used together than the result of selection of a definite article on her part. It is interesting to note that in those cases where *the* and *a* are equally likely in ll. 572 and 578, it is unclear which of the articles she intends, since all that can be heard is a schwa vowel in each of the relevant positions. Of course, since in cases like *a huge puzzle*, [ə] has been transcribed as *a*, perhaps we should conclude that here we have mistaken use of indefinite articles by Sophie. The contexts require specific reference, and she has used non-specifics inappropriately. Since at ll. 497, 505 and 558 it is possible to hear the interdental in [ðə], this would certainly be a plausible analysis. The truth is that we do not have enough data to decide whether she does appreciate the difference between specific and non-specific reference using determiners, but the balance of probabilities is that she does not. Her awareness of the functions of the articles is still sketchy, and indeed her use of them is limited.

Verb-forms

Perhaps the most notable development, in the months since the first sample, has been the appearance of verb inflections, modal auxiliaries and *do*-support. The inflections Sophie has used are *-ed*, *-en*, *-ing* and present tense *-s*; the modals are *will*, *can* and *shall*; and the most frequently used auxiliary has been *do*. The syntactic and semantic importance of these forms cannot be overemphasized for the child's developing language. The inflections (along with auxiliaries, where relevant) code tense and aspect in English; modals generally enable the speaker 'to either qualify the propositions expressed by his sentences with respect to their validity, truth or factuality . . . or to indicate obligation and permission' (Stephany 1985); the *do* auxiliary is used in questions and negatives to carry present and past-tense marking. Clearly by this point Sophie has only begun to acquire the temporal and modal markings that English makes use of, but the set she has developed bear closer examination. We will deal with the temporal markers, those for tense and aspect, together (including *do*), and will then turn to a separate consideration of modal auxiliaries.

Temporal forms

We have already anticipated some of this discussion in chapter 1 (see pp. 21-7 above). There are, however, still a number of questions to be addressed, including:

(a) Apart from irregular pasts, the initial marking used for past was *-ed*; thereafter Sophie developed and used the *-en* overgeneralization we noted in chapter 1. The *-ed* regular markings and *-ed* overgeneralizations were, however, used alongside *-en* forms, from the time when these first appeared. Is it possible to see any reason why this should be the case?

(b) The assumption explicit in the first question is that *-en* and *-ed* forms have the same function in Sophie's language at this point. We have already discussed this in chapter 1, but we will return to the issue here, and in addition ask more generally whether the inflections are being used deictically, to code past, or whether they are aspectual markers. A number of investigators (for example, Antinucci and Miller 1976; Bloom, Lifter and Hafitz 1980; Bronckart and Sinclair 1973) have suggested that early past-tense morphology does not have its usual deictic function of relating a past event to the time of speaking, but instead is being used aspectually to indicate completion. This idea (reviewed by Weist (1985a) under the heading of the 'defective tense hypothesis') has relevance not only for language development *per se*, but also for its conceptual underpinnings.

(c) The appearance of *do*, a semantically empty auxiliary, as a carrier of tense in Sophie's speech, suggests that she is beginning to learn the important syntactic role of auxiliaries in English for interrogative and negative sentences. When did *do*-support begin, and how general is the distribution of forms of *do* in her language at sample 2?

(d) What are the modal auxiliaries she uses, what are their meanings, and can we explain why these items appear first in her development? Does she use items other than auxiliaries (*have to*, *have got to*) with modal meaning?

Progressive. The earliest inflection to appear, as reported for virtually all other English-speaking children (see Brown 1973; Kuczaj 1978), is *-ing*. On the 27.11.79, less than two weeks after sample 1, five verbs – *iron*, *step*, *climb*, *touch* and *fall down* – are used with *-ing* suffixes, in the following utterances:

me ironing that	(describing what Sophie herself is doing)

you stepping mon my satchel	(said to her friend Mary when she stood on the satchel)
Jack climbing mon up there	(said to her mother as Jack climbs on to a cupboard)
Jack touching my hair	(as Jack brushes her hair)
That horsie falling down	(with reference to some toy horses Fran and Sophie are playing with)

The contexts suggest that Sophie is using the *-ing* (at this point without any auxiliary) appropriately to indicate a process, an activity that is in train at the time of speaking. The only exception to this might be *falling down*, in reference to the horse. Once again, this is a circumstance where we would like to have a visual record of the conversational context: we do not know whether the horse was about to fall, or was actually falling, when Sophie said what she did. As it happens, the English progressive can accommodate either of these meanings; with a verb like *fall*, the former (the 'being about to' meaning) is most likely in domestic contexts, as objects that fall tend to do so relatively quickly.

Apart from its early appearance (which is put down to its phonological salience and semantic transparency),[19] the other much remarked feature of children's use of progressive inflections is their non-application of the suffix to inappropriate verbs. There is a group of verbs in English which tend not to take the progressive. The group includes such common verbs as *want*, *know*, *love*, *hate*, *like*, *hear*, *see*;[20] all these verbs may be interpreted as referring to 'states' which are in themselves continuative; one might suppose that the use of the progressive with them is generally redundant. Both Brown (1973) and Kuczaj (1978) observed that children apparently recognize the existence of a distinction between stative and non-stative verbs, because they do not overextend the *-ing* suffix to the stative type. As often is the case with statements about what children do or do not say, it is as well to treat this generalization with caution. On 13.12.79 this conversation took place between Sophie and Fran:

F. what will you give daddy for his Christmas present
S. me not knowing
me not knowing
F. you don't know

This looks as though it is exactly the kind of overextension that Brown and Kuczaj are unable to find in their data. It has to be said that these are the only examples in our data of the inappropriate use of *-ing*, but they nevertheless suggest that Sophie may not have classified verbs into those that allow a 'temporary duration' meaning (and so can have an *-ing* suffix) and those that do not (like *know*), at least at the age of 2;6.

-en and -ed. The first *-ed* suffix other than on *called*[21] appears on 1.12.79, in *Hessy cried party*. This was a reference to a time earlier on the same day

when Hester had cried on arriving at a friend's party. This was not of course the first time that Sophie had referred to a past event, and we should at this point make clear a difference we intend to maintain between 'tense' as a formal marker and 'temporal reference'. Children do refer to past time with bare verb stems, without any inflectional marking. At 1.279 of sample 1, Sophie says *Muffy step on that* of an event that we know happened three days previously. Sachs (1983) has discussed the appearance of what she calls 'temporal displacement' – the child's discussion of events outside the immediate context of the conversation engaged in – and indicated an age of about 32 months for its emergence in the child she was studying. Sophie seems to have done this slightly earlier, but initially with no past-tense marking. The other reason for distinguishing between tense marking and temporal reference comes from the 'aspectual hypothesis' (another term for Weist's defective-tense hypothesis), which claims that early *-ed* markings code for completion, for example, rather than simply locating the action described in the verb as past relative to the time of speaking. There are a number of strands to this argument, which need to be disentangled at the start. First, application of *-ed* suffixes is initially variable in children. They do not move from no use of the suffix, to use in all obligatory contexts, overnight. There will thus be, midway through the period of acquisition, for example, some past events which are marked by an *-ed* suffix on the verb, and some which are not. Second, the majority of past-time references by children are to the immediate past – to events which have happened very close in time to the time of speaking. These two facts are linked by the most influential proponents of the aspectual hypothesis (Antinucci and Miller 1976) into a plausible hypothesis: up to the age of about 2;6, children, because they lack an abstract conception of time, will only use *-ed* forms when (recently) prior situations involve a change of state, the effects of which remain physically present at the time of speaking. The test of this hypothesis depends on a semantic classification of verbs. We have already referred to the stative-dynamic distinction with reference to the progressive. The dynamic class can be further broken down into activity (or atelic) verbs like *cry*, *sing*, *run*, *swim*, and telic verbs (describing actions with an end-point), which can themselves be subcategorized into achievement and accomplishment verbs. The former includes *find*, *lose*, *reach*, and the latter such verbs as *paint*, *draw*, *make*. Weist (1985a) says of the distinction here: 'with achievement verbs the process is bound to the terminal point ... while the process leading to the terminal point of an accomplishment verb can be intermittent'.[22] The classification allows us to go to the data and ask, with reference to the Antinucci-Miller hypothesis, whether or not past tense is marked on children's verbs randomly with respect to semantic classes of verbs. If they are correct about young children's inability to conceptualize the relationship between remote events and the present, then the past tenses that are marked should be restricted to telic verbs that refer to recent events. Antinucci and Miller dealt with the language of children up to 2;6; the age-range of the 'aspectual hypothesis', however, has been greatly extended by experimental work such as that of Bronckart and Sinclair (1973), which suggests that children up to the age of 6 may concentrate, when assigning tense, on the character of an action, rather than when it took place.

Against this background, we can now look in a little more detail at Sophie's *-ed* and *-en* suffixes. We have already indicated our view in chapter 1 that both *-en* and *-ed* are past-tense suffixes on the basis of the range of temporal reference they have in common. We will now look at the case in more detail. Table 4.1 lists the set of *-en* forms (regular and overgeneralized) that Sophie used both between samples 1 and 2 and beyond. Table 4.2 lists the set of *-ed* forms, regular and overgeneralized, for the same time period.

The overgeneralization of *-en* forms is rarely reported for children learning English. There is one account, for a child learning American English (Zwicky 1970), where the forms produced seem similar to Sophie's. Unlike hers, though, they appeared between the fourth and fifth birthdays. The US child, Elizabeth, produced regular *-en* forms, and overextended them, much as Sophie did, but with one exception. A comparison of their *-en* forms, in table 4.3, shows that Sophie differed from Elizabeth in marking regular verbs with *-en* (for example, *touchen*). The other categories are (1) correct *-en* forms; (2) irregular verbs, *-en* marked on present stem; (3) irregular verbs, *-en* marked on past stem.[23]

It is not clear from Zwicky's account whether Elizabeth always, or intermittently, used auxiliaries with her *-en* forms; Sophie, in the period we are considering, did not use them at all. One possible interpretation of the *-en* forms would be that they are precursors of present perfect in the child's speech, just as *-ing* forms without an auxiliary are taken to be precursors of the present progressive. If this was the case, we would expect that the demise of *-en* forms occurring alone is followed by the rise of *have + en* forms; as we shall see when considering sample 3, this is not the case.[24] The *-en* over-regularizations die out before the end of 1980, in Sophie's speech, but they are not succeeded by *have + -en* forms. For a long time, *have* auxiliaries only occur in Sophie's speech with *got*. We would also expect to be able to discern a difference in the functional range of *-en* and *-ed* forms. If the child is going to the trouble to distinguish past and present perfect formally, we would expect there to be some distinction in use. In particular, we might expect *-en* to be restricted to recent events, whereas *-ed* (or indeed past forms generally) were used to refer across a wide range of prior events.[25] Table 4.4 shows the distribution of all past forms (regular and irregular) and all *-en* forms, for part of the period between samples 1 and 2. (For an explanation of the categories, refer to table 1.2 in chapter 1 – p. 22.) It is clear from this that, although the number of past forms is much greater than that of *-en* forms, and although IMM (events that occurred up to 5 minutes before the time of speaking) is the most frequent time reference for both past and *-en*

TABLE 4.1 *Sophie's regular and overgeneralized* -en *forms, 2;5–3;5*

Date	*Form*	*Fre-quency*	*Date*	*Form*	*Fre-quency*	*Date*	*Form*	*Fre-quency*
4.12	broken	8	17.3	letten	1	21.5	fallen	1
10.12	fallen	1	17.3	runnen	2	21.5	eaten	1
10.12	broken	4	17.3	wasen	2	21.5	hiden	1
28.12	taken	1	17.3	putten	1	21.5	walken	1
28.12	broken	1	20.3	touchen	1	27.5	given	1
2.1	broken	4	20.3	putten	2	27.5	buyen	1
17.1	putten	1	20.3	haden	1	29.5	closen	1
2.2	fallen	1	20.3	getten	1	29.5	boughten	1
2.2	putten	1	20.3	see-en	1	29.5	maken	1
12.2	given	1	20.3	rocken	1	29.5	putten	1
12.2	taken	1	24.3	fallen	1	29.5	playen	1
15.2	boughten	1	24.3	broken	2	14.6	taken	1
15.2	builden	1	24.3	given	3	14.6	seen	1
19.2	eaten	1	24.3	maken	1	14.6	putten	1
19.2	riden	1	24.3	putten	2	18.6	fallen	1
24.2	taken	1	24.3	helpen	1	19.6	getten	2
24.2	getten	3	24.3	spoilen	1	19.6	haden	2
26.2	given	1	31.3	taken	1	21.6	given	1
26.2	cutten	1	31.1	maden	1	21.6	bitten	1
26.2	maden	1	31.1	maken	2	4.7	haden	1
29.2	wanten	1	31.3	tippen	1	4.7	wearen	1
29.2	touchen	2	31.3	haven	1	13.7	haden	1
4.3	taken	1	17.4	haden	3	14.7	broken	1
4.3	putten	1	18.4	taken	1	14.7	leaven	1
4.3	haden	1	5.5	haden	1	14.7	haden	1
4.3	stepen	1	5.5	sitten	1	20.7	liken	1
4.3	hurten	1	5.5	?caven	1	20.7	haden	2
6.3	leaven	1	5.5	grown	1	20.7	known	1
6.3	putten	1	8.5	given	6	7.8	seen	1
10.3	putten	1	8.5	haden	1	7.8	stayen	1
10.3	bringen	1	8.5	sitten	2	7.8	haden	1
10.3	comen	1	8.5	letten	1	26.8	haden	1
10.3	drawnen	1	8.5	wrappen	1	11.9	haden	1
11.3	hitten	3	8.5	putten	1	12.9	given	1
11.3	maden	1	8.5	shoulden	1	27.9	haden	1
11.3	putten	1	13.5	haden	2	2.10	haden	1
11.3	getten	2	18.5	haven	2	2.10	given	2
11.3	taken	1	18.5	haden	1	2.10	seen	1
16.3	taken	1	21.5	given	1	14.10	haden	4
16.3	haden	1	21.5	seen	1	14.11	haden	1
17.3	waken	1	21.5	haden	1	2.12	forgotten	4

TABLE 4.2 Sophie's regular and overgeneralized -ed *forms, 2;5–3;5*

Date	*Form*	*Fre-quency*	*Date*	*Form*	*Fre-quency*	*Date*	*Form*	*Fre-quency*
4.12	lived	2	21.5	called	4	10.9	walked	1
4.12	called	1	21.5	finished	2	10.9	banged	1
11.2	called	1	29.5	called	1	10.9	telled	1
22.12	called	2	3.6	finished	1	11.9	called	1
23.12	wanted	1	6.6	locked	1	11.9	banged	1
24.12	called	1	6.6	seened	1	15.9	wanted	1
4.1	called	3	18.6	called	3	15.9	stayed	1
4.1	breaked	1	18.6	changed	2	18.9	flied	1
17.1	called	3	18.6	finished	1	20.9	jumped	1
19.1	called	1	19.6	called	1	20.9	popped	1
21.1	called	1	21.6	called	2	20.9	locked	1
2.2	called	1	21.6	helped	1	20.9	allowed	1
2.2	falled	1	27.6	mended	2	23.9	wanted	1
19.2	drinked	1	27.6	doed	2	27.9	wanted	1
29.2	called	1	4.7	dropped	2	2.10	maked	1
29.2	founded	1	4.7	used	1	14.10	taked	1
4.3	called	2	4.7	tried	1	1.11	whipped	1
6.3	called	1	4.7	called	6	1.11	changed	1
10.3	sawed	1	9.7	called	3	1.11	pushed	1
10.3	called	4	9.7	allowed	1	1.11	bringed	2
11.3	called	3	9.7	wanted	1	1.11	swinged	1
17.3	called	6	13.7	allowed	2	5.11	called	1
17.3	dropped	1	16.7	allowed	1	10.11	throwed	1
17.3	giggled	1	16.7	waked	1	14.11	spilled	1
20.3	called	1	2.8	allowed	1	14.11	squashed	1
20.3	finished	1	2.8	helped	1	14.11	finished	3
20.3	doed	1	7.8	lefted	1	20.11	called	1
24.3	called	1	7.8	falled	1	20.11	comed	1
1.4	called	2	20.8	called	1	26.11	moved	1
6.4	called	1	26.8	washed	1	26.11	looked	1
6.4	dripped	1	26.8	wanted	3	26.11	cooked	1
6.4	dropped	1	26.8	scratched	1	28.11	listened	1
18.4	called	1	26.8	teased	1	28.11	moved	1
18.4	sayed	1	3.9	(re)membered	1	28.11	wanted	1
8.5	called	1	3.9	wanted	1	28.11	squashed	1
13.5	called	4	3.9	blessed	1	2.12	supposed	1
13.5	finished	2	3.9	allowed	1	2.12	wanted	1
15.5	called	1						

TABLE 4.3 Examples of -en *forms used by Sophie and Elizabeth in four different categories*

		Sophie	*Elizabeth*
1	Correct	taken	given
2	Irregular, present stem	maken	baken
3	Irregular, past stem	maden	gaven
4	Regular	touchen	–

TABLE 4.4 Distribution of Sophie's -en *and Past forms in temporal reference categories, 31.3.80–3.6.80*

	IMM	*VREC*	*REC*	*PAST*	*REM*	*VREM*	*UNSPEC*
en	22	4	11	3	4	10	4
Past	41	9	26	9	9	5	12

TABLE 4.5 Examples of -ed *and* -en *marked verbs in aspectual classes*

	Stative	*Dynamic activity*	*Dynamic achievement*	*Dynamic accomplishment*
-en	wanten	rocken walken	putten	spoilen
-ed	wanted	walked drunked	breaked	mended

forms, they are similarly distributed through the rest of the categories. (The correlation between the two sets is 0.87.)

If *-ed* and *-en* are being used interchangeably as far as temporal reference is concerned, we can ask further, in relation to the aspectual hypothesis discussed above, whether *-ed* and *-en* differ in the kind of verb they are attached to – is it the case that *-en* is attached, for example, to telic verbs rather than atelic verbs? On the basis of the information about temporal reference, it seems unlikely, and an examination of the verbs involved shows that there is no preference for aspectual classes. Table 4.5 lists examples of the various classes of verbs.[26] If there is no functional difference, if the two forms are being used with the same meaning, so far as we can tell, why did Sophie have these alternate forms? Are they simply free variants, or is there some factor other than meaning that influences suffix selection for marking past? The first point to note (from tables 4.1 and 4.2) is that the *-en* form is more productive in the sample 1/sample 2 period, whereas *-ed* forms are more productive in the sample 2/sample 3 period. For *-en* for sample 1/2 there are 140 tokens across 44 different lexical verbs. For *-ed* in the same period there are 80 tokens, distributed across 19 verb types (and in fact 54 of the 80 tokens are instances of *called*). For samples 2/3, the figures show a much lower incidence for *-en*: there are 31 tokens for 10 verb types, whereas *-ed* shows 72 tokens across 38 verb types (and *called* only accounts for nine of the 72 tokens).[27] The dominant category between samples 1 and 2, the *-en* forms, was used mainly for coping with irregular verbs: about half the verbs marked for *-en* were irregular: 25 different irregular verbs had *-en* marking on them, whereas during this period only a handful of irregular verbs were used appropriately (though very frequently): *got*, *said*, *found*, *went*, *had* and *came*. All of these, except *got*, have either an *-ed* form or an *-en* form or both, but perhaps the more important point is that for so many irregular verbs Sophie does not use the correct form, but one of the over-regularized forms. For the most part, the present stem (for example, *tearen*) is used rather than the past (*sawed*). It looks then as if, for Sophie as for other children, the *-en* or *-ed* forms are used to cope with the problems of irregularity, and that the *-en* is the dominant form for this purpose until 3;0. After this, the *-en* gradually drops out, and the *-ed* is used, between 3;0 and 3;6. The initial preference for the *-en* form, we may infer from the first verbs to which it was overextended, arose from the problems presented by verbs like *put*, which do not have *any* past marking normally; such verbs tend to end in alveolar stops. She seems to require some overt signal for 'past' on these verbs, and selects *-en* for the marking. (For a similar strategy in Hebrew, see Berman (1983).) To begin with the use of *-en* in overextended contexts is limited to stems which end in alveolar stops. On 29.2 it is extended to the final /tʃ/ of *touch*, and then on 4.3, to a labial stop in *stepen*. We will return to the *-en*/*-ed* forms when we consider sample 3, but for the moment will leave them and turn to auxiliaries, which are the other type of verb modification to emerge between samples 1 and 2. There are two types to examine – *do*-support and modal auxiliaries.

Do-support

The occurrence of positive or negative *do*, *does*, *did*, as an auxiliary form in interrogatives or negatives, begins for Sophie quite early in sporadic, stereotypic forms, as noted earlier in the discussion of wh-questions. These forms (for example, *how do you*), though not subject to internal modification, do appear with a variety of verbs. Negative *don't* appears quite early (22.12.79), but only in *don't know*. The forms are infrequent for some time and either (for wh-interrogative) limited to the wh-forms they occur with or (for yes/no interrogative or negative) limited to certain verbs (*know*, *want*, *mind* are the most common). There is a dramatic increase in frequency, however, at the beginning of May 1980 (about six weeks before sample 2). During April, the average number of *do*-tokens is about 10, distributed across four or five verbs.[28] On 5.5.80 there are 20 tokens, and 10 different verbs. On 8 May, the figures are 24 tokens and 18 verbs, and on 13 May, we find 28 tokens and 12 verbs. There are also beginning to be a proportion of past forms: one on 5.5, five on 8.5, four on 13.5. By 21.5, the numbers are: *do* tokens: 28; verbs: 19; past tokens: 14. The *do*-forms have shown a gradual development since December 1979, when these first appeared. The emergence of a significant number of past forms took five months approximately from first emergence, and there has been a gradual spread of both present and past forms into a range of contexts. As we saw when discussing interrogatives, however, these contexts are still limited, and there seems some way to go yet before a completely productive *do*-support process will be available.[29]

Modals

Sophie began, very shortly after the first sample, to use modal auxiliaries – specifically, *can* and *will*. She thus embarked on the lengthy process of mastering these and similar forms, and their related meanings, which is unlikely to be complete until she gets to secondary school. The learning of modality is complicated by the fact that the kinds of meanings that modal auxiliaries have are also carried by other kinds of verbs. We indicate, for example, our judgement of obligation on someone's part when we say: *he ought to visit his mother*. A similar meaning is carried by another modal *should*, in *he should visit his mother*. In addition, a somewhat stronger view is conveyed by *he's got to visit his mother* or *he has to visit his mother*. Neither *have got to* nor *have to* are, strictly speaking, modal auxiliaries - they do not invert for *yes/no* interrogatives, or form tags as auxiliaries do. So whereas *should he visit his mother* is the appropriate interrogative form for our earlier example, the interrogative of the *have to* sentence is *does he have to visit his mother*. Thus the child has to learn that items that are in one respect positionally similar (*should* and *have to*, which is generally pronounced [hæftə]), and have similar meanings, have different syntactic behaviour in interrogatives. This quite apart from the problems of learning the meanings of the various forms made available in input.

The available information on the development of modals in other English-speaking children, admirably summarized in Stephany (1985), indicates that the first modal auxiliaries to appear are *can't*, *won't*, *can* and *will*; for some children the *have to* form precedes these, whereas for others it is pretty well contemporary.[30] The age of emergence varies, but with the exception of one of the children in Brown's study, Eve, who appears to have been a prodigy and used her first modals at 1;9, most of the children studied have begun to use these forms in their third year, with the time of emergence ranging from

2;2 to 2;11. Sophie seems to fall in the middle of these two points, and in all other respects her behaviour resembles that reported for the other children. In fact she, like four of the seven children examined by Stephany, has a form of *have to* ([hæfə]) as her first modal-like verb pre-modifier.

Sophie's first 'true' modal to appear was *can't*, on 27.11, very shortly after sample 1. It was used with three different verbs, *get*, *put* and *sit*. There are then four instances of *can* on 4.12. By 10.12 there are 11 instances of *can't*, used with five different verbs. It is worth noting that not all the examples of *can't* seem appropriate, from an adult point of view. In one example, Sophie says of a toy car *that can't work*, where *can't* for her seems to carry the same meaning as *doesn't* would for an adult. The same sample sees the first appearance of *will*, in a contracted form, in *I'll sleep over there*. The first appearance of *could* is also recorded in this sample: referring to two of her dolls, in doll's house play, Sophie says *yes her could change her nappy*. Also in the sample for 10.12 are five instances of Sophie's version of *have to* ([hæfə]). By 27.12 there are further examples of *will*.

The next development is the increased frequency of the use of *can*. In the sample for 4.1.80, there are 27 instances. The great majority of these are in sentence-initial position - only two are declaratives. Examples of the use of the forms in this sample are:

can me rubber on there (i.e. use a pencil rubber)
can me play those on your bed
can me play that

All these are requests to her mother by Sophie for permission to act. Even the two declaratives are in fact requests, but with inappropriate *can*-placement:

please me can come shopping with you
please me can play those things

The 'please' is a quite frequent accompaniment to the *can*-initial structures in this sample. The high frequency of *can*-forms, and their general restriction to initial position, continues. On 17.1.80, there are 49 *can*-initial structures, and only six either pre-verbally or standing as the only verb, as in *me can*.

The next distinct modal to appear is *must*, on 12.2.80. There is only one instance, and it comes in a context where it may well be an imitation of her older sister:

Zelda: you must write my letter
Sophie: you must write Zelda letter

At 24.3, however, there are three further instances of *must*, and it appears sporadically thereafter. The samples on 24.3 are:

her must go in the bed
is you going a party, you must dress up
if her like houses you must make

These are appropriate uses of *must*. The interesting question that arises is why she sometimes uses *have to* (for example, *those* [hæfə] *go in same beds*), sometimes *got to* (for example, *me got to put that on again*) and sometimes *must*, with reference to obligation. It is true that *must* does not appear with a first-person subject; however, *have to* appears with both first and third person. It is possible that, for Sophie, *must* represents a stronger obligation; in two of the examples above, which are conditionals, the obligation follows on (a) a social convention she has observed about parties, and (b) the need to respond to someone's perceived wishes. (In the second case, she is again involved in doll's house play and is talking about her 'baby'.) It could be argued here that the obligation to act is stronger than it is when she is saying that two of the dolls she is playing with [hæfə] *go in same beds*.[31] A further modal which can be used to indicate obligation is *should*; this makes its debut on 31.1, in an incomplete utterance which makes it difficult to interpret: *you should want to make* ... It is an infrequently used form from then on, but it does appear, and in more transparent contexts seems to have functions similar to those it would have in the adult language, where its meaning for human agent can range from obligation (*you should leave now*) to recommendation (*you should see her Desdemona*). The obligation or recommendation is either to the hearer (as in the examples), with reference to a third party (*he should pack it in*), or for the speaker (as when Sophie says in reference to a puzzle piece *that go next . . . should really do*).

The last innovation in Sophie's modals before sample 2 is *shall*, which emerges first on 13.5.80. It only appears in sentence-initial positions, as for example (from this sample) *shall me get a lolly*. It is used with first-person subjects only, and is an alternative to *can* as a request for permission or invitation to joint action.

5

Sophie at 3 years 5 months

BACKGROUND

This sample comprises a 540-line extract from a conversation between Sophie and her mother about a fortnight before Christmas. The two-line extract from a carol, quoted by Sophie at ll. 17–18, contains one of those amusing examples of misinterpretation of rote-learned items, which are well known to parents: 'shepherds in the moonlight bright, *washed* their sheep all through the night'. The first part of the sample, to about l. 70, takes place just after Sophie has returned from her next-door neighbour's, where she has been having lunch. In the remainder of the session, but with various interruptions and tangents, Sophie is playing her recorder. She plays from a book called *Recorder in Colour*, which gives colour cues to musical notation, hence the references at, for example, ll. 158 and 160. From l. 265, she begins to play the tune of 'Daisy, daisy', a song which she then wrongly quotes from at ll. 272 ff., and again at l. 321 ff. The correct wording of the relevant verse (older readers will remember) is:

Daisy, daisy
give me your answer do
I'm half crazy
all for the love of you

Sophie's rendering of the second line of this verse is transcribed as 'give me a chance of you'. What she actually says is 'give me a [hæns] of you', which her mother interprets as 'chance'. Whether this accords with what Sophie thinks she is hearing/saying is of course impossible to tell. Sophie's recorder-playing continues intermittently until at least l. 440, when she turns to singing.

Various individuals who have not been referred to in previous samples are mentioned in this transcript; they will be identified as they appear. There is, in addition, one rather obscure reference in the sample that should be explained here, since it cannot readily be handled in marginal notes. At l. 339,

Sophie says 'got my [bʌnjənz] on'. This term 'bunyons' is her pet name for 'bugs' or 'germs'. The exchange actually begins at l. 334, but the reason for her preference does not become clear until l. 339. She will only play a recorder which happens to have her 'bugs' on – one which only she has played (that is, had in her mouth) recently.

SAMPLE 3: SOPHIE AT 3;5.15

S. whŷ/
F. well 'cos it 'might brèak it/
[30-second pause]
S. 'this isn't a 'piano bóok/
F. it's 'got a 'few bits of – – – 'piano music hásn't it/
oh nò/
it's 'more sìnging/
'maybe 'play it on the rècorder/
(unintelligible sequence)
some càrols/
S. nó/
lôok/
[10-second pause]
S. 'look lòts/
look 'lots of * (3 syll.)
F. * did you 'learn some néw carols/ (did you = [dʒʊː]
at schóol/ ('school' = nursery, attended in the mornings)
'what did you 'learn tòday/ (did you = [dɪdʒə])
S. 'shepherds in the 'moonlight bríght/
'washed their 'sheep all 'through the nìght/
F. òh/
S. we 'didn't 'have much 'songs tòday/ (didn't = [dɪnt])
F. dídn't you/
S. nò/
F. 'what did you hàve/
S. 'only have – – thàt many/
F. òh
S. it 'so làte/
F. 'which songs 'did you – 'did you dò/
S. I gòtten/ (whisper) ('gotten' = 'forgotten')
F. oh Sôphie/
you 'can't have for'gotten alreâdy/

S. I hàve/
'was so lông/
I gòtten/ (laughs)
'is it so dárk/
'is it dárk/
F. is whát dark 'love/
S. 'is it dárk - out'side/ (1 syll.)
F. nò/
S. (unintelligible sequence)
I 'thought - you 'coming 'straight after lùnch here/
F. what to fétch you/
S. m̀m/
F. well I 'thought I'd 'leave you to 'watch childrens tèlly/
'did you wátch it/
S. nò/
F. òh/
'didn't Chris lét you/ (Chris is the next-door neighbour)
S. nò/
didn't 'let Matthew 'turn it òn/ (Matthew is Chris's son)
F. ôh/
did you 'have a little pláy/
S. (5 syll.)
we 'had stôry/
F. did he 'read you a stóry/
S. m̀m/
F. whò read you a 'story/
S. Chrìs/
F. àh/
'wasn't Marketta thére/
or 'was she wòrking/
S. yès
F. what 'story did he rèad you/
S. [ɜːm] - [ɜːm] - - - [uː] - [uː] - - [uːwə]
[ɜːm] I gòtten now/
F. the míller/
S. m̀m/
'Windy Mìller/
F. ôh/
S. I 'gotten [ə] rèst/
F. 'I didn't 'know it was in a bòok/
darling lòok (F. is trying to get
'come hère/ S.'s music stand in
you've 'got it 'much too hìgh/ the right position)
and 'too nèar/

'how does it 'go dòwn/
no 'that's ùp/
thère
that bétter/
[8-second pause]
S. 'do thìs/
[10-second pause]
S. 'shall I do thís one/ (shall = [ʃæl])
F. yês/
'why nòt/
it's níce/
S. nò
[8-second pause]
F. are 'these yóurs/ or Hèsters pants/ - - -
S. mìne/ - - -
'Hester got - sōme
'what is thàt one/ (indicating a particular piece of music)
'I do thàt one/
F. whích one 'sweetie/
S. thàt one/
F. yès/
'that's a very nìce one/ - - -
S. shall 'I do thát one/ (shall = [sl])
yès/
shall 'I do thát one/ (shall = [sl])
[S. plays notes on piano]
I 'play it with my còrder/
it su'pposed to 'go on còrder/
(2 syll.)
'where's Gri'selda's còrder/
F. is 'this the 'one that wórks/ (blows recorder)
nò/
'where's the 'one that wòrks/
'on the 'floor thère/
[S. 'plays' the recorder]
F. darling I 'must put some 'new e'lastic in your pyjâmas/
S. m̀m
F. shall I 'take them downstáirs/ (shall = [sl])
S. there's 'some ìn/
F. I knòw/
but it's 'all gone hòpeless/
it 'isn't strètchy any 'more/ ìs it
S. nò/
F. no 'wonder they 'fall òff/ - - -

S. [kən] – I 'want to 'do it hìgher/ – – –
can 'I borrow yoúr 'corder/ (can = [kən])
F. nò/
nò/
S. whý/
F. did 'Sammy come to 'school tóday/ (Sammy is a school-friend of S.'s)
S. nò/
F. whát/
S. nò/
F. nô/
does he 'never come to schóol/
S. nò
cos it's 'his half-têrm/
F. no 'you may nòt touch 'mine darling/ (i.e. F.'s own recorder)
no nèver/
S. whỳ̌/
F. be'cause – it's 'very spècial/ prècious/ – –
S. but a 'jingle came 'off your drèss/ (refers to a dress of F.'s that has a tie with a bell on the end, and also a neck cord with (jingling) beads with bells in)
F. no it hàsn't/
S. yès/
F. it hàsn't
S. it hàs/
'why didn't you 'wear that one todáy/
F. 'cause I 'wore it yèsterday/
S. and you 'didn't wear it anòther day/
F. I 'didn't wánt to/
'don't you lìke 'this one/ – – –
S. 'I want the tìnkle/
F. you 'like the 'tinkle one dó you/
S. m̀m/
[5-second pause]
S. 'why can we 'never – 'why can 'we never 'touch your óne/
F. because it's a spècial one darling/
S. plays the recorder
S. lòok/
it 'doesn't wòrk/ (doesn't = [dʌnt])
F. ôh/
S. 'want to 'do it on the pîano/
F. 'well it shòuld work 'sweetie/

S. dòesn't/ (= [dʌənt])
[8-second pause]
S. no 'that is Grisèlda's/
'cause got thàt/ (that = [næt])
it's 'got thàt/
it's 'got thàt/
'Hester [ɛnt] gòt that/
F. no 'that's Hèster's darling/
Gri'selda's hasn't 'got the 'notes in còlour/ - -
I 'think Griselda's got 'hers in her ròom/
[8-second pause]
S. but 'her got a 'colour one 'like thìs/ - -
F. erm no we 'gave it to Jòssy/ - - -
'we had twò/
[5-second pause]
S. ôh/
F. 'I know 'what we 'must dò/ (very softly)
[10-second pause]
S. I 'don't know 'what to dò/ (whining)
[10-second pause]
S. 'course - - - 'he don't 'go to 'school cause 'his half-têrm/ (S. is referring back to Sammy, l. 119)
[10-second pause]
S. 'where my córder/
F. behìnd you 'sweetie/
S. nò/
my bròwn one/
F. thère/
on the - -
I don't knôw/
there's a 'bit of it 'on my dèsk/
cáreful/
cáreful/
'mind your hèad/
'where's the - - - hère we are/
[5-second pause]
S. d'you 'do it 'this way ròund/
F. 'let me sèe/
S. thát way 'round/ or thàt way 'round/
F. thàt way 'round/
S. (sings) sing beautifully
sing beautifully
F. 'who had that 'little 'guitar at schòol/
S. Lòuisa/ (another school-friend)

F. is it hérs/
S. yèah/
F. òh/ - - -
S. 'why d'you 'never buy 'me a guítar/
F. 'well I don't knòw/
'would you líke one/
S. yès/
F. a 'little guítar/
S. m̀m/
'like Louìsa/
'no a bìg one/
a bìg one/
F. a big one/
you 'wouldn't be 'able to 'play a bìg one/
S. I wòuld/
I wòuld/
I 'would be abl̀e to/
F. 'no it would 'be too bîg sweetie/
S. no 'only - 'some children have 'bigger than mè/
thàt big/
only thàt big/
F. oh I sèe/
what 'like Lòuisa/ -
S. nò/
'like Hèster had/
usèd to 'had/
F. 'that was - 'that was vêry 'big/ (was = [wɒz])
S. nò/
'I - 'I don't mînd/
'[juːz] idiòtic/
'where's my 'piano book góne to/
F. I'm nòt idi'otic/
S. you arè/
'you won't 'let me 'play a gùitar/
lòok/
lòok
F. 'you're chèeky/
S. I 'made it 'go smàller (S. is altering the height of a music stand)
[7-second pause]
I 'want it 'go in a ùpper/
can 'make it 'go - much hìgher/ (*can* = [kn̩])
F. you 'won't be 'able to sêe it/ if it 'goes any hìgher/
S. 'I can 'stand up oǹ it/

F. 'no you càn't/
'it'll brèak sweetie/
'don't be sìlly/
S. 'then – on the ròcking 'chair/
F. 'why do you 'want to 'stand on the ròcking 'chair/
anyway 'when it goes hìgher/ it 'gets awfully
in'clined to fall òver/
'd'you re'member when Hèster did it/
the 'other dày/
and it 'fell òver/ dìdn't it/
'went cràshing down/
S. nō/
'if you 'do it like thîs/ it won't – come dòwn/
F. 'daddy said 'he could hèar you/ – at Màtthews/
d'you knów that/
S. it 'wasn't m̀e/
F. waśn't it/
S. 'it was Màtthew/
F. was 'Matthew shoúting/
S. yès/
F. whý/
'didn't he 'want you to 'have his tóy/ – – –
S. yès/
F. was he 'being naúghty/
S. m̀m/
'and he was crỳing/
F. wás he/
S. yès/
'he is naùghty/
'cause he did – – – (4 syll.)
[10-second pause]
where is Fran, where is Fran, here (to the tune of
I am, here I am Frere Jacques)
F. here I am, here I am (picks up tune)
S. I 'going to 'play thìs one
[30 seconds' recorder 'playing' by Sophie of the song 'Daisy, daisy']
'I did 'daisy dàisy/
F. (laughs)
S. 'that is daísy/
F. yês/
S. nò/
thàt is 'daisy/
F. àh/

[5-second pause]
S. 'shall I 'say thìs bit/
'when it 'goes half cràzy/
'give me a 'chance of yòu/
'half cràzy/
F. mm/
[5 seconds of recorder]
F. lôvely
[further half-minute of 'Daisy daisy' on the recorder]
S. I dìd it/
'what did you 'think from thàt one/
F. I 'thought it was lôvely/ - - -
S. 'shall I 'do it agáin/
[5 seconds of recorder]
'shall I 'do thís one/
I'm going to (3 syll.)
[15 seconds of recorder]
shall 'I do 'this one agáin/
'cause I 'love thàt one/ - - -
this 'much too (3 syll.)
[5-second pause]
S. 'can you 'make it 'go hígher/ (the music-stand, again)
F. not mùch/ nò/
S. whý/
'[hɪ] - - hère we 'are/
'make it 'go - 'little bit hìgher/
a 'little bit hìgher/
'not sò high/
a 'little bit hìgher/
F. whóops/
S. daisy, daisy (sings)
F. is thát 'right/
'that about ríght/
S. nò/
F. like thàt/
S. yès/ - - -
can't rèach/
F. of 'course you càn't/ -
I 'told you 'that would hàppen/
S. 'I can 'stand on 'there without my shòes on/
F. you 'silly gìrl/ (laughs)
S. 'I càn/
F. 'then it'll be 'too lòw/ - - -
S. wòn't/

F. it wìll/ - - -
S. can you 'take off my shóes/
F. ḿm/
S. 'can you 'take off my shóes/ - - -
F. alrìght/
'lift up your fòot/
S. (sings) give me a chance of you
I am half crazy
'it's at 'two o'clòck/
F. are you 'going to 'sing that in 'your [sɜː] - in 'your cárols/
S. yès/
ǹo/
(unintelligible sequence)
I'm half crazy, give me a chance of you (sings)
half crazy
'what one 'was I dòing/ (referring to sheets of music)
'not thàt one/
'not thàt one/
thìs/
'what is thàt one/
'what is thàt one/
F. I 'don't kǹow lovey/
[10-second pause as S. searches]
S. thàt/
thàt/
'that one ìt/
F. yès/
[S. sings 'Daisy daisy', and then plays the recorder for a minute]
S. only 'this one 'works for m̀e/
F. doés it/
S. yès/
F. 'that's jolly fùnny/
S. yès/
[10 seconds' recorder playing]
S. 'got my [bʌnjənz] 'on/
'always it 'has to 'have my [bʌnjənz] 'on/ - - -
'but - 'but it (3 syll.)
[a further 15 seconds' recorder playing]
'who did that 'writing on thère/
F. E'lizabeth I expèct/
S. whý/
F. to re'mind Hèster of 'something/ that 'she was pràctising/
S. 'who's Elìzabeth/
F. 'Hester's re'corder tèacher/
[10 seconds' playing]

S. 'who's Grisèlda's re'corder 'teacher/
F. Miss 'Muxlow I thi̇̀nk/
[S. plays on, for 30 seconds]
S. 'weren't that béautifully/
F. bèautiful/ - - -
S. can 'I ring úp 'somebody/
'and her name is * (1 syll.)/
F. * no dòn't lovey/
because the 'telephone isn't 'working downstàirs/
and I 'need to - 'know if 'that one is rìnging/ - -
so I 'don't want 'you to unplùg it/ - -
tomòrrow/ 'when it's 'been - 'when the 'telephone
down'stairs has been mènded/ - - -
S. whý/
I 'want to 'ring ùp 'somebody/
'and her 'won't be thère to'morrow/
her 'won't be thère/
F. whò 'won't/
S. [əm] - and 'me have 'got to ring ùp/
her 'won't be thère/
F. 'have to 'just try tomôrrow/ and 'hope for the bèst/
S. 'her - 'her wìll be 'there/
'her wòn't be 'there/
'her - 'I'll 'have to 'do it on - on Sùnday/
F. òh/
alrìght/
S. 'that is my ['tɪpɪvɩ] 'play on Sùnday/ (= nativity)
F. what/
S. my ['tɪntɪvɩ] 'play on Sùnday/
F. your ['tɪntɪvɩ] pláy/
S. yès/
my plày/
F. no it's 'on - it's 'next Frìday/
S. òw/
F. dàrling/ - -
we 'don't want twò broken 'telephones/
S. 'how did thàt broke/ (dials telephone)
F. no don't fìddle with it 'sweetie/
S. (3 syll.)
'if it was 'down thêre/ 'it would wòrk/ -
F. mm/
[10-second pause as Sophie dials]
S. 'I just 'put my 'finger thròugh/ and 'phone
úp somebody/ - - -
only 'tènding/

F. mhm̀/
S. tó/ - - -
shall I 'do it 'without thát bit/
[10 seconds' recorder playing]
S. 'that isn't very gòod/
'had to 'get mòre of it/
[25 seconds of recorder playing]
'I didn't stànd on 'nothing/
F. oh/
'don't walk on the iròning darling/
S. I dìdn't/
F. gòod/
[25-second pause, including some recorder]
S. 'what - 'how d'you 'make different músic/
F. I 'don't knòw/
'you put - 'don't walk on my drèss love/
it de'pends where you 'put your fìngers/
which 'holes you còver/ - -
S. 'can I 'put one thére/
F. well trŷ/
'see what it sòunds like/
S. 'see what you sòund like - - 'with it/
[10 seconds of S. playing]
'what did you 'hear of thát/
F. 'well it's - it 'was some 'different nòtes/ wásn't it/ - -
'don't walk on the bòoks sweetie/
[Sophie plays again - 15 seconds]
S. 'what did you 'hear of thát/
F. I 'think I 'liked the 'first one bètter/
[S. continues to play - 20 seconds]
S. 'what did you 'hear of thát/
F. [ɜː] 'that was very nìce/
[15 seconds of the recorder playing]
S. 'shall I - 'shall I 'make a fuńny music/
'shall I 'make a fuńny music/
F. mȟm/
[S. plays for 5 seconds]
S. 'I only 'know a pèrson says 'this/ (laughs and plays briefly)
F. 'rather naughty bòys/
[25-second pause, with intermittent recorder]
F. 'just going to 'get some wàter lovey
[15 seconds' recorder]
S. mummy/
'what did you 'think of thàt/
F. 'I thought 'that was vèry nice/

S. can you 'make it 'go úpper/
F. 'more stíll/
S. yèah/
F. (2 syll.)
I 'wonder if Griselda did her còncert to'day/
we'll 'have to 'ask Hèster/ wòn't we/
S. (2 syll.)
nòw/ – – –
'what shall I dò/
F. 'what d'you meán/
S. which 'one shall I 'do on the còrder/ – – –
F. I don't knòw/
'you chòose/
[S. searches through music]
S. 'why don't I 'have thàt one/
F. alrìght/
[S. plays]
S. 'what did you 'think of thàt/
F. I 'thought that was 'very gòod/ –
'you've been 'playing the re'corder 'very wèll/ – – –
S. I 'getting hard wôrk/
F. m̂m/
S. 'have you – 'did you 'buy some – 'did you 'buy something for mé/
F. nò/
'what were you thìnking of/
S. I 'wanted you to 'buy some swèeties/
F. some swêeties/
S. yès/
F. nò/
S. yês/
F. nò/
S. yès/
there is 'shop at Bàrnett's/ (Barnett's is the local toyshop)
they 'sell some at Bàrnett's/
F. dó they/
S. yès/
F. I 'thought what we 'might do while 'Hester's doing her recòrder/
S. yéə/
F. was to 'go – 'doing her dàncing/
was to 'go and 'get you some tìghts/
and then 'go and 'watch the 'end of 'Hester's dàncing/
'would you líke that/
S. m̂hm/

some swèets/
F. whát/
S. 'you – 'you can 'get – my tìghts/ and 'I
can 'get – swèets/
F. (laughs)
S. yes/
[S. sings]
'is it – 'when is it 'going to 'be my dáncing/ – – –
F. your '[də] – on Thûrsday 'love/
S. I 'thought it 'going to be todày/
I'll mìss it 'all/
F. 'no you wòn't/
today's Wèdnesday/ isń't it/
S. yès/
F. or 'is it Tùesday/
I don't knòw/
[S. sings]
S. 'shall we 'go down to – Bárnett's/
F. ǹo/
'cause we're 'waiting for 'Hester to come bàck/
[S. sings]
S. while 'Hester at's còrder/ 'I'll 'buy some swèets/
'and while 'Hester at dàncing/ you'll 'get some tìghts/
F. mhm̀/
S. 'that's a 'good idèa/
[S. sings]
F. shall we 'take your púshchair/
S. yès/
while – 'Hester at schóol/ 'we can 'buy – 'I can
buy some swèets/
F. 'she'll be 'back any mìnute lovey/
S. oh/
'when her's at schóol/ – – 'I – 'I'll buy
some swèeties/
yes/
and 'when her at còrder/ 'you buy some tìghties/
F. 'tighties and sweéeties/ (imitates S.)
'silly vòice/
S. (laughs)
tíghties/
and swéeties/
'can you 'get those 'right nów/
F. nò/
S. 'straight awáy/

F. whát/
the swéeties/
n̂o/
S. yês/
'cause I lìke 'those/
F. 'I dare 'say you dô/
S. I càn go/
I shàll know
'who said I shàll know/
F. yòu did/
S. 'no yòu did/
shall 'I do a 'trick on yoú/
F. yès/
S. 'give me your hànd/
'that is your thúmb/
'that is your lìttle 'finger/
'that is your thùmb/
and 'that is your thùmb/ (laughs)
S. can you 'do that to mé/
F. 'there's your thúmb/
and 'that's your líttle finger/
and 'that's your – míddle finger/
S. nò/
'that's your thùmb/
and thàt's your 'thumb/
F. ôh/
'you've got 'lots of thùmbs/ háve you/
S. and thàt/
and thàt/
and thàt/
you sée/
F. 'this takes a 'long tìme/

DATA SUMMARIES: SAMPLE 3

(a) MLU(m) = 4.47 (range = 1-11)
(b) TTR = 0.26

(c) LARSP

Stage I (0.9–1.6)	*Minor*		*Responses*		*Vocatives*	*Other*	*Problems*	
	Major	*Comm.*	*Quest.*	*Statement*				
		'V'	'Q'	'V'	'N'	Other	Problems	
	Conn.	Clause				Phrase		Word
Stage II (1.6–2.0)		V *X*	Q *X*	SV **8**	A *X*	DN **12**	VV **6**	
				SO	VO **1**	Adj N **1**	V part **2**	-ing
				SC	VC **1**	NN **1**	Int *X* **2**	
				Neg *X*	Other	PrN **5**	Other **1**	pl
Stage III (2.0–2.6)		*X* + S:NP	*X* + V:VP **2**	*X* + C:NP **2**		*X* + O:NP	*X* + A:AP	-ed **4**
		V *X Y*	Q *X Y*	SVC **3**	VCA	D Adj N **2**	Cop	-en **3**
		let X Y		SVO **5**	VOA **1**	Adj Adj N	Aux^{M8}_{O16}	
			VS(*X*) **4**	SVA **3**	VO_dO_i	Pr DN **4**		3s
		do X Y		Neg *X Y*	Other	$Pron^{P34}_{O3}$	Other **3**	gen
Stage IV (2.6–3.0)		*XY* + S:NP	*XY* + V:VP **8**	*XY* + C:NP **3**		*XY* + O:NP **6**	*XY* + A:AP **5**	
		+ S	QVS **7**	SVOA **6**	AA *X Y*	Np Pr NP	Neg V **5**	n't
			Q *X Y* +	SVCA	Other	Pr D Adj N	Neg *X*	
		V *X Y* +	VS(*X* +)	SVO_dO_i		c *X*	2 Aux	'cop **4**
			tag	SVOC		*X*c *X*	Other	'aux **2**
Stage V (3.0–3.6)	*and*	Coord.	Coord.	Coord. 1	1 +	Postmod. clause	1 1 +	
	c	Other	Other	Subord. A **2** 1	1 +			-est
	s			S C **5**	O **2**			-er **3**
	Other			Comparative		Postmod. phrase	1 +	-ly

Verb valency analysis

Total verb types: 23 *Total verb tokens:* 50

	Type	*Tokens*	*Frames and realizations*				
1.	BORROW	1	S	–	O		
			Pronp		DN		
2.	BUY	1	S	–	O		
			Pronp		DN		
3.	COME	1	S	–	A		
			DN		Pr DN		
4.	CRY	1	S	–			
			Pronp				
5.	DO	10	S	–	O		
			Pronp		DN	[3]	
					N		
					Pronp		
			S	–	O	A	
			Pronp		DN	adv	
					Pronp		
			S	–	O	A	
			Pronp		Pronp	adv	
						DN adj	
				–	O	A	
					Pronp	Pr DN	
6.	FORGET	3	S	–			(2)
			S	–	A		
			Pronp		adv		
7.	GO	3	S	–	A		
			Pronp		Pr N		
			S	–	A	A	
			Pronp		Pr N	*Clause*	
			A	S –		A	
			where	D Adj N		Pr	
8.	GOT	5	S	–	O	(3)	
			Pronp		Prono		
			PN				
			S	–	O		
			Pronp		Prono		
			S	–	O	A	
			Pronp		D Adj N	Pr N	
9.	HAVE	2	S	–	O		
			Pronp		N		
					Adj Pr Pronp		

	Type	*Tokens*	*Frames and realizations*					
10.	KNOW	1	S	-	O			
			Pronp		*Clause*			
11.	LET	2	(S)	-	O	*Clause*		(2)
			Pronp		Pronp			
					PN			
12.	LOVE	1	S	-	O			
			Pronp		DN			
13.	MAKE	4	(S)	-	O	*Clause*		(4)
14.	PLAY	2	S	-	O	A		
			Pronp		Pronp	Pr DN		
			S	-	O			
			Pronp		DN			
15.	REACH	1		-				
16.	SAY	1	S	-	O			
			Pronp		DN			
17.	STAND	2	S	-	A			
			Pronp		P Pr Pronp			
			S	-	A	A		
			Pronp		Pr Adv	Pr D N Adv		
18.	TAKE	1	S	-	Part	O		
			Pronp			DN		
19.	THINK	2	S	-	O			
			Pronp		*Clause*			
20.	TOUCH	1	A	S		A	–	O
			why	Pronp		adv		DN
21.	WANT	2	S	-	O			
			Pronp		DN			
			S	-	O	*Clause*		
			Pronp		Pronp			
22.	WEAR	2	A	S	-	O		A
			why	Pronp		DN		adv
			S	-	O	A		
			Pronp		Pronp	DN		
23.	WORK	1	S	-				
			Pronp					

PRONUNCIATION

Sophie continues occasionally to pronounce [ð] as [d], or as [n] initially in *that*, *there*. Additionally, [θ] is pronounced as [f] in *thumb*, and there are occasional rare tongue-slips as at l. 311, where *take* appears as [keik]. But singleton consonants and consonant clusters now seem to be for the most part under control. She even produces a correct [pj] sequence for the initial cluster of *piano* at l. 217 (see above, p. 73). The area where problems still arise for Sophie is in the pronunciation of polysyllabic words. We see once again in her realization of a word like *recorder* as [ˈkɔːdə], or *forgotten* as [ˈgɒtən], and *tomorrow* as [əˈmɒroʊ], a tendency to omit unstressed syllables in words of three syllables. And at ll. 374 ff. we see two different attempts at the production of *nativity*, which exhibit the omission of the initial unstressed syllable of the target together with consonant metathesis (transposition) and substitution. In the first effort, [ˈtɪpɪvɩ], the initial consonants of the second and third syllables are transposed and a labial substituted for a [t] at the beginning of the second syllable. The second attempt at *nativity* transposes [t] and [v], but also interestingly adds a nasal (presumably from the missing unstressed syllable) to the 'beginning' of the second syllable. The productions suggest that Sophie has a fair grasp of the syllabic structure of the word she is aiming at, but does not have available for production a complete specification of the features of consonants that appear at the various positions in this structure. We have already mentioned the indications from Smith's diary (Smith 1973) that Amahl had a particular strategy for coping with unstressed syllables in words of two or more syllables: at stage 27, which began when the child was 3;5 (that is, roughly the same age as Sophie at sample 3), he did not omit these syllables, as Sophie does, but used a single form, [riː], as the initial unstressed syllable of words like *adaptor* ([riːˈdæptə]), *conductor* ([riːˈdəktə]), etc. In addition, there are two examples in the diary of similar errors to those shown by Sophie in her pronunciation of *nativity*: at stage 27, Amahl has a variant pronunciation of *animal*, [ˈæmələn], which involves consonant metathesis. And a little earlier, during stage 25 (3;3–3;4), there is a pronunciation of *bicycle* as [ˈbaikisəl], which has a consonant metathesis of a similar kind to that in [ˈtɪpɪvi], namely, stop and fricative changing places in the second and third syllables.[1]

The only other point to be made concerns some odd (by comparison with adults) features of Sophie's placement of the nuclear tonic. The clearest examples are:

l. 144 'why can 'we never 'touch your óne/
l. 228 'I can 'stand up òn it/
l. 396 'I didn't stànd on 'nothing/

The first example would normally have the tonic marked on *your*. The misplacement presumably arises from Sophie's awareness of the general rule in English (Crystal 1985) that for the most part the tonic will fall on the stressed syllable of the last word in a sentence consisting of one tone-group. But there are exceptions to this – when *one* occurs used pronominally with a possessive determiner, for example, as here, where the tonic would normally move forward to *your*. The second example shows Sophie placing the tonic where it would only normally occur contrastively, in a sentence like *I can stand on it* (as opposed to under it); but there is no contrast, and she has failed to realize that verb + adverb sequences like *stand up* require the tonic on *up*. The third example is less clear. We might expect the tonic to fall on *nothing*, unless she wanted to use the tonic on *stand* to emphasize that it was being used contrastively (*I didn't stànd on nothing*; *I did kìck something though*). It is not clear from the context what the contrast would be with, though it is not possible for us to say that she is not using the tonic placement contrastively. She is certainly capable of using contrastive tonic placement in what we would consider an appropriate way, as at l. 393:

shall I ˈdo it without thát bit/

Unfortunately there is very little research on the development of children's prosodic features in relation to lexis and syntax acquisition between 3 and 5 years of age, so it is difficult to know whether or not Sophie is typical. The very slight evidence here suggests that she is beginning to experiment with the informational possibilities of variation in tonic placement, but has as yet a limited grasp of what these possibilities are.

GRAMMAR

The MLU(m) for a 100-utterance subset of this sample (from l. 28) is 4.47, whereas the figure for the complete sample is 4.68. These values put Sophie into Brown's stage V, for which coordination is the major expected process of sentence construction. The age-range predicted by Miller and Chapman (1981) for an MLU value of 4.47 is 43–46 months. The predicted age-range for an MLU of 4.68 is 47+ months (with no upper limit given). Although we may conclude from these figures that Sophie is advanced for her age,[2] two points should give us pause. First, another analysis on the data, of a different sample of 106 utterances, yielded an MLU value of 4.94. Second, although some difficulties involved in applying Brown's rules for MLU counts have been apparent in earlier samples, they have become potentially more serious here. Earlier, the problems have been those which anyone who has ever attempted an MLU count is familiar with (and which are listed in detail in Crystal 1974): for instance, when is an utterance such as *mm* by the child a 'filler' (and hence not counted) and when is it a response like *yes* (and so to be counted); is *Christmas tree* a compound (one morpheme) or a construction (two morphemes)? Now of course even decisions on these issues will affect the MLU figure arrived at: including *mm* as a one-morpheme utterance will slightly depress the MLU value, whereas counting *Christmas tree* as a construction will slightly inflate it. We might suppose, however, that for the data we have examined so far, the variation introduced by different decisions on these issues (if other investigators examined the data) would be within acceptable limits. But once we address data in which the child begins to link clauses more extensively, as in sample 3, the potential for variation becomes greater. As Crystal (1974: 295) puts it, we are faced with the problem of 'deciding where one unit of speech ends and the next begins'. Take the sequence at ll. 487–8:

S. while 'Hester at's corder/ 'I'll 'buy some 'sweets/
'and while 'Hester at dancing/ 'you'll get some tights/

Without some working definition, it is not easy to see how one decides that this sequence is four 'utterances', two 'utterances', or one. (A similar kind of problem arises of course for any attempt at a grammatical characterization of the sequence, and we return to the issue below.) As such sequences become more common, so it seems likely that the MLU value assigned will vary from analyst to analyst.

The TTR for the sample of 106 utterances referred to above is 0.26; a TTR for 50 utterances from this set is 0.39. The original Templin norms were based on 50 utterances, and this value is certainly closer to Templin's norm than the TTR from the larger sample. But as we advance through the Sophie samples, this ratio is in itself beginning to look rather uninformative. (The TTR of 0.26 was based on 136 lexemes and 515 tokens.)

The LARSP profile

As before, we will start from the 50-sentence sample that was used for the LARSP analysis, but bring in examples from elsewhere in the full sample, where relevant. A visual comparison of the profile charts for samples 3 and 2 is not as straightforward as that between profiles 2 and 1. The differences seem more marginal. We will see, however, that even apparently minor profile differences can be indices of change since sample 2; other differences are masked by this way of looking at the data, but emerge from the valency analysis, and the other analytical subheadings that consider in more detail verb-forms, articles, etc. We begin with further developments in complex sentences between samples 2 and 3.

Complex sentences

We saw in sample 2 that Sophie was making use in a limited way of some of the constructions traditionally referred to as complex sentences. How much further has this aspect of her syntactic ability extended in the period since sample 2? One area of change, which is not obvious from a visual inspection of the modified LARSP profiles, is the appearance in sample 3 of constructions exemplified in the following utterances, and characterized in Crystal et al. (1981) as *Complex VP* constructions:

didn't let Matthew turn it on
you won't let me play the guitar
can make it go much higher
I made it go smaller

Make and *let* are two of the four catenative verbs that Palmer (1974: 199) refers to as 'causative'. (The others are *have* and *help*.) The term 'catenative' refers to the close syntactic and/or semantic link between the first and second verbs in the utterances above - links which do not hold in sequences which also have two verbs, such as *he left wondering about his chances*. *Make* and *let* are distinguished from *want* (also a catenative) in terms of the different constructions in which they occur. In Palmer's terms, constructions with *make* and *let* (and *have*, *help*) can be schematized as NP_1 V NP_2[(NP_2)V]. This can be shown with one of our examples:

I	made	it	go	smaller	
NP_1	V	NP_2[	(NP_2)V	X	]

The parenthesized NP_2 inside the bracket indicates that *it*, which is the object of *made*, is also the subject of *go*.[3] Even though these constructions are not entered at Stage V, it is clear that they could fit our earlier definition of complex sentences, with a main and a subordinate clause, but the dual function of the unit between first and second verb requires us for catenatives like *want*, where the unit following *want* is part of the subordinate clause:[4]

I	want	daddy to go	
NP_1	V	[NP_2 V	]

Apart from the *make/let* examples, and one other instance (*I thought you coming straight after lunch here*), most of the complex sentences in sample 3 fall outside the 50-utterance set chosen for the LARSP profile. This is another reminder, if any were needed, of the difficulty of selecting samples that are representative of the child's usage at a particular point in time. A list of the other utterances from this sample in which we might want to recognize complex constructions, or their precursors, appears in table 5.1.

We will deal with these complex constructions in turn, but first we should address issues of segmentation, which we have been able to ignore in the two previous samples. As Sophie's utterances become longer, there are increasing problems in the provision of consistent procedures for identifying the divisions between constructions. Although we cannot hope to solve these problems finally, it is important to air them and to indicate the (inevitably *ad hoc*) solutions adopted. We can use as an example the sequence mentioned in the discussion of MLU:

1.487 while 'Hester at's còrder/ 'I'll buy some swèets/
and while 'Hester at dàncing/ 'you'll get some tìghts/

TABLE 5.1 Complex sentences in sample 3

1. *Relative*
   I only know a person say this
2. *Causal adverbial clause*
   he don't go to school 'cos his half-term
3. *Complementation*
   I thought it going to be today
   who sayed I shall know
   I thought you coming straight after lunch here
4. *Coordination*
   I ring up somebody and her name is XX
   I put my finger through and phone up somebody
   you can get my tights and I get some sweets
   I want to ring up somebody and her won't be there tomorrow
   that's your thumb and that's your thumb
5. *Temporal adverbial clause*
   while Hester at's corder I'll buy some sweets
   and while Hester's at dancing you'll get some tights
   while Hester at school I can buy some sweets
   when her's at school I'll buy some sweeties
   and when her at corder you buy some tighties

The issue that needs to be decided for syntactic analysis (particularly when our view of developmental change is to be based on that analysis) is whether there is a single complex construction here, made up of four clauses linked by subordinative and coordinative devices, or two separate (subordinative) complex constructions, one to each line. How is the decision to be arrived at? One assumption, following on the inclusion of prosodic information in the transcript, might be that we could use this to segment long utterances. But it will not work. The use of prosodic features as heuristics for segmentation will, if we apply procedures consistently, lead to unwanted distortions in our analysis. A brief review of the issues should make this clear. Suppose we consider pause as the only boundary marker for constructions.[5] This would lead us to consider ll. 487–8 above as representing a single construction, whereas l. 497 would consist of two constructions:

ˈwhen her's at schóol/ – – ˈI – ˈI'll buy some swèeties/

Although there are certainly good reasons for including pause markers in the transcription (see above p. 17), pause on its own is not going to be much help for segmentation. We might turn then to the other prosodic features marked in our transcript, tone-unit boundaries and nuclear tones. It is apparent even from the examples that we have looked at so far that tone-unit boundaries will not be of much help for segmenting ll. 487–8 into *two* complex constructions, since we are ignoring some tone-unit markers in allowing the only alternative segmentation to be a *single* construction. If we were using tone-unit boundaries alone to segment, then we would have to allow a further option, of four separate single clauses.[6] Is it then possible to use nuclear tone to indicate syntactic coherence? This suggestion is a little more promising, but ultimately it too has to be abandoned. It is true that we could argue that in the utterance of l. 497 the rising tone of the first tone-unit might be held to indicate incompleteness and so to link the first tone-unit with the second, which has a falling, 'conclusive' tone (see, for example, Crystal 1969: 216). But there are two problems here. First, there will be constructions which exemplify the same tonal structure, but which we would not want to associate grammatically. So, for example, if we look at ll. 523–4:

l. 523 'that is your thúmb
'that is your lìttle 'finger/

the prosodic characteristics are similar to l. 497 (two tone units, rising tone in the first and falling in the second), but we cannot see a grammatical link between the two simple clauses. Second, there will be cases where the rising tone + falling tone sequence does *not* arise (as in l. 487),[7] but we would still want to recognize a grammatical link between the simple clauses.

This catalogue of problems should be enough to preclude the systematic use of prosodic features to make grammatical decisions. It is more fruitful for us to consider the prosodic and the grammatical as independent systems which do make intermittent contact; however, neither is wholly determined by the other.[8] The rejection of prosodic criteria for segmentation does not do away with the problem, though. We need to set up a consistent approach to utterances like those at ll. 487–8, which will become increasingly more common as Sophie gets older. From an analytic point of view, we need to record not only the increasing diversity of coordinative and subordinative links between two clauses, which began to develop in sample 2, but the chaining together of clauses into longer and longer constructional sequences. In order to assess Sophie's development by comparing successive language samples, there seems little alternative at present to the procedure we have adopted, which is to analyse the complex sequences in two stages:

(a) Identify a complex construction represented by a two-clause sequence, and assign it to its appropriate stage V complex sentence category,
(b) Where a contiguous sequence of items identified under (a) exist in a child's utterance between two adult utterances, represent the sequence separately using these symbols:
s,c for subordinator, coordinator

S,M for subordinate clause, main clause
for the boundary of a complex construction identified under (a).

Thus ll. 487, 488 are analysed as follows:

(i) l. 487 = subord A
l. 488 = subord A
(ii) The sequence is represented as sSM csSM

This procedure will allow us to characterize changes in clause-linking devices over time and to determine the relevance to development of sequences of complex clauses of varying lengths. We can now return to the utterances listed in table 5.1.

Relatives

We begin with the single item under this heading, which occurs at l. 420:

ˈI only ˈknow a ˈperson says this

Strictly, this should probably be assigned to a category 'Ambiguous', since it is not possible to tell from its internal structure or unequivocally from the context whether it is a subord: O structure (like (1) below) or a construction incorporating a relative clause modifying 'person', but with the relative marker omitted (like (2)):

1. I only know [a person says this]
2. I only know a person [ø says this]

The occurrence of the tonic on *person* could be argued to favour the relative-clause interpretation, as could Fran's response at l. 421. Sophie has made 'a funny noise' on the recorder (ll. 417 ff.) and Fran at l. 421 seems to be acknowledging an identified referent (or referents). It is possible that the 'person' Sophie refers to at l. 420 is one of these referents. Let us assume that this is the more plausible interpretation, and consider first of all relevant information from the literature on relative-clause development, which, though extensive, has little on production data. (For an enlightening review, see Hamburger and Crain 1982.) One informative account based on longitudinal spontaneous data is Limber (1973). He reports (from records of three US children) that relatives on 'empty' NPs like *thing* or *one* appear at 2;9, whereas relatives on common nouns like *ball* appear at about 3;0. He also notes that all relatives in his data are object relatives, and that those on common nouns are infrequent. Limber does not mention the omission of obligatory relative markers in his data, but it would not perhaps be surprising if a child overgeneralized from the regular omission of a relative marker where the head of the relative clause is an object, as in *the girl I know*, *the man you saw last week*, to omit the marker where the head of the relative clause is a subject (as in Sophie's *a person says this*). In their discussion of the development of (restrictive) relatives, Hamburger and Crain suggest that two factors must be present for a construction that is not an accurate adult-type relative to count as a prototype of a relative clause. Syntactically, there must be a verb within a noun phrase, and in addition the relative clauses should be interpretable as placing 'a restriction on the set referred to by the noun phrase'. In Sophie's [a person [says this]], the first requirement is met. But it is not so obvious that this sentence meets the second requirement, since, except in a rather trivial sense, it is not clear that relativizing 'empty' NPs like *person*, particularly when they are indefinite, effects a restriction on a set.[9] However, more fruitful discussion of the nature and function of Sophie's relative clauses will await more extensive data from her. What we can say is that her 'relative' conforms in its appearance after the emergence of other complex constructions, in relativizing the object of the main clause, where this object is an 'empty' NP. It seems to be unusual, however, in having a subject as its head (though see note 9) and in omitting the relative pronoun.[10]

Causal adverbials

The LARSP profile analysis is not set up to distinguish between functionally different types of adverbial clauses. The distinct functions are signalled by the connectives that introduce these clauses, and an account of complex sentence development which omitted reference to function would be misleadingly one-sided. Within the LARSP sample, the new connective to appear is |*cos*:[11]

l. 166 he didn't go to school cos his half-term

Sophie omits the subject and verb from the *cos* sequence, so strictly speaking this is not a complex sentence, but both the connective and the reason proffered for Sammy's absence from 'school' suggest that we should consider the construction as a possible causal adverbial. The initial discussion was at l. 119 ff., where Fran first asks about Sammy's absence. Sophie provides a reason at l. 126, where the clause introduced by *cos* does include subject and verb, and she then repeats this for no obvious reason at l. 166, but this time the attempt to incorporate the '*cos* clause into a complex sentence appears to affect the syntax of the subordinate clause. Despite the fact that the reason provided by Sophie for Sammy's absence is highly implausible (half-term holidays are for the whole school, and are not granted to single pupils),[12] Fran does not comment. Bloom, Lahey et al. (1980) record the emergence of complex sentences with causal relationships and connective *cos* at 32 months, with *cos* as the next connective to appear after *when*. Although the order of emergence of these items does fit our data, the ages do not seem to match too well.

One other point which is worth emphasizing with reference to causal relations between sentences in children's language is made by Hood (1977) (reported in Bowerman 1979). The early and (in Hood's data) productive use of *cos* to indicate a causal relationship is in marked contrast to reports on experimental studies which indicate that the child's grasp of causal relations is still developing by the age of 7 or 8 (for example, Piaget 1959). The explanation for the discrepancy is, according to Hood, because the experimental studies have concentrated on physical or logical causal relations between sentences, whereas the relations expressed in early spontaneous speech tend to be 'motivational or psychological' (as in the Sophie examples we have quoted).

Complementation

We saw in sample 2 that Sophie used complements accompanying the verbs *know* and *watch*. We find in sample 3 a limited extension of this pattern, to *thought* and *sayed*. In the two examples accompanying *thought*, there are errors in the dependent clause, where the past auxiliary is omitted. The complement-taking verbs that Sophie uses fit with those reported elsewhere (Bloom, Lahey et al. 1980; Limber 1973). Of the verbs used, *think* (as Limber points out) cannot normally be used without a nominal complement. As in the data provided by Bloom and colleagues, Sophie does not appear to use *that* as a complementizer with these verbs.

Coordination

In sample 2 we saw the first examples of coordination, both phrasal and sentential.[13] Coordination was not frequent, however, nor is it in this sample. It is a little difficult to tell whether Sophie is or is not unusual in this respect, because, despite a large literature on the topic, there is very little on the statistics of coordination (though see below). A good deal of the discussion has concerned the relationship between the facts of language development and linguistic theory, and investigators have been interested in the relative order of appearance of phrasal and sentential coordinations, and the character of these coordinations, in order to relate them to rules or schemas for coordination in the adult grammar. The dominant methodological approaches have been comprehension testing and elicited production, and there is little analysis of spontaneous production data. However, some information can be gleaned from Tager-Flugsberg, de Villiers and Hakuta (1982) and Bloom. Lahey et al. (1980). First, we can assume that the incidence of coordination up to a point at which the MLU(m) level is 4.25 (for Sophie, somewhere between samples 2 and 3) is low (as a proportion of all structures). (Of course, we have been led to expect by Paul (1981) that the proportion of complex sentences in samples from pre-school children will on average be about 0.10.) A count by Tager-Flugsberg and colleagues on the Brown corpora finds just 360 'well-formed coordinations' (of which 108 are sentential), up to the point at which each child reached an MLU of 4.25. The periods reviewed for each child were: Adam, 20 months; Sarah, 17 months; and Eve, 7 months. Since we know that the minimum amount of data available from these children was two hours of recording per month (Brown 1973: 51), it follows that Tager-Flugsberg et al. found only about four coordinations per hour in these transcripts, of which 2.45 are sentential.[14] The second point to emerge from these figures on the Brown corpora is that there is individual variation in the use of the coordinative construction across children. The figures indicate these average sentential coordinations per month:

Adam	3.35
Sarah	1.35
Eve	2.51

Of Sophie's five sentential coordinations listed in table 5.1, one shows an appropriate subject deletion in the second clause:

I put my finger through and phone up somebody

Two of the others show anaphoric reference between the second and first clauses:

I ring up somebody and her name is (1 syll.)
I want to ring up somebody and her won't be there tomorrow.

The remaining two show neither of these linkage features:

you can get my tights and I get some sweets
that's your thumb and that's your thumb

Since the two clauses in the first example refer to separate events with distinct agents, whereas in the second example the deictics indicate two separate items, the contexts constrain the syntactic possibilities. No deletion or gapping is possible in the first example (except possibly the main verb, but that produces a very strange-sounding coordination - *you can get my tights and I some sweets*), and no anaphor in either case. We can reasonably suggest on the basis of these examples that Sophie is sensitive to the pragmatic constraints that control the syntactic options in coordinations.[15] But once again, we await more data.

Temporal adverbials

The final heading in table 5.1 includes clauses linked by *while*, *when*, which do not appear in the LARSP sample, but are found elsewhere in sample 3. We have already seen specifying clauses linked to a main clause by *when*, but the *while* is new. It looks as though Sophie's use of *while* at l. 487 is an imitation of her mother's introduction of the item at l. 461; indeed when Sophie uses *while* at l. 487 she uses a very similar 'period of time' in the *while* clause -

Hester at's recorder - compared with her mother's *while Hester is doing her recorder*. The other *while* clauses Sophie uses, very shortly after the first, are concerned with the same (or similar) events. And she very soon switches to *when* clauses (l. 497) to specify the time of the action in the main verb, which suggests that she sees the two connectives as synonymous. There is a good deal of support for her view in the language she will hear. It is true that, leaving aside the concessive use of *while* (as in '*while I am prepared to condone violence, I am not*, etc.'), we can contrast the *while* and *when* as durational vs. punctual, as in *while John was gardening, Millie was reading* vs. *when John arrived, everything stopped*. However, *when* can be substituted in the first example with very little change in meaning (though the reverse is not true). The aspectual distinction which is available between the two items is neutralized in many contexts, and it seems unlikely that Sophie will have grasped the rather subtle interaction between the connective chosen and the verb forms in the clauses linked, which conveys where necessary the temporal connection between the events of the main and subordinate clause. We saw that in clauses containing 'because', the association between the events or states referred to was only loosely causal. Again, in these temporal clauses there is no reason to assume that because Sophie is using *while*, she understands that the event or state in the main clause (a) has duration[16] and (b) that its duration is contained within (or is coextensive with) the limits of the (also durational) event or state in the subordinate clause. She certainly understands that there is a temporal association, but is unlikely as yet to have worked out its full implications.

A comparison of sample 3 with sample 2 complex sentences shows some advance on Sophie's part. As the range of complex structures available to her expands and we are able to examine in some more detail the structure and functions of these items, what begins to be apparent is the heterogeneity of the structures included under the 'complex sentence' heading. While it is true that her utterances are becoming longer and that one reason for the length increase is the higher incidence of multi-clause sequences linked in various ways, the grammatical constructions and the problems they pose for the child are very different in complementation, say, as opposed to coordination. In learning about complementation, the child has to learn that certain verbs govern clauses which follow and which have either a particular structure associated with them, or a limited range of structures. So *think*, for instance, can be followed by *that + finite clause* or simply *clause*, whereas *want* can never be followed by *that*, but must have a non-finite clause with an infinite marking the verb. For coordination, on the other hand, the syntactic relationship is less restricted, and at its simplest can be defined as *clause and clause*. There are, however, contextual conditions which affect how the second clause may be linked to the first, or whether clausal coordination is appropriate. It is also true that the functions of the various constructions are very different, and the analyst may need to consider this, to achieve an appropriate developmental perspective which will link constructions which happen to be included under the heading of 'complex sentences', to other non-complex constructions which are functionally similar. There are obvious functional links, for instance, between relative clauses and phrasal post-modification of nouns, and between temporal adverbials and phrasally realized temporal specification, which should not be ignored.

A more detailed consideration of 'complex sentences', going somewhat beyond the bare facts of the syntactic profile, has indicated some of the changes between samples 2 and 3. Other differences are also hinted at by the profile chart, but require some further elaboration. There is an increase in sample 3 in the number of auxiliaries, and in verb phrase expansions, but we will deal with these under the verb-forms heading below. We now turn to interrogatives, an important feature of the sample 2–sample 1 comparison. Are there any changes here?

Interrogatives

Although the proportion of interrogatives in the LARSP set of sample 3 is smaller than that of sample 2, the number overall in the sample is quite high. Because the appearance of apparently well-formed interrogatives in sample 2 marked an important change from sample 1, we paid some attention to them in the sample 2 commentary. What changes have taken place in interrogative structures since, and what can we make of these changes? In table 5.2 we have listed interrogative 'schemas' for sample 2 and sample 3. Included in these lists are both *wh*-initial and auxiliary initial structures. At first glance, it is not easy to see differences between the two samples. Closer examination, however, reveals subtle changes which may be interpreted as reflecting a rather gradual development over the period between 3 and 3½ years.

1. Whereas in sample 2 the occurrence of modals was limited to sentence-initial position, sample 3 includes wh-interrogatives with pre-subject modals:

   which one shall I do on the 'corder
   what shall I do
   why can we never touch your one

   In fact modals have been turning up for some time in this position – since 4.7.80, about a fortnight after sample 2. The modals represented since then in wh-interrogatives (always in small numbers, with at most five instances in a sample) are *could*, *couldn't*, *shall*, *should*, *can*. Another instance of the distributional extension of auxiliary forms is the appearance of *did* with *who*, where in sample 2 the auxiliary was omitted.[17] And *did* also now occurs with *how*,

TABLE 5.2 *Interrogative schemas, samples 2 and 3*

Sample 2			*Sample 3*		
Wh-word	*Auxiliary*	*Subject*	*Wh-word*	*Auxiliary*	*Subject*
	is	this		is	it
	are	those			
	do	this/it		do	you
	does	it			
	–			did	you
	can	our/me		can	I/you
	shall	me		shall	I/we
who	–	you	who	did/'s/past tense	NP/NP/I
what	∅/pres tense/ are/is/did	NP/PP/ NP/NP/her	what	shall/is/did	I/NP/you
where	are	you	where	's/–	NP/NP
why	's/did/didn't/ is/are/have/do	he/you.her. PN.it/me/ it/you.me/ it/me	why	didn't/don't/ can	you/I/we
which one	do	it	which one	shall	I
–	–		how	did/do	you/you
–	–		when	is	it

which, though not occurring in sample 2, did occur before sample 2, but only in the sequence *how d'you* (see p. 106).

2. The introduction of a new *wh*-initial item. Sample 3 sees the appearance of a *when*-initial structure. As it happens the first *when*-question also appeared in the sample for 4.7.80:

   when you go somewhere why do Jill look after us

   when-questions appear intermittently in samples between 4.7 and sample 3.
3. In some cases we can see in sample 3 an extension of subject range which, together with the verb changes, can be argued to signal a more productive use of interrogative structures by the child. In sample 2, *where* occurred only in the sequence *where are you*; it is

now followed by different NP subjects. In fact in sample 3 there are three wh-words - *who*, *what* and *where* - that take NP subjects, as against one in sample 2. Of course the majority of subjects are still pronouns (though the pronouns used are for the most part now the correct subject pronouns - see below).

There are changes here then (some of which have been in train for some time), which can be seen as representing progress since sample 2. In evaluating them, it is important to realize that they constitute a relaxation of the constraints on interrogative schemas available to Sophie in sample 2. But it is only a restricted relaxation, and there are two points to emphasize which may help to put the child's achievements with interrogative structures into perspective. First, for a child whose verb-forms now include a wide range of modals, *do*-support, full auxiliary + *-ing*, and auxiliary *have*, the range of auxiliary items represented in pre-subject position is very limited. We would expect future development to involve a much wider differentiation of pre-subject auxiliaries. Second, the long haul towards adult competence will surely bring more complex NP structures in subject position in questions. The slight changes between samples 2 and 3 are perhaps a hint of this, and we will watch out for this development.

This is perhaps the place to mention tag questions, even though none appear in sample 3. Tags did, however, suddenly occur in Sophie's speech on 20.10, when she used three of them for the first time. They then appear with some regularity, variety and frequency, up to and beyond 2.12. As this is a significant development since sample 2, we should not ignore it simply because sample 3 fails to represent it, and we can summarize development up to 2.12 in table 5.3, simply by listing different tags that occur from their first occurrence on 20.10. It is noticeable from the outset that Sophie has a range of different tags available. If we consider simply the different auxiliaries represented, there are 11 types (*aren't*, *can't*, *couldn't*, *doesn't*, *don't*, *didn't*, *haven't*, *isn't*, *wasn't*, *won't*, *wouldn't*). If we consider auxiliary + pronoun sequences, there are 28 different types represented up to 2.12.

The grammar of tags is generally considered complex in English. The main problem faced by the child in learning how they are formed is the choice of auxiliary in the tag. In the simplest case, the tag auxiliary is the negative form of the auxiliary used in the main clause to which the tag is attached.

he can come, can't he
she is a singer, isn't she

Where there is no auxiliary in the main-clause verb-form, the child has to learn that a *do*-form appropriate in tense and number is used:

he made the apple pie, didn't he
she likes swimming, doesn't she

TABLE 5.3 Tags occurring between 20.10.80 and 2.12.80 in Sophie's speech

20.10	aren't you	1.11	don't I
	didn't I		don't they
	aren't I		can't I
	don't they		don't you
	haven't I		haven't you
	can't I		didn't they
			don't we
5.11	isn't it	10.11	couldn't we
	don't you		
	doesn't it	14.11	didn't we
	wasn't it		couldn't we
	didn't we		don't you
	wouldn't I		haven't you
	aren't I		haven't I
	aren't you		won't I
			don't we
			isn't it
20.11	couldn't her	26.11	haven't I
	couldn't I		don't I
	don't I		can't we
	isn't it		isn't it
	aren't they		
	don't it	28.11	aren't I
	won't it		haven't you
	wasn't her		isn't it
	didn't you		isn't her
	don't we		
	aren't we		
	haven't we		
	won't you		

Do-support is also used where catenatives precede the main-clause verb:

he has to leave at nine, doesn't he

Although it is probably most common for tags to reverse the polarity of the main clause, either as in the examples quoted or in cases where the main clause is negative and the tag positive (***he can't come, can he***, ***she isn't a singer, is she***), a same-polarity option also exists: ***he can come, can he***, or ***she isn't a singer, isn't she***. In all the cases we have quoted, the grammatical requirements for a tag hold (a sequence of matched auxiliary ± negative + pronoun), but the functions of the tag can vary. In the less common same-polarity cases, positive + positive cases are said to indicate 'the speaker's arrival at a conclusion by inference, or by recalling what has already been said' (Quirk and Greenbaum 1973: 195). Another way of putting this is that in the positive + positive case the speaker is asking for confirmation of a proposition he has good reason to presuppose is true (or at least, better reason than in the positive + negative case). The negative + negative case, rare in adult speech, does not appear either in Sophie's speech or in the reports of tag use by other children, so can safely be ignored.

Another factor relevant to the function of tags is their intonation (see above p. 18). A rising tone on the reversed polarity tag indicates that the speaker is requesting information or confirmation from the hearer, with respect to the main-clause proposition. A falling tone indicates the speaker's expectation that the hearer will agree to the proposition in the main clause. (In the positive main clause + positive tag, the tone on the tag is always rising.) Sophie's tags here all have falling tone.

With this brief description as background, we can now look in detail at the tags for one of the samples close to sample 3. The sample summarized here is that for 20.11.80. We will examine the syntactic characteristics of these items, and consider how they fit into Sophie's discourse. There are 17 tags in the sample, and they are listed, along with the conversational extracts in which they are embedded, in table 5.4.

The first point of note about table 5.4 is that all of Sophie's tags are negative, with the main clause to which they are attached being positive. In a study of 36 nursery-school children's use of tags (age-range 2;10–5;7), Berninger and Garvey (1982) found a two-to-one preference overall for the positive + negative sequence in main clauses plus tags. So Sophie's preference is not surprising by comparison. However, Todd (1982), in a longitudinal study of his daughter's tags, reports no negative tags up to the age of 5;3, even though tags began to be produced at 3;2. So his child, Audrey, would always produce sequences like *we're 'going hòme àre we*, or *'he looks sìlly dòes he*, with a falling tone on the tag. This is the odd feature, of course. As we have seen, if the tags with these examples had a rising tone they would seem quite normal. With a falling tone they sound odd: as Todd says, 'omission of negation in tags attached to affirmative declaratives is correct in adult speech only when the intonation on the tag is rising, or at least non-falling'. In terms of the age at which tags begin to appear, Audrey and Sophie are comparable. Both, however, appear to have produced tags somewhat in advance of the children in Brown's study, from the information given in Brown and Hanlon (1970). So far as it is possible to tell (from their table 1.3), Adam's first tag appeared at 3;11 and tags were relatively infrequent until 4;6. At 4;6, in a sample of (it would appear) 700 utterances, he produced 16 tags, and the next month, in a similar sample, 32. Sophie's figure of 16 tags for the 20.11 sample appears in approximately 300 utterances. On the basis of frequency alone, then, Adam at 4;7 might seem to be using tags similarly to Sophie at 3;5. Age is a notoriously unreliable guide to

TABLE 5.4 Tags and their environments for 20.11.80 sample

1.	F.	well I don't ˈknow that ˈshe'd really ˈwant a children's present/ wóuld she/
	S.	ˈher mìght/
		and ˈalso ˈher could plày with it/ còuldn't her/
	F.	well ˈgranny doesn't ˈplay with ˈgames very mùch sweetie/
2.	S.	ˈI could ˈgive her a ˈpack of càrds/ còuldn't I/
	F.	m̀m/
3.	S.	ˈhave to ˈput it on the bòttom/ dòn't I/
	F.	m̀m/
4.	S.	it ˈvery sòft/ ìsn't it/ (*isn't* = [ɪnt])
	F.	m̀m/
5–6	S.	ˈthose are ˈvery shàrp ˈscissors/ àren't they/
		ˈthis one is mìne/ ìsn't it (*isn't* = [ɪnt])
	F.	m̀m/
7.	S.	sailing off through night and day (sings) dòesn't it/ (*doesn't* = [dʌnt])
	F.	it ìs/
		like ˈMax's bòat/
8.	S.	ˈotherwise it ˈwill be bùtter/ wòn't it/
9.	S.	Griselda was ˈfighting with thàt pair/ wàsn't her/ (*wasn't* = [wɒnt])
	F.	m̀m
10.	S.	ˈher could ˈplay it with Hìlda/ coùldn't her/
	F.	m̀m/
11.	S.	ˈthese are mìne/ àren't they/
12.		you sàid/ ôh/ ôh/ dìdn't you/ (*didn't* = [dɪnt])
	F.	m̀m/
13.	S.	we nèed them/ dòn't we/
	F.	ḿm
	S.	we nèed them/
14.	S.	ˈwe're just ˈhading a ˈlittle chàt/ àren't we/
	F.	*laughs*
15.	S.	ˈwe got ˈsome new m̀ilk/ hàven't we/ (*haven't* = [hænt])
	F.	yès/
16.	S.	we ˈhave to ˈsit in a hìgh ˈchair/
	V.	dó you/
	S.	ˈat a gàtes one/ dòn't we/
17.	S.	ˈthat bìg one/
		you ˈwill bo càrcful/ wòn't you/

language ability in children, as we have already seen, so perhaps Adam and Sophie are comparable in their MLU. However, Adam's tags are said (Brown and Hanlon 1970: 43) to start *after* stage V, which he leaves at an MLU of 5.2 – somewhat in advance of Sophie's MLU figure for sample 3.

The only British English data we have for tags come from the Bristol project (Wells 1984), where the appearance of tags is located with reference neither to age nor MLU, but to the sequence of development of syntactic structures in this large sample study. Wells locates it at his stage VII, and confirms Brown and Hanlon's prediction that the first main clause + tag sequence comes later than the first well-formed polar (or *yes–no* interrogative).[18] This is not particularly helpful, however, as it is some time since we saw the first of these structures in the Sophie data. Perhaps a more interesting comparison is between the structures Wells lists as typical of his stage VII, and the type of structure found to co-occur with the onset of tags in the Sophie data. Wells gives as criterial for stage VII the filling out of the range of interrogative structures, the addition of a second auxiliary, and the emergence of the first complex structures. These are exemplified as follows:

Interrogative:	Where did you find it
Two auxiliaries:	We'll have to buy a plaster for it
Complex:	I need water because I haven't had water for a long time

No full comparison is of course possible without having samples from the Wells data comparable to Sophie's; nevertheless these examples do not look too dissimilar to the language we have seen from Sophie in samples 2 and 3. We saw the interrogative structure in sample 2, and the auxiliary and complex-sentence structures are available by sample 3. So the superficial comparison that is possible indicates that Sophie's level of ability is not unlike that of the Bristol children at the point of emergence of tags.

What of the grammatical characteristics of Sophie's tags on 20.11? We will consider auxiliaries first. These fall into three main groups:

1. Repetitions in the tag of the main-clause auxiliary or copula: nos. 1, 2, 5, 6, 8, 9, 10, 11, 14, 17 in table 5.4. This constitutes the majority of the items.
2. *Do*-support in the tag for tense-marked verb or catenative in the main clause: nos. 3, 12, 13, 16. The tag in 16 is somewhat unusual in this set in that it is a tag 'at a distance' from its main clause, which is *we have to sit in a high chair*. Sophie is talking about having her hair cut at a particular hairdresser's, which she refers to as the 'gates one'. The main clause is responded to by her father with *do you*, and she then produces the *don't we* tag, which is presumably dependent on main-clause *have to*.
3. There are three tags remaining which do not fit into either of these categories: nos. 4, 15 and 7. Nos. 4 and 15 have tags which are appropriate for a copula and an auxiliary, respectively, which have been omitted in the main clause:

 it ˈvery soft/ isn't it
 ˌwe got ˈsome new mìlk/ havèn't we

The second example constitutes of course an exception to the general rule she appears to be following that main verbs occurring without auxiliaries require *do*-support in the tag. However, since *got* is such a frequent item in input, marked with *have* auxiliary, it is perhaps not surprising that she treats it as a lexical exception to *do*-support and provides the appropriate auxiliary in the tag. She is consistent in this behaviour: all other cases of *haven't* as tags listed in table 5.3 occur with main-clause verb *got*, which is not marked with an auxiliary in positive declaratives.

The final term, *doesn't it* in no. 7, is the only item not explicable in terms of the grammatical context in which it occurs. The contextual notes for this sequence indicate that when Sophie is saying *sailing off through night and day*, she is holding a pen, on the side of which is a ship which appears to move when the pen is moved. The full sequence is:

S. 'show that to 'Granny Yorke/
'sailing 'off through 'night and day/ dòesn't it/
F. it is̀/ like 'Max's bòat/

The name 'Max' in Fran's response is a clue to what Sophie is talking about. Her 'sailing off . . .' is a quote from Maurice Sendak's *Where the Wild Things Are*, where Max, the main (human) character, is depicted sailing off to the land of the wild things. Although this explains the reference, it is not clear why, in the grammatical context, Sophie chooses *doesn't it* rather than *isn't it* as a tag. This, however, represents the only error she makes in the sample.

In all there are nine separate tags: *aren't*, *couldn't*, *doesn't*, *don't*, *didn't*, *haven't*, *isn't*, *wasn't*, *won't*.[19] The tags are used with a range of pronouns and Sophie demonstrates an awareness of the co-occurrence between pronouns and particular verb-forms by using *aren't* with *we* and *they*, and *isn't* with *it*; and by using *don't* with *I* and *we*, and *doesn't* with *it*. So far as the other aspect of pronoun choice in tags is concerned, its agreement with subject NP, she also shows by the following pairings, in which she is not simply repeating a subject pronoun in a tag, that she is following the appropriate pattern:

No.	*Subject NP*	*Tag pronoun*
5	those	they
9	Griselda	her
11	these	they

More data would of course be required before we could be sure that Sophie was in control of the subject NP–tag pronoun agreement rule, but these examples suggest that she is on her way.[20]

It has been frequently pointed out that the various aspects of agreement between tags and the declaratives on which they depend make this a relatively complex area of the grammar. Nevertheless it is an area of which Sophie has a reasonable command by the age of $3\frac{1}{2}$. The most important grammatical prerequisite for tag development is clearly the mastery of a range of auxiliary verbs, with the differentiation of the personal pronoun system being an important secondary consideration. As we saw in chapter 4, Sophie had already begun to develop her auxiliary system, and this development has continued between samples 2 and 3. She has also extended her personal pronoun system over this period. These grammatical advances, though necessary for the development of tags, are not of course a sufficient reason for their relatively sudden emergence at the time they do. This remains something of a mystery.[21]

Valency analysis

There is some indication of an increase in the number of verb types represented in a 50-utterance subset of sample 3, where we find 23 different lexemes as opposed to 19 in sample 2. It is at least possible that verb-type differentiation is a relevant index of change between 3;0 and 3;6.

Arguments

A count of arguments per verb token for sample 3 provides a figure of 2.02, which is in fact a decrease from the sample 2 figure of 2.48. So there has been little change when constructions are looked at in these terms. If we again compare verb overlap between the two samples, we find that the eight verbs which are common to the two analyses are: COME, DO, GO, GOT, HAVE, KNOW, TAKE and WANT. There are no surprises here – these would be very frequently occurring verbs in any sample. Nor are there any gross differences in valency structure for these verbs between samples 2 and 3. There is no similar change, for common verbs or for verbs generally, to that observed between samples 1 and 2 in the accretion of adverbial elements. We can now look at these elements in some detail, as an area of the grammar which is generally ignored in accounts of children's language development.[22] What adverbials are used, and are there any changes between samples 2 and 3? We can begin by looking at those verbs that samples 2 and 3 have in common, that occur with adverbials. Table 5.5 lists these verbs and the utterances in which they occur.

The first point to emphasize about these examples is the heterogeneity of the term 'adverbial' as we are using it, across the two samples. It can either consist of a single element or a phrase, with a variety of realizations. Examples:

One-element realizations:

adverb:	*now*, *again*, *back*
adjective:	*higher*
question word:	*why*, *where*

TABLE 5.5 Verbs common to both samples 2 and 3 which occur with adverbials (valency subsamples only)

Verb		*Sample 2*		*Sample 3*
COME	(1)[a]	once our came back from somewhere	(1)	but a jingle came off your dress
DO	(6)	you do it all by yourself can our do it again me did it now what are these pictures doing here	(10)	I want to do it higher want to do it on the piano d'you do it this way round shall I do this one again
GO	(9)	what goes in this hole sometimes me don't go to the teacher me always go with Maggie it does go there where does this go it doesn't go that way go this way do it go this side	(3)	it supposed to go on 'corder he don't go to school 'cos his half-term where's my piano book gone to
GOT	(5)	why have it got flowers on	(5)	but her got a colour one like this
HAVE	(4)	why did her have two sweets why did her have a runny tummy	(2)	–
KNOW	(1)	–	(1)	–

[a] Numbers in parentheses indicate total number of valency frames for each verb.

phrasal and other realizations:

NP: *this way (round)*
PP: *like this, from somewhere, on 'corder, to the teacher, on the piano*
Clause: *cos his half-term*

This heterogeneity is reminiscent of the well-known diversity of items within the traditional grammatical category of adverb, as applied to English. It seems possible that the structural variability seen here reflects a functional diversity, and we now need to consider the roles played in valency structure by what we have labelled adverbials.

The straightforward view of adverbials (see, for example, Lyons's characterization of adjuncts (1977: 435)) is that they are optional or omissible expressions, in grammatical terms, which specify a time, place, location, person, etc. relevant to the action of the verb. Their optionality is relevant only to the grammatical status of the sentence they occur in, and is checked by asking whether a sentence which is grammatical with the adverbial included remains so when it is left out. The simplest case is that of the temporal adverbial in a transitive sentence such as *Mary left Sam yesterday*, where the NPs *Mary*, *Sam* are required by the verb *leave* in order for the sentence to be grammatical, whereas yesterday is optional with respect to grammaticality. But the simplest case is not well represented in our data. Of the utterances listed in table 5.5, perhaps only one, *me did it now* (l. 453), resembles the *Mary left Sam yesterday* example. The rest of the examples tend to emphasize how difficult it can be to set up a simple binary distinction between 'central' (usually NP) elements and 'peripheral' (usually adverb or PP) elements. We saw in sample 1 that Sophie was already using prepositional phrases for indirect objects with the obvious divalent verbs like *put* or *give*. Such elements would be regarded as 'central' (the term used by Matthews, who discusses these issues in detail (1981: 123 ff.) or as verb 'elaborators' (Allerton 1982: 57 ff.). But it is not only verbs which in English have indirect objects realized as prepositional phrases which show a close link between verb and adverbial. So, for example, as Allerton (1982: 62) points out, a verb of motion like GO requires a directional adverbial, as in *Lily has gone to Haifa*. Since Sophie has already shown that she is sensitive to the valency requirements of verbs like PUT and GIVE, we might expect to find even in sample 2 that her utterances with GO include an appropriate adverb. It does turn out that all but one instance of GO, in each sample, have adverbial elements. A glance at the examples in table 5.5, however, reveals that the statement of relationship between GO and its adverbials needs refining: it is not simply a matter of a motion verb being specified as to the direction of the motion. GO is not used even by Sophie simply as a verb of motion, or at least motion by a human agent. In a number of the cases in sample 2 where she is referring to the puzzle she and her mother are doing, GO has a meaning something like 'fit', and adverbials such as *in this hole*, *there* are more locational than directional, while adverbial NPs such as *that way*, *this way*, could be interpreted as either locational or manner. The third NP adverbial in sample 2, *this side*, is more obviously locational. Other non-directional adverbials are *with Maggie*, and *on 'corder*. If *with Maggie* occurred with GO in a similar adult utterance, it would be argued that a directional element has to be reconstructed from the context for this to be understood. As it happens, the direction in this instance is available when Sophie uses this adverbial at l. 509. The other example, *it supposed to go on 'corder*, appears to be an idiosyncratic and non-adult use of GO, meaning something like 'be played'. However, it clearly requires the adverbial provided.

Whatever the more complex statement of GO and its required elaborators would look like, it seems clear that in most instances the verb does expect adverbials, and also that Sophie is sensitive to this requirement from as early as sample 2, and is able to supply the appropriate forms. If we examine other verbs common to samples 2 and 3 in table 5.5, we see that there are no obvious differences in valency structure between the two samples. It is also clear that there is a gradation in this set of verbs between verbs like GO, which require adverbials, through DO, which has them about half the time, to GOT, which rarely uses them.

If we now turn to a comparison of all verbs in valency samples 2 and 3, can any differences be discerned? Have the realizations of the adverbials changed, or is there an increase in the range of functions they perform? In sample 3, as in sample 2, we find adverbial question words (for example, *why*). Temporal adverbials are present in both samples, but the set shows more variety in sample 3 (*now*, *straight after lunch*, *today*, *another day*, *never*). There is a causal adverbial clause (discussed above), which is new in the later sample, and also phrases of comparison such as *like this*, (*bigger*) *than me*, which are novel. There are also phrases like *with my 'corder*, *on 'corder*, *on the piano*, which are clearly adverbial, but a little more difficult to assign function to. As before in this chapter, then, we find the differences between the two samples to be in the elaboration in sample 3 of structural types already represented in sample 2.

Deixis

We noted in the commentary on sample 2 the appearance of a possible *this/that* contrast in Sophie's conversation, but also came to the conclusion that the basis for it was unlikely to be the spatial proximal/distal distinction that has formed the framework for experimental approaches to the comprehension of this pair of items. The data in sample 3 seem to support these conclusions (in so far as is possible for production data without a visual record). *That* is still used more frequently than *this* (about four times as often); both items are used as pronouns and determiners, and there appears to be no restriction on their positions in clause structure - both appear in subject and object position.[23] The clearest example of a contrastive use of *this/that* seems to be at ll. 323 ff., where Sophie is searching through her music for the sheet that she wants:

S. what one was I doing
not that one
l. 325 not that one
this
what is that one
what is that one

Here at l. 326 she uses *this* to refer to the sheet of music she wants. It is not easy to see, in the context of turning over sheets of music, a near-to-speaker/

away-from-speaker spatial basis for the choice of the two forms, though certainly the choice of *this* for the crucial piece of music could be assumed to be speaker-centred. But it is the relevance of the piece for the speaker, rather than its spatial proximity, which governs the choice, if our assumption is correct. There is also evidence that the contrast is not really controlled by Sophie, as for example at ll. 282–3:

S. shall I do this one again
cause I love that one

Here she seems to be referring to the same piece on both occasions, in which case the use of different demonstratives would be inappropriate.

There are also signs in the sample of extended uses of *this/that* for discourse purposes. In particular, Sophie uses *this* to anticipate something that is about to take place, and *that* to refer back in the conversation (cf. Fillmore 1975: 71). So, for example, at l. 265 she says:

S. that is daisy/

with reference to a piece she has just played; or again, l. 350, after she has again played her recorder for a time:

S. weren't that beautifully/

At l. 420, her *this* refers to something which she then plays:

S. I only know a person says this/

But, again, there are signs that she does not yet control the use of a form when she uses *that* instead of *it* in l. 375:

that is my [tɪntɪvɩ] play on Sunday

She seems to have overgeneralized the *that is* schema, which she is using increasingly in this sample, to refer to previous events or objects, to an event that is yet to take place. This is not surprising: what she has to learn about discourse uses of *this* and *that*, and the appropriacy conditions for the use of *its* and existential *there's*, is complex. It would be possible to say *there's my* [tɪntɪvɩ] *play on Sunday*, but only in a context where, for example, potential Sunday activities were under discussion by the participants in the conversation.[24] Despite the appearance of some restricted uses of *this* and *that* as discourse deictics, Sophie still has a great deal to learn in this area.

One other topic which is worth mentioning in this section concerns the deictic verbs of motion *come* and *go*. The conditions governing the use of *come* vs. *go* are complex in the adult language, but a minimum requirement for the use of *come* is that it indicate motion towards the speaker, whereas *go* is used for motion to a location distinct from the speaker.[25] The child's development of an appreciation of the conditions governing the use of *come* and *go* has been examined experimentally by Clark and Garnica (1974) and

Tanz (1980). In the study by Tanz, no subject under 4 years of age achieved criterion for her *come/go* experiment, and of 19 subjects over 4;0 (the top end of her age-range was 5;3), only six demonstrated knowledge of the contrast. In sample 3 Sophie provides one example of *come* which is appropriate, when at l. 40 she says:

I thought you coming straight after lunch here

She is talking about her mother appearing at the location she, Sophie, was at, and the choice of verb indicates that she has some knowledge at least that speaker location is relevant to its selection. But on the available data there is very little to be said other than that. It is certainly not possible for us to contradict the comprehension study evidence.

A similar conclusion emerges from looking at Sophie's use of *here* and *there* in sample 3. *Here* is linked appropriately with *come* in the utterance at l. 40 above, and *there* appears at l. 342, linked with *that*:

who did that writing on there

So there is once again appropriate use of items which, when they are specifically contrasted in an experimental context, cause problems for children of Sophie's age (more than half of Tanz's 3-year-old subjects were not able to cope with the *here/there* contrast). We do not, however, in the production data available, have any analogue in the use of the contrastive experimental situation; in addition, the co-occurrence of *come* with *here*, and *that* with *there*, is common in the language directed at the child. So we have to conclude that more evidence is required before we can be sure about the child's grasp of these items. But it is also necessary to underline the differences between the assumed basis of the child's comprehension, when successful in the experimental situation, and the uses that we see in production. Otherwise we can misinterpret the comprehension-production relationship (see above pp. 2ff.). The experimental situation (for example, Tanz 1980: 83) concentrates on the proximal/distal basis in the immediate environment of the speaker for the investigation of the child's understanding of *here* and *there*. Tanz gave her subjects sentences such as:

The plate over here has the penny under it
The plate over there has the penny under it

The sentences were 'spoken' by two dolls, one of which stood next to each plate. Sophie's use of *there* at l. 342 could be said to be with reference to object location in the immediate environment, as in the experiment. The use of *here* at l. 40, however, is different to the experimental *here*, since it concerns motion to the speaker from an outside location. The general point is that careful attention to the contexts of use in production may indicate that our production analysis is tapping rather different abilities to those being addressed in comprehension.

Personal pronouns

A comparison of the use of personal and possessive pronouns across the three samples we have considered appears in table 5.6. The table represents the dimensions of the system as follows:

1. personal pronoun vs possessive determiner vs possessive pronominal;
2. first, second and third person, singular and plural (where relevant);
3. subject/object distinctions for personal pronouns (where relevant);
4. gender distinctions for third person.

Although facts about frequency or errors are not available from the profile, it is apparent from it that there have been some changes between samples 2 and 3:

1. The differentiation of subject and object pronouns, apparent in sample 2 for *he/she*, and somewhat earlier for *I/me*, continues with the addition of *we* to Sophie's repertoire.
2. Possessive determiner use is extended to *her*, by the time of sample 3, and perhaps also to *their*. However, as this only occurs in a line of a carol (l. 18, *washed their sheep*), we cannot be too confident. *Our* has now (temporarily, presumably) disappeared from Sophie's repertoire as *we* has become available as a subject pronoun.
3. The least controlled dimension, at this point, is that of the possessive pronominal, for which *mine* is the only attested example.

Apart from the minor changes and the obvious deficiency, one error - that of substituting *me* for *I* - has been all but eliminated by sample 3 (though see l. 365). The tendency to substitute object for subject pronoun is still present, however, but shifted from first person to third, where *her* is almost exclusively used for female pronoun subjects (see, for example, the sequence about telephoning a friend, from l. 361 on). There is further evidence here that the case-marking problem is being solved item by item, though in fact the she/her distinction is the last one to be achieved, at least for the pronouns. We can see this from table 5.3, where a number of different tags are listed: the only error for case is with *her*, which perhaps remains recalcitrant because of its frequency and prominence in the conversation between Sophie, her mother and her sisters. (See note 18 of chapter 4.)

Articles

Once again, the articles *the* and *a* tend to be infrequent in the sample, although, as we can see under other headings (deixis, possessive determiners), there is no shortage of items (*my*, *its*, *that*) in Sophie's repertoire to serve a determiner

TABLE 5.6 Personal and possessive pronoun profile, samples 1–3

	Personal pronoun		Possessive (determiner)		Possessive (pronominal)	
Singular						
1	I	me	me		mine	
	√/(√)/√)	√/√/√/	–/√/√/		–/√/√/	
2	you		your		yours	
	√/√/√/		–/√/√/		–/–/–/	
3	he	she	his	her	his	hers
	–/√/√/	–/√/(√)/	–/√/√/	–/–/(√)/	–/–/–/	–/–/–/
	him	her	its			
	–/–/(√)/	–/√/√/	–/–/–/			
	it					
	–/√/√/					
Plural						
1	we	us	our		ours	
	–/–/√/	–/√/–/	√/√/–/		–/–/–/	
2	you		your		yours	
	–/–/–		–/–/–/		–/–/–/	
3	they	them	their		theirs	
	–/√/(√)/	–/√/(√)/	–/–/√/		–/–/–/	

Sample 1/sample 2/sample 3/
√ = present in sample
(√) = present in recent sample
– = not present in this or any recent sample

function. This sample also includes *some* and *much* as determiners. There are some slight signs, however, of advance, with fewer errors of omission, one new type of error, and one possible example of an appropriate non-specific use of *a* followed by a specific use of *the*. The instances of *a* are similar to those seen in sample 2 (with two exceptions), for example, *this isn't a piano book*, *why d'you never buy my a guitar*, *that's a good idea*. The first exception is an error at 1.417, *shall I make a funny music*, where *a* is used inappropriately with a mass noun. It is possible that the inclusion of *some* into the determiner system (for example, 1.450, *I wanted you to buy some sweeties*) has precipitated this error by making Sophie unsure of the application of other determiners. Alternatively, such an error may simply reflect the freeing of *a* from a purely collocational usage, and its use by Sophie as a choice in an independent system which she has only begun to grasp.

The second exception is not so much in the use of *a*, but in Sophie's use of *the*, once *a* has been used to introduce a referent. At l. 131, Sophie (discussing a particular dress of her mother's that she likes) says, *but a jingle came off your dress*. The dress continues to be the topic of conversation up to l. 141, where Sophie refers to the dress again, saying *I want the tinkle*. Although the two lexical items are different, it is possible that this is an appropriate use of *the* to indicate a referent made specific for speaker and hearer by an earlier introduction into the conversation. But we cannot be sure: 'tinkle' may refer to the dress, in which case the use of *the* in l. 141 is simply another example of the 'larger situation' image of the definite article discussed in chapter 4. It is certainly the case that the other uses of *the* in sample 3 fall under this heading:

l. 149 the piano
l. 232 the rocking chair

The use of articles remains limited, and we have to conclude that Sophie's awareness of their functions is probably little advanced on sample 2.

Verb-forms

The different forms which appear in samples 1, 2 and 3 can be compared by means of a profile of English verb-forms such as that used in table 5.7. Like all profiles, this is selective: it does not, for example, in items 7–11 distinguish between alternate forms of *is* and *was* with *-ing*, nor between full and reduced forms of *is* and *have*. It does, however, comprise 33 forms, covering inflections, auxiliaries, modals, some catenatives and various forms of the copula. Items 1–4 are present and past-tense forms; (UVF or unmarked verb-form refers to stems with no inflection, which are *usually* present tense). Items 5 and 6 are for verbs which have *-en* or *-ing* inflections, but no auxiliary. The next five items (7–11) cover present and past progressive forms, and present and past perfect forms (*have* + *got* is listed separately, for reasons we return to later). The next two items are present and past forms of *do*-support (12 and 13), and they are followed by ten modals (14–23). Items 24–26 are three of the most common catenatives: *have to*, *going to* used for future reference, and *used to* for past habitual actions. Item 27 is *been*, used without an auxiliary, and finally items 28–33 are various forms of *be* used as a copula. If any item is present once in a sample, it is marked in table 5.7 – there is no frequency information included in the profile.

The dramatic changes in verb-form use between samples 1 and 2, discussed in chapter 4, are graphically represented in the profile. The changes between samples 2 and 3, as we might expect from the comparisons we have already made in other areas of the language, are more subtle. If we simply look at incidence, then the items that appear in sample 3 that were not present in sample 2 are past progressive (8), *won't* (17), *should* (21), *would* (22), *might*

TABLE 5.7 *Verb-form profile, samples 1–3*

	Forms	*Sample 1*	*Sample 2*	*Sample 3*
1.	UVF	√	√	√
2.	Third singular	–	√	√
3.	Regular past	–	√	√
4.	Irregular past	√	√	√
5.	*-en*	–	√	√
6.	*-ing*	√	–	–
7.	is + *-ing*	–	√	√
8.	was + *-ing*	–	–	√
9.	have + got	–	(√)	√
10.	have + PP	–	–	(√)
11.	had + PP	–	–	–
12.	do + V	–	√	√
13.	did + V	–	√	√
14.	can	–	√	√
15.	can't	–	√	√
16.	will	–	√	√
17.	won't	–	–	√
18.	shall	–	√	√
19.	must	–	√	√
20.	could	–	√	(√)
21.	should	–	–	(√)
22.	would	–	–	(√)
23.	might	–	–	(√)
24.	have to	–	√	√
25.	going to	–	√	√
26.	used to	–	–	√
27.	been	–	√	–
28.	is	–	√	√
29.	am	–	–	√
30.	are	–	√	(√)
31.	was	–	–	√
32.	were	–	–	√
33.	'cop	–	√	√

√ = present in sample.
(√) = not present, but present in recent sample.
– = not present in this or any recent sample.

(23), *used to* (26), *am* (29), *was* (31) and possibly *have* + past participle (10; see below for discussion). What the profile does not reveal is any information about frequency changes between samples 2 and 3, and also the elimination between the two samples of errors in verb-form use, such as the *-en* over-generalization discussed in the previous chapter. In addition, it is necessary to supply functional information – extensions of use in sample 3 of forms that are common to the two samples. These points will be taken up in the discussion.

Temporal forms

We will return first to the *-en* and *-ed* forms, and particularly to the virtual elimination of the *-en* overgeneralization from Sophie's repertoire by sample 3. Other topics to be covered are the adverbial specification of temporal forms, and changes in modal use between samples 2 and 3.

-en *and* -ed

As we noted earlier (see p. 000), the *-en* overgeneralization (forms like *putten*, *getten* used without an auxiliary) occurs initially about three months after sample 1. The form continues to appear almost to sample 3, although it is most frequent around the time of sample 2, and its use then declines. In attempting to account for any systematic error by a child, there are three issues that should be examined. First, is it possible to identify the *source* of the error. Why did the child adopt this particular morphological strategy? Second, we need to try to explain why the error *persisted*. This particular form lasts for nearly a year, in the face of data from the child's language environment which plainly would not reinforce it. And thirdly, we have to address the issue of why the child finally *eliminates* the error. We have already dealt with the issue of *source* to some extent in chapter 4, but we will now look at it in more detail, with particular reference to Berman (1983), because there seem to be parallels between Sophie's behaviour with *-en* and a widespread early error in Hebrew. For the root *r–d–m* (*fall asleep*) in Hebrew, which has present tense *nirdam*, children form * *miradem*. Berman's original explanation for this was the traditional one of overextension from an available pattern. Hebrew has a number of verb conjugations. The root *r–d–m* belongs to the *nif'al* set, whereas the *k–b–l* verb root is from another conjugation, *pi'el*, which forms present tense *məkabel* (generally pronounced by children *mikabel*). Since many of the verbs in the *pi'el* conjugation are familiar from an early age (verbs like *play*, *walk*), it seems plausible that Hebrew-speaking children would overextend the pattern for *pi'el* present tense to *nif'al* verbs.[26] Berman, however, proposes what she describes as a 'rather different explanation' for errors of this type. She wants to analyse use of the *m-* prefix for *nif'al* verbs 'not as an overextension of this morphophonological pattern to inappropriate lexical items', but rather as a device which is adopted by young children very early on, in order to 'mark the distinction between present tense and other forms of verbs'. The children, in her view, want to mark present tense as distinct from the imperatives and infinitives they have been using, and 'construe prefixal as the marker *par excellence* of present tense, so that they assign this marker both to verbs where the grammar requires it, and to inappropriate cases'. Now this is not actually a different explanation *to* overextension, but an explanation *of* overextension that the Israeli children adopt. The term overextension is a descriptive one, while Berman's 'interim strategy' for present-tense marking is an attempt to explain the child's adoption of this particular pattern. Sophie's *-en* overextension can be thought of in similar terms. The source of the suffix is, in general, clear enough.[27] It could be argued that Sophie's initial use of the *-en* suffix on irregular verbs is an attempt to mark for past tense, lexical items (like *put*, *bought*, *build*, etc.) which either do not have a marker for past tense, or where she does not recognize that a stem is already marked for past, or where she does not know the past-tense form. She has understood that there is a form/meaning relation between the *-en* suffix and a non-present state or action (and also, to judge from overextensions in table 4.2, a similar one for the *-ed* suffix) and is inclined to mark this, even where it is not called for in the adult system. As with the Hebrew children's marking present tense, it seems important for Sophie, once she has realized that there is a present/non-present distinction, to signal the non-present on all relevant occasions.

It is possible that there are further parallels between Sophie's use of *-en* and the *m*-prefix overextension in Hebrew, though since we have no chronology of the life-span of the form in an Israeli child it is not possible to make exact comparisons. Berman notes that the *m*-prefix error, like the *-en* overextension, is transitory. She emphasizes that it is 'restricted to child speech and ... is not found at later pre-school age', unlike other forms, which are not normal usage, but persist into the school years. For Sophie, *-en* eventually disappears, but *-ed* overextensions continue. We know that in other English-speaking children these morphological errors continue into the early school years (see, for example, Bybee and Slobin 1982). But even though the *-en* error is certainly a temporary phenomenon for Sophie, it does last in her speech for nearly a year. To try to account for this persistence, and the eventual elimination of the suffix as an overextension, we need to scrutinize the *-en* and other related forms over the relevant period. Why does it persist, particularly when the child clearly can use *-ed* forms, and why does she finally give it up?

The 'unlearning' of overextension errors is a matter of some interest for current language-acquisition theory (see, for example, Atkinson 1985; Mazurkewich and White 1984; for an earlier discussion see Braine 1971). It is an important claim of modern learnability theories that the child only learns language from 'positive' instances. That is, the child learning English is provided only with 'grammatical' sequences by his speech community, and receives no information on what is ungrammatical. The importance of the 'positive data only' principle for the linguist lies in the perceived relationship between linguistic theory and language acquisition. Generative grammar has always seen as a crucial task the explanation of how children acquire language.

If it is the case that children receive no correction in their input, then the theory has to be constrained so that it can achieve its explanatory task using rules that can be constructed according to universal principles (the child's innate endowment), interacting with positive data. A crucial issue here, empirically, is what counts as positive and negative data. Atkinson (1985) suggests that if we widen the search for negative data (beyond overt parental correction), we may well find that there are ways in which parents inform children that some forms are counter-indicated, even though the parents are not engaging in explicit correction.

How might Sophie's overextensions be relevant to these issues? An important contribution to the debate would be a demonstration that negative data are available.[28] One possible source of such data would be the nature of maternal responses to Sophie's use of *-en* overextensions. Is it possible to identify occasions on which Fran corrects, even implicitly, the form that Sophie uses? There are occasions on which this happens, as we can see in these two examples:

(a) (5.3.80) The topic is pirates, which have been the subject of work at school:

S. ˈpirate is ìn it/
F. whát/
S. ˈpirate is ìn it/
F. whìch ˈpirate is ˈin it/
S. rèd ˈpirate/
F. is in whát/
S. is - he hìden it/ (hiden = [ˈhaɪɕə n])
F. ˈhiding in whát/ dàrling
S. ˈhis sìlver/
F. ˈhis sílver/
S. m̀m/
F. oh he's hìdden it/

Fran's misunderstanding initially comes from the repetition early in the excerpt of *in it*, and from Sophie's use of the present-tense stem in her pronunciation of *hiden*. In the eventual reinterpretation (l. 12), Fran gives the appropriate grammatical form for the present perfect of *hide*, with the verb with the *-en* suffix being pre-modifed by an auxiliary.

(b) (7.8.80) Sophie is here engaged in some language play with no obvious contextual reference:

S. you ˈhaden a mòuth/
F. ˈwho had a mòuth/
S. bùs/
and he bìte it/

In this example the response is immediate and provides the correct form for a past-referring use of *have*.

The frequent occurrence of examples of discourse like either (a) or (b) could be useful information to Sophie, letting her know (a) that *-en* suffixed verbs are normally accompanied by auxiliaries or (b) that it is inappropriate to add *-en* to irregular verbs to mark past. Since examples of type (a) are strictly relevant only for 'correct' uses of *-en*, it is type (b) we should concentrate on. How extensive are they? It turns out that there are other instances of the same type in our data, but they are outnumbered by responses that could not be interpreted as giving 'correcting' information at all, or could give it only very indirectly. So, for example, in the same for 4.3.80, where there are five instances of *-en* suffixes without auxiliaries, there is only one of type (b):

S. ˈme hurten my tòe/
F. you ˈhurt your tóe/

The other four sequences containing a Sophie *-en* suffix do not provide the same kind of feedback:

F. ˈwhat hàppened/
S. ˈJack stepen on my tòe/
F. òh/
ˈis it bétter now/
S. nò/

and

S. ˈwhere my mán/
ˈme haden a màn/
F. your ˈlittle ˈlego màn/
S. yés/

Here there is no information to be gleaned from the response as to the status of the verb-form. There are other responses by Fran that, if they do anything, would seem to reinforce the use of *-en* as a past-referring form; for example:

1. (20.7.80) S. ˈme haden ˈthat when ˈme was a bàby/
F. ˈyes you dìd/
2. (27.5.80) F. ˈwho gave you that pùzzle/
S. ˈnobody given it to mè/
ˈhow did yoù get it ˈthen/
S. ˈme just bùyen it/
F. díd you/

Although it is true that, if we take all the data used as examples, there are some instances of negative data, taken overall the discourse sequences cannot be unequivocally interpreted. There is no neat solution here, it seems, to the problem of how Sophie removes her *-en* overextensions.

If we are no nearer explaining the disappearance of Sophie's *-en* overextensions through 'correction', nor are we any closer to satisfactorily accounting for the persistence of the form throughout 1980. Recall that we suggested that Sophie used *-en* as a past marker initially on verbs that either do not mark in English for past (*put*), or might not look to her as if they did (*bought*). We might speculate that her reason for choosing *-en* in the first place was because it seemed to her to refer to past, but there is no obvious phonological reason why she should transfer it from the frequent 'correct' *-en* forms – *fallen*, *broken*, *taken* – to verb stems ending in alveolars (though see note 27). It has been noted that English-speaking children are generally less likely to mark verbs with -t and -d stem-finals which require *-ed*, when they start using regular past. Sophie's behaviour is at variance with this general tendency, and for the explanation that has been proposed for it. In his updated discussion of operating principles for language acquisition, in relation to cross-linguistic evidence, Slobin (1985) discusses a constraint on the operation of the principle EXTENSION, which he refers to as affix-checking. When a verb already has a phonological shape similar to a past tense (like *put*, *hurt*), the child will tend to see this as a past-tense marker (by comparison with a *schema* that has already been established for past tense) and resist adding a 'further' past affix. 'Children orient to the form of a verb in relation to this schema, rather than add a suffix to modify its meaning.'

Not only does Sophie's early addition of *-en* on to verbs like *put* and *bought* serve as a counter-example to the principle of affix-checking, but her dual overextension for past does not fit either with the characterization given by Slobin to the operating principle of extension itself:

If you have discovered the linguistic means to mark a Notion in relation to a word class or configuration, try to mark the Notion on every member of the word class or every instance of the configuration, and try to use the same linguistic means to mark the Notion. (Slobin 1985; 44)

The term 'Notion' here is a 'general term for nodes in Semantic Space'. For the *-en* and *-ed* overextensions by Sophie, the Notion is pastness. The coexistence of *-en* and *-ed* overextensions appears to be a counter-example to the operation of the extension principle, as stated, since two forms are being used, apparently, with the same semantic import.

However, to return to the history of the *-en* extension in Sophie's speech, it has to be emphasized that she quite soon appears to free herself of this restriction to stems with final alveolars, and begins to generalize the ending. The two suffixes coexist with each other and with irregular pasts, and it is Sophie's growing ability to use the latter correctly that eventually superannuates the *-en* overextension. However, despite Sophie's use of *-en* with stem-finals other than alveolars, it is possible to see some phonological conditioning of her variable use of the suffixes that is related to the initial

TABLE 5.8 *Verb types and* -en/-ed *suffixes*

Irregular stems – -en *and* -ed	*Regular stems –* -en *and* -ed	*Irregular stems –* -en *only*	*Irregular stems –* -ed *only*
break	help	bought	do
bring	stay	build	drink
come		cut	fly
fall		get	saw
leave		had	say
make		hide	throw
take		hit	tell
wake		hurt	
		let	
		put	
		ride	
		sit	
		buy	
		drawn	
		run	
		wear	
		(seen)	
		(should)	
		(was)	

restriction of *-en* to alveolars. We can see this in table 5.8. This shows the distribution of verb types under four different headings:

1. those irregular verbs for which Sophie used both *-en* and *-ed* marking;
2. those regular verbs for which she was prepared to use both suffixes;
3. those irregular verbs to which Sophie only applied the *-en* suffix;
4. those irregular verbs to which she only applied the *-ed* suffix.

First, it is apparent that, so far as verb types are concerned, the *-en* suffix is a strategy for dealing with irregularity,[29] and that despite the relaxation of the initial alveolar constraint, it is, over the whole period, a strategy for dealing with irregulars with stem-final alveolars. This is not a categorial rule, but it is a general tendency. Second, the irregular verb types that are restricted to *-ed* overextensions are fewer in number, and tend to be those that end in vowels. Irregular verbs with stem-finals other than alveolars or vowels can be marked with either suffix. This rather straightforward phonological conditioning goes some way towards accounting for the variability in application of the suffixes over the period when they are both being used.[30] The demise of the *-en* is inevitable once Sophie appreciates that the irregulars with stem-final alveolars are either unchanged for past reference (*put*, *cut*), already marked for past (*made*, *had*) or require vowel change (*rode*, *hid*). The pattern between samples 1 and 2 is for these irregular verbs to be overmarked with *-en*; between samples 2 and 3, correct irregular forms become more likely.

Although we can *descriptively* approach the problem of the persistence and elimination of *-en* forms with reasonable success, the mechanism by which the child maintains and discards erroneous forms is still not entirely clear. The availability of the natural history of the suffix does, however, reveal the interaction at a relatively early age between the child's morpheme-recognition device and the problems posed for it by a specific natural language. The apparent functional similarity in English between *-en* and *-ed* forms, and the existence of a subgroup of strong verbs which do not mark for past, conspire to mislead the child temporarily.

Present perfect

When does Sophie differentiate past from present perfect? These are two distinct forms in English, at least in their paradigm cases, which we can exemplify by contrasting *he walked* and *he has fallen*. The formal differences here are obvious; it should, however, be apparent from earlier discussion that specifying the functional differences is not so straightforward, in particular because the forms can be used to refer to the same past event, especially if it is relatively recent, from different speaker perspectives. The child's differentiation of the two is not then helped by the fact that the paradigm form of the present perfect is rarely available in input. In positive declaratives the *have* auxiliary is contracted to *'s* or *'ve*, and for all regular verbs the past participle form is formed in the same way as the past tense, by the addition of *-ed*. The child is more likely, then, to be faced with the problem of distinguishing between *he's walked* and *he walked*, in situational contexts which are not conducive to maximizing the meaning difference between the two.

In the verb-form profile for sample 3, *have* + past participle is marked as not present, but as having occurred in a recent sample (see also table 5.7). In samples prior to this, however, *have* appears with a restricted range of past participles, and since these forms are available, the possibility needs to be investigated that Sophie develops some awareness of the differences between past and present perfect. But first we need to explain why we distinguish *have* + *got* from other present perfect forms.

Fodor and Smith (1978) argue that *have got* in English is functionally distinct from other perfects in only having a stative present meaning relating to possessions and attributes. In an analysis of data from Wells's Bristol project, Fletcher (1981) found that *have got* was the most frequent 'perfect' form that appeared in 3;3-year-olds, and there was some indication, when data from individual children were examined, that some children would use *have got* without using other perfect forms. Whether children are realizing the functional distinctiveness of *have got*, or whether frequency together with relevance is the crucial factor in children's lives at this age, it seems sensible for analytical purposes to keep *have* + *got* and other perfect forms distinct.

What is the course of development of present perfect forms for Sophie? We see in table 5.7 that although *have got* forms do not appear in sample 2, they are present in a previous sample close to the date. So, for example, on 5.5.80 (more than a month before sample 2) Sophie's conversation includes these examples:

S. and me haven't got dirty feet

and

F. Zelda's got shoes on
S. haven't
F. yes she has
S. her haven't

It is at this point the negative auxiliary only which accompanies *got*. In positive declaratives, *got* appears unaccompanied by an auxiliary. Given the relative brevity of the contracted auxiliary which would normally appear in input with *got*, this is scarcely surprising. The development of auxiliaries with past participles up to sample 3 and beyond is set out in table 5.9. The notable features of this are as follows.

1. The predominance of GOT as the stem most frequently co-occurring with *have* forms, and the limited range of other irregular lexical types.
2. The first occurrence of a regular past participle with a *have* form would appear to be on 2.10 (Sophie and Fran are discussing the construction of a puzzle):

   S. that goes after/
   when you've finished body/

   Apart from FINISH, there are only two other *-ed* past participles recorded in the next four months, and generally they are very infrequent. A note of caution should be sounded, however, about interpreting the utterance on 2.10 as containing a (contracted) auxiliary, because of the initial consonant of the verb. The phonetic sequence [ju:fɪnɪʃd] may be conventionally transcribed as *you've finished*, but this is another example of how an orthographic transcription may mislead our analysis, since past and present perfect are homophonous, for *finish*, for all except third-person forms. So it is possible that this example on 23.1.81 is the first instance of Sophie using a form of *have* with a regular past participle:

   S. mummy your flowers have nearly died

3. The use of *have* forms in declaratives (contracted and negative forms) is extended to *yes–no* questions by 9.7.80, and to WH-questions by 14.10.80:

   S. have you found the top for it

4. The first appearance of *been* with a form of *have* is on 20.11, but *been* has been common on its own as a verb since before sample 2, as a precursor of *have* + *been* forms,[31] much as *got* in declaratives is a precursor of *have* + *got*. For example (discussing a doll):

   F. where did you put her down
   S. her been in my bed somewhere

Because of the absence of *-en* and *-ed* past particples up to sample 3, and the very restricted set of irregular participles with which the forms of *have* co-occur, it would be reasonable to interpret present perfect, for Sophie, during the second half of 1980, as a primarily lexical matter – there are certain past participles with which she uses the *have* auxiliary primarily, though not exclusively, for stative meaning. It is clear that even at the beginning of 1981, when she is 3;7, she is only beginning to differentiate past and present perfect, and that acquisition of the distinction is some way off. (We assume in making this assertion that we will take the child's ability to mark the *same* regular verbs for past and present perfect as the best evidence for differentiation.)

Temporal specification

In a discussion of the relationship between temporal adverbials and temporal marking on verbs, Crystal (1966) points out that, in his (adult) corpus, tense co-occurs with temporal adverbial in one in every four clauses. This is by way of underlining his claim that it is not tense-forms alone which convey the relevant time-relationship for a clause, but the tense form 'with or without adverbial specification which gives unambiguous indication'. One interprets a given tense form in a particular way either because the key to the interpretation is given in the form of an adverbial specifier, or because the absence of such a key is itself equally clear as a pointer to which time is being referred to' (Crystal 1966: 5). In this case, then, it is of considerable interest to anyone investigating language-learning, since the child's appreciation of temporal-form distinctions may depend on adverbial co-occurrence, and a narrow focus on the verb-forms themselves could miss this. There are adverbials, for example, that co-occur with present perfect forms, but not with past. In the sentence *I've watched TV since eight*, the adverbial *since eight* emphasizes the duration of the action into the present, and could not be used with a past form. There is no sign of this or similar specification, how-

TABLE 5.9 Forms of have + *past participle, sample 2 to sample 3 and beyond*

Date	*Auxiliary + irregular past participle*	*Auxiliary* + -ed
9.7.80	(Y) GOT 3	
	(Y) FOUND	
2.8	GOT	
7.8	GOT	
26.8	DONE	
	BOUGHT	
	DONE	
10.9	(N) GOT	
23.9	(N) GOT	
	(N) DONE	
27.9	GONE	
2.10	GOT	FINISHED
14.10	(Q) PUT 2	
	(Q) GONE	
1.11	(NQ) GOT 4	
	GONE 2	
6.11	(N) GOT	
14.11	GOT 3	
	DONE 2	
20.11	(NQ) GOT 6	
	BEEN	
	DONE	
26.11	GOT 4	
	GONE	
	THROWN	
28.11	GOT 4	
23.1.81	(N) GOT	DIED
	(Y) COME	FINISHED
	(N) WENT	
27.1		STARTED
6.2	HAD	FINISHED
	GOT	
	BOUGHT	

N Auxiliary occurs in negative form.
Q Auxiliary occurs in *what*-question.
Y Auxiliary occurs in *yes-no* question.

ever, in Sophie's language at this point, but this kind of co-occurrence, or errors in its use, would clearly be of great interest in Sophie's future language development. The discussion above of adverbials in samples 2 and 3 indicates that Sophie's control of temporal adverbials is at present rather rudimentary.

The issue of temporal adverb development is linked to a recent chain that temporal systems in child language are based on and evolve through a sequence of temporal concepts. Weist (1985a, 1985b) elaborates a series of configurations of temporal concepts which depend on the notion of speech time (the ST system), event time (the ET system) and reference time (the RT system). Initially, the child's system only has speech time, and verbs are unmarked for tense. The child (like Sophie in sample 1), does not use tense to relate an event to the time of speaking. In the third year, when children expand their temporal system to include ET, they use tense (initially, past vs present) to signal the deictic relation with ST. (We might surmise that Sophie fits into this framework somewhere between samples 1 and 2.) It is with the development of RT by the child that temporal adverbials become relevant (or, to put it another way, it is the temporal adverbials that alert us to the availability to the child of RT). Initially, the reference time is restricted to either ST or RT. So a child's *yesterday me went school* has ET = RT, and *now me playing* has RT = ST. Weist estimates that the restricted RT system is available at about $2\frac{1}{2}$-3 years. What he calls the 'free reference time' system is said not to emerge until 4-$4\frac{1}{2}$ years of age. Evidence for its emergence comes primarily from the use of *before* and *after* as temporal adverbials. In a sentence like *he saw Lily before the summer ended*, the *before* clause is the reference time - the temporal background or setting, for the event of seeing Lily. The past tense in the main clause indicates that this event is prior to the time of speaking. Even by sample 3 there is no indication that Sophie uses adverbial clauses of this type, and we must assume that the free RT system will be (as Weist indicates) a later development.

Modality

The verb-form profile in table 5.7 suggests some change in modal types over the period between samples 2 and 3. The forms to have appeared in the interim are *won't*, *would* and *might*. These first occurred in samples for the following dates:

won't	27.6.80
would	20.8.80
might	27.6.80

Of these three, *would* and *might* do not actually occur in sample 3, but are used intermittently from the above dates onward. One form with modal meaning, which occurs in sample 3, but is not listed in the verb-forms profile, is *have got to*. Other features relevant for the discussion, but not revealed by the profile are change in frequency, such as the increase in occurrences of *shall*-forms (from 4 to 18 between the two samples), and functional spread - extensions of the meanings of modals. The most frequent modal throughout this period continues to be *can*, often in pre-subject position, as we saw in sample 2. But from quite early in the period after sample 2, the number of *can*-forms in declaratives increases and they are used with other than first- and second-person subjects. For example:

4.7.80	H.	can I have that cot for my dolly
	S.	no you can had your own bed
	S.	me can look after her
	S.	he can lie on that bed you can lie on this bed
20.8.80	S.	I can wear that
15.9.80	S.	I can do it all by myself this time
20.10.80	S.	I can put on these socks
	S.	and you can't polish these

Identifying any changes in the functions of *can* (or any other modal) requires some framework within which the function can be considered. Recent discussions of modal meaning – both those concerned with acquisition (Pea and Mawby 1981; Stephany 1985) and those which deal with the adult language (for example, Palmer 1979) – distinguish three kinds of modal meaning. *Epistemic* modality is (in Stephany's words) concerned with the 'validity, truth or factuality of propositions'; *deontic* modality is concerned with obligation and permission in relation to actions. The third kind of meaning, *dynamic* modality, is generally held to refer to volition and ability in relation to actions. One of the complications of examining the acquisition of modals is that individual modals can be ascribed to more than one of these categories of meaning, depending on a number of factors – tense, whether or not the modal is negated or occurs in an interrogative, whether the subject of the verb is first, second or third person, and on the extra-sentential context. For example, *can*, when it refers to ability, is normally assigned to the dynamic meaning category, and all of Sophie's uses of *can* with first-person subject can be regarded as 'ability' uses. We might, then, want to say that *can* is a 'dynamic modal'. But other uses in the set of examples are not so obviously to do with ability. In the pair *he can lie on that bed* and *you can lie on this bed*, Sophie is suggesting that these actions be followed by the subjects of the verb. The recommendation in *you can had your own bed* seems even stronger. These meanings seem to be more deontic than dynamic; and the most frequent *can* use, in utterance-initial position, in requests for permission, seems to be deontic by Stephany's definition.

If we compare the uses of *can* in sample 3 with those in sample 2, we see that dynamic 'ability' use and the deontic 'suggested action' uses are new. The extension in use is of course connected with the wider syntactic contexts in which the modal appears – in declaratives and with third- as well as first- and second-person subjects. This brief review for *can* suggests that merely noting the incidence of *can*, or other modals, will fail to pick up developmentally relevant information, and that it is necessary to examine syntactic contexts and functions in some detail, if the course of acquisition of these important items is to be mapped reliably.

In Pea and Mawby's (1981) study of six children, aged from 28 to 34 months, *can* was also the most frequent modal use, and in the majority of cases it was used for 'deontic permission'. Another common modal (40 per cent of the total) was *could*, which was exemplified in the sample 2 discussion in the utterance *yes her could change her nappy*. It is not easy from the context (Sophie is talking about two of her dolls) to be entirely clear about the meaning of *could*, but it seems unlikely that the reference is to a past ability (as in *she could run a mile when she was young*). Rather, the reference is to a possible event. This use of *could* is much clearer in examples between samples 2 and 3. So on 21.10.80, when Sophie and her mother are discussing whether some clothes and other items should be sent to a jumble sale, a pair of shoes are found, and she says *I could have these* and, later, *I could have these look awfully pretty*. Since these uses of *could* refer to possible events, we may want to consider them epistemic. But if we look at one of the modals that is new since sample 2, used in the same sample as the *could* examples and with reference to the same topic, we can perhaps see a case for distinguishing dynamic and epistemic possibility. In *those might fit me*, it is clear that the possibility of the event only is indicated, whereas in the *could* sentences the subject is involved in the potentiality of the event or state. The distinction is clearest if we compare reasonable paraphrases of two of the sentences:

those might fit me	*it is possible that those will fit me*
I could have those look awfully pretty	*it is possible that I will be able to have those look awfully pretty*

The past ability use of *could* does, however, appear between samples 2 and 3, in the negative (where it is of course easiest to discern). For example, on 15.8.80:

S. Jack couldn't do it (with reference to a game Sophie gave to him earlier in the year)

S. her went to Jack's party and her couldn't do it (same game)

Of the other frequent modals listed by Pea and Mawby for their children (the oldest of whom, at 34 months, is rather younger than Sophie in sample 2), *have to* (deontic obligation) and *will* (dynamic volition) have been used by Sophie since sample 2. In general, it is still deontic and dynamic uses of modals that are most common for her, and true epistemics (concerned with the modality of propositions) are by comparison rather rare. Once again, we have seen some changes between samples 2 and 3, in frequency of use of forms and diversification of use; but in this crucial area of the language, there is still a great deal to be learned. Although the interpersonal uses of various modals seem to be quite well grasped, the epistemic use of modals - the reflection in the language of an individual's view of the possibility, actuality or necessity of events or actions - remains an area to be developed.

6
Conclusions and Prospects

The period of development reviewed in samples 1–3 covers just over a year of the child's life. None the less, it will be clear from the previous three chapters that, although much remains to be learned, this is an important period for grammatical development: considerable progress has been made in the organization of syntactic structures and the elaboration of a range of grammatical systems. It remains for us to try to draw some general conclusions about the course of language-learning as we have seen it over this period (albeit in a single child) and consider the likely course of her future development, so far as we can predict it.

GENERALIZATIONS IN MORPHOLOGY AND SYNTAX

It is impossible for us to account *in general* for the changes in linguistic performance that occur over the period which has been examined. There is nothing less than the totality of language under scrutiny here, and it is not feasible even descriptively to do more than pick out the salient features of change. Since the main focus of the description has been grammar, however, it is perhaps appropriate to make some general observations about the apparent differences between Sophie's learning of verb morphology and of the syntax of auxiliaries, over this period. Although she is able relatively early to segment verbs into stem and suffix and generalize the suffix to new stems, the learning of auxiliaries, and particularly of auxiliary inversion in questions, proceeds in a slow and gradual fashion. Of course all this is relative; by the age of $3\frac{1}{2}$ there is certainly a good deal that Sophie knows about English auxiliaries. But the evidence of table 5.2, for example, is that such change is piecemeal and restricted. Why should one regularity or subregularity in the language (the *-ed* or *-en* suffixes) be learned with comparative ease, whereas another causes greater difficulty? Part of the answer is that the syntactic regularity of auxiliary inversion may not be so transparent as its characterization in the adult grammar makes it appear. We will approach this issue by re-examining the effects of characteristics of motherese (especially clarification) on children's language-learning. In chapter 1 (see pp. 38ff.), we considered the demonstrated relationship between mothers' auxiliary-initial utterances and children's auxiliary growth, and suggested that this effect was something worth pursuing.

The most intriguing aspect of the Gleitman, Newport and Gleitman (1984) data is the nature of the explanation they adduce. They propose that the child's learning is the result of an interaction between the child's learning biases and incoming information. There are two parts to this argument. First, it is claimed that it is the initial position of the auxiliary in *yes/no* questions, together with the fact that it is 'non-contractible and stressed' in this position (see, for example, Wanner and Gleitman 1982: 19), which accounts for the observed learning effects. In addition to this phonetic hypothesis, there is a further argument, which links the findings of Gleitman and colleagues to the broader context of current language-learning theories (for example, Wexler and Culicover 1980). For these learnability theories to work, they require that the learner hear data of moderate complexity: it must be at least complex enough to provide information about transformational relationships in the language. There is no point in having the input so simple that the relationship between, for example, *will you eat your toast* and *you will eat your toast* is never available to the child. She needs this kind of data in order to appreciate the structure dependence of the rule in English that moves the first auxiliary of the declarative form to a position in front of the subject NP for the interrogative. Within the theory we are considering, she will expect structure dependence by virtue of her innate resources, but she will need evidence as to how this is instantiated. Thus, more complex input, which lays bare the relationships, will be of more use to her than arguably simpler input in which only declaratives, say, appear. The *yes/no* question–auxiliary growth relation, it is suggested, carries the further possibility that the more the mother introduces this form into the input, the more likely the child is to intuit the question–declarative relationship that will be a crucial part of her grammar. In a field notably lacking in explanatory hypotheses that can be addressed by data, the attraction of this elegant linkage of learnability theory, linguistics and language-acquisition data is very obvious. But if Gleitman et al. are to be seen to be right about the route children take from sound to syntax in respect of auxiliaries, two important conditions must be maintained: it has to be the case that the auxiliaries in input *are* clarified (that is, stressed and uncontracted) and, in addition, there should be evidence that children make the syntactic generalization that the elements in pre-subject position and those in post-subject position belong to the same category. We will consider these issues in turn.

The idea that auxiliaries in initial position are uncontractible and stressed is, without any specific data provided, somewhat implausible. If adults were to provide such auxiliaries, it would be quite unlike their behaviour in speech to other adults. And as we saw in chapter 2, there is some doubt as to whether speech to children is 'clarified' generally, in a way that makes its phonetic characteristics different to that of adults speaking to their peers. Adult speech does use forms of auxiliaries that are quite different to a citation form. Consider, for instance, *have*. We might expect the following range of forms, from most careful to least careful, in the pronunciation of a sentence orthographically transcribed as *have you got a match?*: [hæv - həv - əv - v]. That is, the phonetic realization of the sentence-initial auxiliary may be as reduced as a labio-dental fricative of brief duration. Similar variants can be listed for other auxiliaries:

Orthographic transcription forms	Phonetic variants
will	[wɪl - wəl - əl - l]
can	[kæn - kən - kn]
shall	[ʃæl - ʃəl - ʃl - ʃ]
do	[duː - də - d]
did	[dɪd - d]
is	[ɪz - z]
am	[æm - əm - m]
are	[aː - ə]

These are the forms we can expect in adult-to-adult speech. What happens in speech to children? The data we have available are from Fran speaking to Sophie, and were initially analysed in Malan (1983). It comes from the period of sample 1 when Sophie was 2;4–2;5, and it indicates that the majority of auxiliaries used to the child are unstressed: the proportion of initial unstressed auxiliaries is 82 per cent, which is a remarkable figure in relation to the hypothesis of Gleitman and colleagues. If we look at the most common sentence-initial auxiliary *shall*, all but one of its occurrences fall into the unstressed category, with *shall we* realized as [ʃl̩wiː] or simply [ʃwiː], in some cases. When initial *are* (which accounted for 13 per cent of initial auxiliary forms) was realized, it was contracted to a brief, unstressed [ə]. Forms of *have* and *do* also tended to be reduced, with *have* realized as [həv] or [əv], and *do you* realized as [dʒuː]. Malan's analysis suggests that, for this mother-child pair at least, initial auxiliaries in mother–child speech are as prone to reduction and contraction as medial auxiliaries (and as we know they are in adult–adult speech).

This information pertains only to a single English mother–child pair, at a time when the child involved in the conversations is two months older than the oldest child in the Newport, Gleitman and Gleitman (1977) experiment. It cannot then be said, as it stands, to contradict their findings. But if it turns out that, in general, English-speaking mothers do not clarify their auxiliaries to children, then the phonetic aspect of the account of the positive correlation between maternal use and auxiliary growth collapses (though the 'positional' part of the argument remains).[1] And more generally, the non-clarification of auxiliaries in input seems to support the position taken by Bard and Anderson (1983) on the characteristics of the speech parents use. The first part of the conclusion to their paper runs as follows:

> The work reported here was originally intended to protect language acquisition theories against the complications attendant on considering the problems of speech recognition in the linguistically naive. It has not fulfilled this aim, because parental speech is not easier to decipher, word for word, than ordinary conversational speech, but very dependably harder to decipher. (Bard and Anderson 1983: 288)

We would not want to go this far, on the basis of the available data on auxiliaries. But it is useful for our purposes to consider, as Bard and Anderson do, the wider implications of non-clarified input. If the child has to deal with fast speech from early in his language development, then where there is phonetic variability in a form like an auxiliary, either in a particular position or when we compare initial and medial positions, we might expect generalization problems. Particularly for the grammatical generalization for auxiliaries to be made across medial and pre-subject position, the child must as a minimum be able to recognize that the phonetic shapes representing a specific form are in some sense 'the same'. If we then consider that for some forms, like *can*, the phonetic shapes are (objectively) similar across positions, with [kən] or [kn̩] as likely representatives, whereas others like *will* tend to have different forms ([wɪl] or [wəl] pre-subject, [əl] medially), we can hypothesize that one variable affecting the acquisition of the grammatical generalization that links medial and pre-subject auxiliaries will be the phonetic character of the items. It is clearly not the only relevant variable, but it is one that is generally ignored, except of course in Gleitman and colleagues' explanatory account.

But if auxiliaries are not clarified in input, where does this leave their account? The twin claims are that stressed auxiliaries in initial position 'provide useful input data for noticing auxiliaries and beginning to construct, in combination with declaratives, the canonical position of auxiliaries' (Gleitman et al. 1984: 74–5). In other words, it is the phonetic character of the auxiliaries in initial position that leads the child to link them to the medial auxiliaries. But is there any evidence that this kind of generalization has taken place? Certainly Gleitman et al. do not provide any such evidence. The only datum we have is that of the correlation itself (between maternal *yes/no* questions and auxiliary growth). We are not even informed of the raw scores on which the correlations are based, much less which auxiliaries are used by the mother, and which by the child. Nor do we discover how the auxiliary growth referred to is split between medial and pre-subject position.

Once again, the study of a single child can neither refute nor confirm Gleitman and colleagues' arguments, but it is certainly worth considering the

Sophie data to see how they bear on the issues and whether they suggest further enquiry. If we look at sample 2, which is roughly six months after the time at which Malan looked at the phonetic character of Fran's auxiliaries, what forms do we find Sophie using, in which positions? Table 6.1 shows the distribution of auxiliaries in sample 2, in pre-subject and medial positions. Again, if the picture in table 6.1 turned out to be in any way a representative one, then caution is necessary in making claims about generalization. The only candidate would appear to be DO, and even then it is not used in the past in *yes/no* questions. In addition, its occurrence in pre-subject position is limited to certain kinds of questions, notably *why*-questions.[2] If our criterion for generalization is to include not only appearance of the same forms in medial and pre-subject position, but in *yes/no* and wh-questions, in a range of wh-questions, and with a variety of subject NP structures, then clearly generalization has only just begun. It is perhaps relevant to the promising start Sophie has made that the phonetic character of a number of DO forms (particularly negatives) is relatively invariant across positions.

Once again, a close examination of the data suggests asymmetry and gradualness, along with partial generalization of a single form. It simply reinforces the picture of the gradual development of the auxiliary system that we have already built up in chapters 4 and 5. But, in the light of the discussion here, it should be more obvious why the acquisition of this syntactic regularity is a rather slow business. It is because an adult-based description of auxiliary inversion, focused on orthographically represented data,

TABLE 6.1 Auxiliaries and their structural positions in sample 2

	Pre-subject		
	yes/no *questions*	*WH-questions*	*Medial*
BE	are	's is	–
HAVE	–	–	's[a]
DO	do does	do does did didn't	does[b] doesn't don't didn't
CAN	can	–	can't
WILL	–	–	will
SHALL	shall	–	–

[a] With *got*.
[b] Emphatic use, in declarative.

drastically oversimplifies the learning problem for the child. The road from sound to syntax is likely to be lengthier for the child than a reliance on adult-centred descriptions based on orthography would have us suppose. And for adequate descriptions of the child's behaviour (the only sensible basis for attempts at explanation), a more realistic appraisal of the characteristics of child speech and child-directed speech is required. This means both finer descriptions and more attention (in the case of auxiliaries at least) to the phonetic facts.

WHAT HAPPENS NOW?

Recommendations for caution in assessing the extent of Sophie's syntactic generalizations, however, should not be allowed to obscure the extent of her achievement as we have seen it since sample 1. Whatever the basis in terms of syntactic representation for the behaviour that has been examined, Sophie's language at the age of $3\frac{1}{2}$ exhibits a variety of clause types and a range of phrasal constructions. It is clear that part of her future development will involve the extension of substitution possibilities in schemas such as those for the interrogative (see table 5.2). In addition, we would expect to see, if we followed her development through, those features of verb-modification (see table 5.7) which are either first beginning to develop in sample 3 - the present perfect - or which do not appear in sample 3 - past perfect, or modals + *have*, or modal negation. It is easy to overlook, in the context of what the child has done, how much there is still to do when we consider normal adult utterances such as *he must have decided to go*, *it can't have been easy*, *he might not have wanted to*. The area of modality is one in which - both in terms of the types of forms just exemplified, and the functions of particular modals - development continues from now until the early school years (see, for example, Perkins 1980: ch. 7; Wilding 1984). In addition, the period between now and the early school years will see for Sophie the further development of complex structures such as temporal and causal adverbial clauses, relativization and complementation.

It is important, though, to emphasize the *gradual* nature of the changes we might expect to see. Once we have identified in any area of the grammar a structure emerging for the first time, further changes in its form or function may be relatively subtle. Changes in form may require a more 'delicate' syntactic framework than the ones we have used so far to assess differences between samples, and identifying functional extension will require attention to context (linguistic and otherwise). It would be very difficult, on the basis of the data we have seen, to define discrete stages in Sophie's acquisition of wh-questions - other than a stage when they do not appear in the data, and a stage when they do. Once they begin to appear, as table 5.2 indicates, changes may require detailed attention to individual auxiliaries, and subject NPs, and their co-occurrence.

In similar fashion, if we were to examine the future development of Sophie's relative clauses, we would be interested in a range of factors relevant to their description, but it is not easy again to see how we would interpret the development in terms of identifiable stages.[3] We would be required to consider at least the following points.

Position

Does the relative clause tend to occur in subject position or in object position? The comprehension studies that we have already referred to (see pp. 6ff.) tend to include relatives embedded into both subject and object position, for example (relative in subject position) *the lion that bumps the cow jumps over the elephant*; (relative in object position) *the lion jumps over the cow that bumps the elephant*. Some experimenters (for example, Sheldon 1974) have found that certain kinds of relatives in subject position are easier for 4-year-olds to comprehend than those in object position. However, in production, object position is more popular. This was true in Romaine's study (1984: 42), and appears also to be the case in a sample of ten American children's conversations, at 7 years of age, that we had the opportunity to analyse.[4] These children provided on average three relative clauses per hundred utterances; of the total of thirty in the sample, only three were in subject position.[5]

Focus

A further structural dimension to consider is the function of the relativized item. This can be illustrated from the US data:

relative as subject:
  there's no friends of mine *that* walk to school
relative as object:
  and it was not my bike *that* I have now

Other functions of the relative pronoun, not attested in the US data, but occurring in Romaine's Scottish data are:

relative pronoun as object of a preposition:[6]
  the house in *which* I live
relative pronoun as genitive:
  the person *that's* foot is touched

It is also possible for the relative pronoun to function as indirect object, although this does not occur in either the US or Scottish data:

I saw the boy *that* I gave the book to

Alternative or non-standard forms

In both the Scottish and US data, occasional examples show inappropriate pronouns in the relative clause; the extra pronoun is normally co-referential with the relativized NP; for example (US data):

they're putting the other ones what they made it in the Dukes of Hazzard

Wider functional considerations

There are two points to be considered which will be relevant to any assessment of the child's capabilities with respect to relative clauses – the nature of the modification that the child's relative clause achieves, and the potential for structural alternatives to fulfil the same role. It is usual in linguistic descriptions of the relative clause to characterize their role in modification as either ***restrictive*** or ***non-restrictive***. These terms are glossed by Quirk et al. (1972: 858) in terms of the identification of the referent provided by the modification. If the modification (in the case we are considering, the relative clause) is used to identify the noun it modifies for the hearer, then it is restrictive; if the modification gives additional information about a noun which is already identified, it is non-restrictive. A clear contrast is provided by these examples:

the man who you saw at the bus-stop is dead
George, who is a taxi-driver in his spare time, fell asleep

This distinction is generally clearly represented in the data from the 7-year-old US children. A number of clauses fall within the Quirk et al. definition of restrictive in the US data; for example:

and it was not my bike that I have now
he's the only one what buys them
but there was a big bee that wasn't invited
and then Henry took the food he was cooking off the stove

The clear restrictive clauses are in the majority, but there are one or two clear non-restrictive cases; for example:

so we never got to keep my grandma's dog, who's named Heidi

In addition there are a number of unclear cases where it is difficult to know which term to apply; for example:

they can't watch that because it's a Bozo show that's on in the morning

The second point that is relevant to a full description of relative clauses in the child's development concerns alternative structures that can perform the same function. The most obvious alternative is nominal post-modification, but there are others. For restrictive relatives, a post-modifying NP may serve as an equivalent:

that's the one that's in kindergarten → that's the one in kindergarten
my grandma that is in Richland Center → my grandma in Richland Center

It is possible that post-modifying NPs are less complex and appear earlier in development than relative clauses. There is, however, no data on this issue for 4 to 7-year-old children. It is worth pointing out that if the child, in the second example, had wanted to talk about his Grandma that *was* in Richland Center – that is, she has died or moved somewhere else, but this is still the way he is identifying her – a relative clause is the only way to include the past tense. A post-modifying NP can generally be seen only as a substitute for a relative with present tense. This may seem a minor point, but adds yet another dimension to our examination of the development of relative clauses and related structures. How do children include tense and aspect into the descriptions incorporated in relative clauses for specification?

We have deliberately chosen a complex example, but similar points about form and function could be made about many areas of the grammar. Of course we would not want to lose the major features of Sophie's, or any child's, future development in a welter of detail. But without a realistic appraisal of the language-learning task, we run the risk of providing explanations for children's language which rely on an over-simplified view of what the child's learning task is.

One of the aims of presenting the data in samples 1 to 3, and the analyses and commentaries, has been to allow a realistic appraisal of what the child learns of her language during a critical period for development. It is this data *in its totality* which needs to be explained, and which must form the raw material for any satisfactory theory. The reader can continue the assessment of Sophie's language development by considering sample 4, a conversation between Sophie and her mother shortly before her fourth birthday, which appears in the Appendix.

Appendix Sample
Sophie at 3 years 11 months

This session follows a by-now familiar pattern, with Sophie and her mother conversing at home around a set of topics which include food, an alphabet book, going to the country, television programmes, and friends (e.g. Quinty, l. 11). A good deal of the first part of the session revolves around the alphabet book - a series of pictures organized in sequence according to the initial letters of the objects they represent - and it is interesting to see, from l. 69 on, how Fran handles the problem of naming the letters. She tends very often to use a phonetic label for them, and wherever this is done a phonetic representation appears in the transcript. For example, she introduces the letter A (at l. 69) in the way that it is normally pronounced in a recitation of the alphabet (phonetically [eɪ]). At l. 76, however, she calls the letter [ə], which is another of the phonetic values that it can take. Similarly, she refers to the letter B both as [biː], and (when she is talking about occurrences of the letter B in the plural) as [bʌz]

SAMPLE 4: SOPHIE AT 3;11.[15]

F. no you dìdn't dis'turb me/
did you 'have a 'nice 'tíme though/
S. m̀m/
F. gòod
'what did you dò/
S. 'horrible thìngs/
F. I 'don't belìeve you/
you 'always say that/
S. 'I . . . dìd/
F. díd you/
S. 'I had to 'look after Qùinty/
to 'get him insîde/

F. whý/
S. just dìd/
F. whát/
'when you were 'playing outsíde/
S. m̀m/
'I took . . . 'I had to 'get him ìnside/
F. 'did you mánage/
[unintelligible sequence]
S. he'll 'go a 'different way than m̀e/ (referring to Quinty)
F. oh dêar/
'did you mánage in the 'end/
S. yès/
F. is 'he a 'naughty bóy/
S. 'no he wàsn't (*wasn't* = [wɒnt])
he 'got in the 'end with mè/
F. òh/
gòod/
S. when thāt . . .
'mummy here's anòther dog/ 'coming alòng/
(looking out of the window)
a smàller 'dog/
óne/
twō/
let's 'see that nóse/
F. whòse 'nose/
S. yoùr 'nose/
F. 'why d'you 'want to see my nòse/
[unintelligible sequence]
S. can I 'see what's in thère/
F. eg̀g/
S. I lòve 'that/
F. mḿ/
S. I lòve 'that/
F. d'you líke 'kippers/
S. m̂m/
F. gòod/
[unintelligible sequence]
S. 'how nìce/
F. gŏod/
S. 'mummy I've 'made it as 'small as 'they can gò/
(folding tissue paper)
they 'can't – 'I can't 'make them any smàller/
F. whàt 'can't you/
'what can't you 'make any smáller/

S. thèse/
F. òh/
S. ˈmummy ˈlook how ˈmany tìssues I've ˈgot/
F. oh ˈwhat a lòt/
ˈhow many have you gòt/
S. eìghteen/
F. eîghteen/
[S. counts, accurately, to fifteen and then 'sings' some of the numbers]
S. eìghty/
F. eíghty/
S. tìssues/
F. oh gosh ˈthis is a ˈlong stòry/
S. ˈhow d'yòu know/
F. aˈbout Zòzo/ (S. and F. begin to look at the book)
ˈZozo the mònkey/
S. ˈcan you rèad it to me/
F. I'll ˈread sòme of it/
ˈthere he's ˈdrawing À/ (A is pronounced [eɪ])
a bìg A/
S. for cròcodile/
F. and ˈthere's a lìttle A/
ˈA beˈcomes an . . . àlligator/
S. ˈwhat's a àlligator/
F. it's ˈlike a cròcodile/
here's [ə]/
ˈwhat's . . . ˈwhat's . . . fór/ – –
ǎpple/
S. àpple/
F. ˈthat's rìght/
ˈlook at all the ˈdifferent ˈplaces where [æ̀] comes/ – – –
and ˈthere's some [bʌz]/ (i.e. instances of B)
a ˈbig B́/ (B is pronounced [biː])
ˈwith a bèak/
ˈfor a ˈbird with a bèak/
and a lìttle B/
[bə] fór/ – –
ˈwhat's that ˈinsect càlled/
[Sophie makes a buzzing noise]
a bèe/
[Sophie buzzes again]
and ˈthat's a [kə] for/
S. I ˈdon't knòw/
F. cràb/

S. 'what's a cráb/
F. cràb/
'it's a 'kind of fìsh/
'shell - what 'we call shèllfish/
'there we àre/
[ə́]/
[bə́]/
[kə́]/
oh càb/
'that's an 'American 'word for tàxi/
oh you 'know what thàt is/
[də] fór/ - - -
S. Àlison/
F. whát/
S. Àlison/
F. Ălison/
S. yès/
F. 'it's a dînosaur/ (S. laughs)
S. you 'know that bìg one/ - -
F. ḿm/
S. in L - in Lòndon/
(2 syll.)
enòrmous one/
F. 'in the múseum/
S. ǹo/
a f - frìghtening 'one/
you 'weren't wàtching it/
F. 'where did you sèe it/
S. on 'television in Lòndon/
F. òh/
S. while 'you were 'doing your pàcking/
F. òh/
S. for gòing/
F. 'where were we gòing/
S. 'back to cou - còuntry/
F. 'where were yòu then/
S. 'with my dàddy/ - -
F. òh/
S. 'case I stùrbed you/ (i.e. *disturbed*)
F. òh/
'that's what we 'call a dròmedary/
* 'like a càmel
S. * 'what's thàt/
F. 'it's an 'animal a 'bit like a càmel/
that's an [ε] for/

S. dìnosaur/ (laughs)
F. 'it's an èlephant/
'it's a 'very funny 'drawing of an èlephant/
S. mummy why is (unintelligible sequence)
F. 'that's an êar/
lòok/
they've 'made it 'look like an eàr/ hàven't they/
the E/ (E pronounced [iː])
S. 'why don't – 'why don't they do 'that for èlephant/
F. well it's the 'same lètter/
But 'that's a bìg one/ and that's a lìttle one/ is̀n't it/
they 'don't lòok quite the 'same/ dò they/
that's a [fə] for . . . fîre/
ańd/ – – –
S. 'why is it 'fire . . . on fǐre/
F. I 'don't kǹow/
perhaps 'somebody 'dropped a màtch/ d'you thìnk/
S. m̀m/
F. and 'that's a flôwer/
and á/ – –
what's 'that (2 syll.) up thére/
S. a tòg/
F. Sŏphie/
(S. laughs)
S. tògofiler/ – – –
tògofiner/
F. so 'what letter does 'that begìn with then/
S. tògofiner/
F. 'that's a gòose/
S. ǹo/
dògofiner/ (laughs)
F. and a gòldfish/
'that's a 'nice drawing of a g̀oldfish/
S. it's hòrrible 'fish/
F. iś it/
òh/
'now we've 'got sèven letters/
S. béd/
F. m̀m/
S. sáck/
gèrbils/
F. nò/
càge/
S. càge/
and bèd/

F. and thére's a/ --
S. hòuse/
F. and [hə́] for/
S. hoùse/
F. '[h] for hòuse/
and 'little [hə] fór/ ---
hòrse/
[10-second pause]
F. and 'that's for ìce/
ìcicle/
'that's an 'animal 'called an igùana/
'don't you líke that/
S. 'cover he's fàce/
F. oh whý/
(S. laughs)
'don't you líke it/
S. * no he's
F. * he's 'rather a 'friendly igùana/ --
S. 'what are gúanas/
F. gúanas/
'it's a 'sort of 'lizard . . . ànimal/
grèen animal/ ---
oh 'what's happened to the fìre/
S. 'I got a hèadache/
F. oh dârling/ -
háve you/
S. m̀m/
can we 'have some 'cucumber for [ɜːm] lúnch/
F. cúcumber/
yèah/
'if you wànt to/
S. 'cos I nèed some/
I 'need a còol bit/
F. you 'need some cùcumber/
dó you/
S. 'cos I 'need the 'cold bit to 'spread on my (1 syll.)/
and it 'goes awày/
F. oh Sòphie/
S. 'cos it dòes mummy/
F. ỳes/
but 'who on 'earth have you 'seen putting 'cucumber on their fàce/
S. whát/
F. 'who have you 'seen put 'cucumber on their fàce/

S. Gris̀elda/
'she had a – 'Jane took it awày/
'why you 'putting 'newspaper iǹ/ (F. is tending the fire)
F. 'trying to 'get a 'bit more of a 'flame on this fìre/
(S. laughs)
(S. sings an improvised song about burning her fingers)
S. 'can you go ón/
F. 'with the bóok/
yès/
S. 'I can sèe it/
F. whòops/
hàng on/
[8-second pause]
S. múmmy/
'where does that – 'flame go úp to/
'does it go 'up to 'Father Chrístmas/
F. whát/
S. that flâme/
F. the bóok/ – –
S. nò/
the flâme/
F. 'does it 'go up to 'Father Chrístmas/
S. yès/ – – –
F. it 'goes up 'through the chìmney/ (S. laughs)
'only at 'Christmas it 'goes up to Father Chrìstmas/
and you 'send – 'did you 'send your 'letters up thére/
'up the chímney/
díd you/
'that's an 'animal 'called a jàguar/
a 'bit like a tìger/
S. thát/
F. 'that's called a jàck-in-the-'box/ – – –
and a – kangaròo/
S. [kə] (whispers)
F. kangaròo/
'going to 'manage to 'learn your 'letters/
before you 'go to the Réd House/
S. nò/
F. whát/
S. nò/
F. nò/
Ì see/ – –
S. 'I don't 'want to 'learn my lètters/
F. dón't you/

S. nò/
F. 'you'll 'have to with 'Mrs Sỳred/
S. nò/
F. you wìll/
S. múmmy/
'I don't 'want to 'go to 'Red House Schòol/
F. dón't you/
'what do you 'want to dó/
S. I 'want to 'go to plàygroup/
F. for 'ever and éver/
S. yès/
F. till you're fourtéen/
S. yès/
F. 'just do 'gluing and 'sticking for 'years and yèars/
S. m̀m/
'till I'm thirtèen/
F. 'there's a 'lamb and a làdy/
'what's she 'licking that begins with [l̀ə]/ - -
S. a lòllipop/
F. a lòlly/
yès/
oh 'that's a dìfficult 'one/
'that's a sàilor/
they 'obviously 'call him a 'mariner in Amèrica/
S. Mum 'what's thát/
F. his bâg/
and there's a mòuse/
'eating mìnts/
there's a nàpkin/
and a nòse/
lòok/
'there's a '[nə] for nòse/
S. it's a nòse/ ìsn't it/
F. m̀m/
and an óstrich/
S. my 'pants are 'going up my bòttom/
F. oh 'dear oh dèar/
S. I'm 'getting them òut/
F. alríght/
S. yès/
F. 'there's a pènguin/
S. 'penguins are sìlly/
F. 'penguins are sìlly/
whý/

S. that's a kànguin/
F. oh S̀ophie/ (S. laughs)
'that's called a qùail/
S. 'that's a pàil/
F. 'what's thàt lady/
S. 'that's a pàil/
F. 'she's a qùeen/
S. 'that's a (3 syll.)
F. and a ràbbit/
S. and 'that's a pàggit/
F. oh Sòphie/
a snăil/
S. a pàil/
F. 'what's thát/
S. 'silly bìlly/
'that's a pea 'thing/ (laughs)
'that's a pèa 'thing/
F. a 'table with a tèa-pot on/
S. a p̀ea thing
F. 'there's a tènt/
an 'Indian tènt/
S. 'that's a ... pìndian 'tent/
F. he's 'gone to 'buy some dòughnuts/
oh dear m̀e/
lòok/
he's cròss/
[5-second pause]
S. 'why does he 'put them all òut/
F. an umbr̀ella/
S. 'why does he 'tip them all òut/
F. 'cos he's a mònkey/ (both laugh)
'there's a vàlentine/
S. can 'I do 'one of thóse/
F. a válentine/
it's prètty/ isń't it/
d'you 'think you could máke one 'one day/
'like thát/
'beautiful as thát/
S. yès/
F. 'that's a 'walrus with whìskers/
S. that's a pàlrus/
F. 'that's a 'man with a mùstache/
S. 'that's a ... tàurus/
F. iś it/

[10-second pause with some S. laughter]
F. 'there's Father Chrìstmas/
S. nò/
pàther 'Christmas/ (laughing)
F. and a yàk/
S. 'that's a-tàk/
F. and a zèbra/
S. and a [ziːbə]/
F. 'now he's 'going to 'eat the dòughnuts/
S. he 'made them 'into lètters/ dídn't he/
F. m̀m/
S. 'what are dóughnuts/
F. 'sort of càke/
have you 'never hád one/
S. nò/
F. 'I must màke some 'one day/
S. 'how d'you màke them/
F. you 'make the dòugh/
'rather like 'making 'bread dough I thìnk/
'I've never màde them
and 'then you frỳ them/
[5-second pause]
S. he's 'silly that mònkey/
F. 'don't you líke him/
S. nò/
F. òh/
'what a shàme/
S. shall we 'read it agaín/
F. nò/
(S. laughs)
are 'there some 'other Zózo books/
S. whát/
F. òh/
'didn't he - I 'think that 'man did 'that
funny 'animal 'book of yòurs/ dìdn't he/
the 'baby ànimals/
S. whích/
F. d'you remémber/
the 'one about the còw/ and 'where were her bàbies/
and the hèn/ and 'where were hér babies/
d'you remémber/
S. yes/
F. the 'one with the 'funny 'cut-in-half páges/
S. yès/
F. oh the mìlk/

S. whát milk/
395 F. the 'milk must have 'boiled by nòw/
[25-second pause; S. sings, and then F. asks a question which is not intelligible on the tape; S. responds to the question]
S. whát/
F. did 'Thomas come to 'playgroup todáy/
S. nò/
F. 'why nòt/
400 S. 'only Bèn/
he's 'still not bètter/
F. oh dèar/
'poor little chàp/
S. but whò 'bit him/
405 F. a dòg/
S. whòse 'dog/
F. hìs 'dog/
S. whát/
F. hìs 'dog/ I thìnk/
S. [unintelligible sequence]
410 F. nò/
I 'don't think it wàs/
S. it mìght be ['hi:z] dog/ 'which is a 'one like ['hi:z] dog/
F. yès/
'could be thàt/
415 S. I'm 'waiting for our bàby/
F. yóu are/
S. yès/
F. òh/
S. I 'want to 'see if it's a gírl or a bòy/
420 F. 'so do Ì/
S. whỳ/
F. wèll/
what 'else could she bè/
'could it bè/
425 if it 'wasn't a * 'boy or gìrl/
S. it could be a ['sɒrɪə]/
F. oh/
(S. laughs)
S. it could [ɒv] be a ['tɒrə]/
F. a tǒy
430 S. yès/
F. in'stead of a bàby/ (S. laughs)
perhaps you'd 'all prefèr that/
S. a tòy/
mùmmy/

'it's a 'toy inside the 'baby's tùmmy/
F. ís it/
[1 minute of S. humming and singing to herself while playing with toys, while F. is otherwise occupied]
S. but múmmy/
F. yès love/
S. 'on bùnny/ (S. is referring to a TV programme)
'you see – you 'know the 'new pérson/
F. the whó/
S. you 'have a 'new pèrson/
F. at plaýgroup/
S. nò/
on tèlevision/
F. oh yès/
S. you sèe/ he 'had a prècious/
and it 'was a ròund thing/ that 'had pòckets in/
'like thàt/
'all the way roùnd/
cìrcle/
and you sèe/ 'there was 'this bùtton/
and a thíng/
and . . . and (3 syll.)
F. 'start agàin 'Sophie/
'start agàin/
S. and you sèe/
you 'know the 'new pérson/
F. the nèw 'person/
S. 'not at plàygroup/
F. ǹo/
S. on tèlevision/
F. whát/
just nòw/
S. yès/
F. m̀m/
S. [əm] – [əm] – 'he – 'he had his 'own ròom/
and – 'he – 'he had a 'pointy thìng/
and a machìne/
you sèe/
F. a machìne/
S. and – and 'he heard he sày/ 'if you 'push that 'button agàin/
and the 'man dìd/ and you sèe/
and – [əm] – 'he – and 'he – –
and 'all the 'paper 'flied out insìde/
and 'flied through 'all the (1 sỳll.)/
and 'all of it 'flied òff/

F. alĺ of it/
S. yès/
F. òh/
'cos it 'was a wìnd machine/
S. yès/
F. 'didn't they 'manage to 'save ańy of the 'paper/
S. nò/
F. réally/
S. ǹo/
it 'was 'all gòne/
F. 'where tó/
S. it 'all wènt/ 'over to 'this bìrd/
and it 'was on thère/
and it 'all went 'down thère/
[10-second pause]
S. 'where's my bâg/
F. 'your bâg/
'what with your dòlly/
S. yès/
F. 'where did you 'put it dòwn/
S. I've 'got some 'snotty in my nòse/
F. oh dèar/
'where did you pùt it 'sweetie/
you 'brought it ìn/ díd n't you/
S. yès/
F. well 'where did you pùt it/
S. 'we'll look in the hàll/
F. hère it is/
lòok/
'right next to the sòfa love/
'right besìde you/
S. beside my (1 s̀yll.)
lòok/
'something in a dìary/
F. òh/
[10-second pause]
S. mummy/
shall I 'tell you what 'daddy just . . . 'tried to dò/
the children/ 'they tried to 'stop daddy 'picking his nòse/ – – –
'rude bòy/
'Prince Chàrles/
[a break of almost 2 minutes while S. 'writes in her diary'; she occasionally talks to herself while doing this, mostly unintelligibly]
S. 'I want to 'go to a nûrsery/

to plàygroup/
F. you 'can't go to 'playgroup for 'ever and èver/
S. whý/
F. 'you're already the 'oldest 'person thère/ arén't you/
pràctically/
ǹo/
'Mary's a 'bit òlder than you/ is̀n't she/
S. 'she's fòur/
F. 'yes she's fòur/
but 'you're very 'nearly fòur/
aŕen't you/
(S. laughs)
'shoe makes a 'funny noiśe/
or 'was it 'your fòot/
[10-second pause]
F. shall I 'pull up your 'other sóck/
'aren't your 'legs cóld/
S. nò/
F. úp/
S. I 'don't wànt them 'up/
'that one's 'shorter than thàt one/
F. 'perhaps that 'leg's lònger/
(S. laughs)
nó/
could 'that not bé/
S. 'I want to 'wear my Alexànder 'skirt/
F. dó you/
we'll 'have to 'get it oùt one day/ wòn't we/
if it 'stays as 'cold as thìs/ I 'think we'll 'have to 'get àll the
'winter clothes 'out again/
'what a bòre/
S. 'Hester Yòrke/ (very loud)
(laughs)
'Hester Yòrke/ (very loud)
'when is 'daddy 'going to 'come báck/
F. quite sòon/ I 'think lòve/
S. at 'eight o clóck/
F. nò/
I 'hope he'll be 'back at òne o'clock/
S. 'mummy he's 'going to be 'back at eìght o'clock/
F. iś he/
(unintelligible sequence)
S. he s̀aid/
I'm 'going to 'eat m̀ud for 'lunch/

I'm 'going to 'get a pìcnic/
I'm 'going to stèal 'one/
F. whát/
'go for a 'picnic and eat múd/
S. nò/
he's 'going to 'steal a pìcnic 'thing/
F. oh dèar/
I 'don't know 'what to 'do about thàt/
[1-minute break while S. plays a game and talks to herself]
S. 'I've wòn/ (very loud)
'I've wòn/
'I've put 'two – 'thirteen 'letters 'down on m̀y one/

ANALYSING THE DATA

In addition to performing the standard analyses on this data, as exemplified in chapters 3–5, it may also be useful to examine more specific features of the data. The guidelines below give page references for information on analyses and relevant discussions, and line references to relevant instances in sample 4.

1. Calculate an MLU(m) for this data, beginning at l. 52 and using the next 100 utterances. How does this value compare with the MLU(m) quoted for sample 3? How does it compare with the mean values for MLU(m) for 4-year-olds quoted in Miller and Chapman (1981)? Calculate another MLU(m) starting from Sophie's last utterance (in l. 567), and working back for 100 utterances. How similar is this value?
2. Construct a LARSP profile for 50 of Sophie's major utterances, beginning at l. 203, and compare it with the LARSP for sample 3. More generally, consider as many of Sophie's utterances as possible that could be described in terms of complex-sentence constructions, and tabulate them as in table 5.1. Read the discussion on pp. 151 ff., and consider whether there has been any development between the two samples. These are some examples from the data that may be helpful (this is *not* an exhaustive list):

Relative:	ll. 412, 448;
Complementation:	ll. 54, 215;
Coordination:	l. 473 ff.

3. List valency frames for 50 clauses in the sample. Refer to table 5.5 and the discussion of it (pp. 169 ff.) and compare verbs that are common to samples 3 and 4, and their adverbials.

4. Table 5.7 gives a verb-form profile for samples 1–3. What is the profile for sample 4? Does it present changes over sample 3? Would modification of the profile be required in order to record some of the changes you have found between the two samples?
5. Using table 5.6 as a guide, determine whether there is any change in sample 4 in the representation of the personal pronominal system. At l. 412, there is pronunciation of *his* by Sophie as [hiːz] (which we transcribed [hiːz]). This is a novel error, in that *his* was used in earlier samples, but correctly pronounced. What could be the significance of this error (see Chiat 1981)?
6. In the discussion of temporal specification (pp. 186 ff.), we discussed the late development of the RT (reference-time) system in children's temporal language. Is there any evidence in sample 4 that Sophie has begun to develop a free reference-time system? (Consider the conversation about daddy's return from l. 548 on, in particular.)
7. By far the major part of the analysis and discussion has centred on Sophie's language. It would, however, be interesting to know whether the nature of the language her mother uses has changed at all, over the period in which we have seen considerable developments in the child. Samples 1–4 provide ample data for the application of similar analyses and profiles to the speech Fran directs at Sophie.

Notes

1 METHOD AND EXPLANATION

1 There are exceptions, however. See, for example, Huttenlocher (1974), in which the relationship between comprehension and production in very young children is investigated.

2 Two examples covering quite different topics are Bridges (1980), on active and passive word-orders, and Ruder (1982), on children's understanding of the verb *open*.

3 Of course we know very little about the temporal sequence of processing steps in the young child's perception of linguistic information. The use of 'next', 'then', etc. in this discussion is purely a stylistic convenience and has no significance necessarily for the order of processing steps by the child. We know from experiments with adults that at least some speakers process from acoustic signal to meaning from the time they start hearing an utterance (see Marslen-Wilson and Tyler 1980 for a summary of this work), and it is at least possible that this is true for children as well.

4 That is, morphologically speaking; grammatically, it would be possible to reduce to three by linking *'s* and *-ing*.

5 Reversible active and passive sentences are ones in which subject and object are generally interchangeable in practice: boys can hit girls, and vice versa; a non-reversible passive sentence would be *the girl was hit by the bus*. In the real world, buses knock people down, and not the other way around.

6 The argument here is independent of whatever the basic analytical units turn out to be for the child or the adult. Here I am making the simplifying assumption that they are morphemes, as traditionally identified.

7 The question of identifying the units which are the basis for children's language use is addressed by Clark (1974) and Ingram (1975). A discussion of comprehension which bears on points raised here is Clark, Hutcheson and van Buren (1974).

8 It is a measure of Leopold's scrupulousness that, having assigned the task of data collection to his wife while he was away, he was concerned enough about her transcriptions to issue a cautionary note to the reader (Leopold 1939–49, Vol. 4: 2).

9 The amount of time taken depends of course on the length of the sample and the nature of the analysis. A complete syntactic analysis of an hour's sample (using the LARSP procedure described in Crystal et al. 1981) could take half a day (including orthographic transcription. A phonological analysis that necessitated a broad phonetic transcription could well take much longer.

10 That is, as a separate morpheme which the child has recognized as a constituent of the two forms. On the basis of the evidence available, it is quite possible that the child has learned two unitary forms, *taken* and *given*, without further analysis.

11 There are, however, experimental studies which demonstrate the value of the technique for preschool or clinical populations (for example, Nelson, Carskaddon and Bonvillian 1973).

12 For more detailed discussion, see Crystal et al. (1981: 57–8).

13 In Halliday's words, the label 'mathetic' refers to 'language enabling the child to learn about his social and material environment, serving him in the construction of reality' (Halliday 1975: 75).

14 See Howe (1976, 1981) for detailed discussion of the issues raised here.

15 One point to note here is that, for Labov and Labov, contracted auxiliaries were counted as inverted. Thus examples like *what's he doing* would be interpreted as having an inverted auxiliary. This is a problematic assumption (see above p. 15), and they may have overestimated the child's facility with this rule.

16 For discussion of Piaget's theories in relation to language development, see Donaldson (1978) and Piatelli-Palmarini (1980).

17 There are some notable exceptions to this stricture, for example, Johnston and Slobin (1979) and Tanz (1980).

18 For a view of the relevance of cognition for language development, see Campbell (1985).

19 It is also likely that some of the characteristics of motherese are highly culture-specific. English-speaking mothers raise the pitch of their voice and exaggerate intonation when addressing their infant (Gleason 1975; Garnica 1977). However, Ratner and Pye (1984) report that when Quiche Mayan mothers in Guatemala talk to their babies, *low* pitch appears to be the norm, and they frequently reduce their voice to a whisper.

20 In Hockett's view (1955) frequency-norm phonological analysis 'insists on accepting . . . any utterance which is produced by a native-speaker and understood, or understandable, by other native-speakers'. The fast forms of ordinary conversation are thus taken as data for analysis on the same terms as more clarified form.

21 The mean words per minute score was arrived at by averaging over a five-minute segment for each condition.

22 See also Gleitman et al. (1984), which reanalyses the original data of Newport et al. and also Furrow and Benedict, and concludes that the relationship between yes/no questions used by mothers and the growth of auxiliaries in children still holds.

4 SOPHIE AT 3 YEARS

1 The importance of this area of the grammar for linguists interested in language acquisition should be obvious, and we have discussed it in chapter 1 at some length. One reason for this interest, however, bears repeating: in the context of a variety of language acquisition theories – cognitive, interactional, social-psychological – the issue of the child's progress from non-inverted to inverted wh-questions seems to be interpretable as a purely linguistic problem. So, for example, the transition from *why you ate my bissie* to a later *why did you eat my bissie* is in the main a matter of the child's ability to cope with the complexities of *do*-support, and is unlikely to be explained in terms of modifications in maternal input, or particular features of cognitive development. Wh-questions are thus seen as a test-bed for theories of rule acquisition.

2 We are of course assuming, here and elsewhere, the classic and still most widespread analysis of auxiliary-positioning in interrogatives, which stems from Chomsky (1957) and claims that initial or pre-subject auxiliaries in interrogatives are the result of a transformation that moves them from pre-verb position. This is certainly the line that most of the child language literature studying the issue has followed, along with the theoretical discussion of explanation in language acquisition. There is, however, an alternative linguistic account of 'inversion', in terms of a context-free phrase structure grammar, in Gazdar, Pullum and Sag (1980). In this account, auxiliaries are generated directly, by PS rules in initial or pre-subject position in sentences, just as they are generated in pre-verbal position, and the question of a transformation of subject–auxiliary inversion does not arise. *Pace* the extremely complex question of the relationship between language-acquisition data and linguistic theory, such an account actually appears to fit the Sophie data better than an inversion account, as we will see below. See also Kuczaj and Maratsos (1983).

3 The values on which these proportions are calculated are estimated from the graphs which appear in Labov and Labov (1978: 22–3). The reason why the mean of the four production values for different types of wh-questions is not 0.40 (the value derived from the graph for *all* wh-questions – ibid.: 22) is presumably because there were values for other types of wh-question not included in the graph on p. 23, which breaks down the overall figures by question type.

4 Note also that there are *no* other 'do-support' examples in data from the child at this point.

5 This is of course a misnomer as a functional label, but is used as the common designation for the structural type. Most of the forms are *can*-initial, and are used by Sophie at this point as requests for action on her mother's part, or for permission for Sophie herself to act. They are not used to get information.

6 For convenience, this discussion of sample 2 interrogatives does not restrict itself to the subsample used for the LARSP analysis.

7 These are the only such examples in sample 2, but other samples close to the same time contain similar errors. Two days later we find:

where did my pink bathroom be
why did granny's be where Zelda been

The first example suggests that Sophie's idiosyncratic form of *do*-support, for interrogatives containing copulas, extends to question-types other than *why*.

8 Thus it may well be that for this specific area of the grammar, an account similar to that of Gazdar et al. (1980), formulated in terms of auxiliary/copula insertion rather than inversion is more appropriate. This, in turn, would suggest that *a priori* arguments about the relevance of structure-dependent rules for acquisition (see above p. 23) for references) may need to be reconsidered.

9 There may be parallels between the kind of strategy we are suggesting the child is using at this point for forming interrogatives, and what Matthews (1981: 187) refers to as 'collocational schemata' – linear concatenations of either lexical items or phrases, which may result in what look like constructions conforming to adult rules (for example, complex sentences), but which are not rule-governed for the child. Since it is not our intention to provide a formalism for the data presented, and since Matthews's exposition is highly schematic, it is not possible to pursue the potential similarities in any detail. See also Ingram (1975).

10 It will be noticed here that we are relying crucially on the surface data in this account for describing the coordinations that appear in sample 2. The discussion here distinguishes *he given one to Hester and two to us* (as phrasal), from an example like *Sophie will go to the cupboard and get a toy* as clausal. But some transformational accounts would treat them as sentences of similar provenance. The first would be derived from *he given one to Hester and he given two to us*, with subject and verb omitted in the surface structure by a rule of conjunction reduction. Similarly, *Sophie will go to the cupboard and get a toy* would derive from *Sophie will go to the cupboard and will get a toy*, and so on. As usual with children's speech, we do not have data which would enable us to select one description as *the* correct account of the facts. For the moment then, we will stay with the surface structure account distinguishing phrasal/clausal coordination as being the one that makes least assumptions, though we may later wish to revise our view, given other evidence. There is a further kind of coordination involving ellipses in the second clause, where the second clause exhibits what is known as 'gapping' (see Jackendoff 1971), which, if it turns up in the data, cannot be handled satisfactorily under our surface structure categories. An example would be *Sophie took the apple and Zelda the orange*.

11 This perhaps requires some explication, because of the way Paul's data are reported. Her early stage IV children have a MLU range of 3.00–3.50, with a predicted age 34–37 months. Some of these subjects apparently produce sentences with two clauses conjoined, but such structures are more reliably found in the next group up, with MLU range 3.51–4.00. Sophie's various MLU estimates place her in the lower half of Paul's later stage IV range. See also Tager-Flugsberg, de Villiers and Hakuta (1982: 211), where an MLU of 3.80 (derived from the Brown children) is suggested for the emergence of sentential coordination.

12 For more detailed discussion see Hakuta, de Villiers and Tager-Flugsberg (1982).

13 The study by Nelson (1976) looks at adjectives in predicative position as well as attributive, and so includes in the adjective class possessives and past participles. Our interest here is only in the attributive function, and primarily in what are called here 'lexical' adjectives.

14 Of course the same point could be phrased 'in her extended clause structures', and related to the LARSP analysis. The valency approach does, however, have the advantage of allowing us verb-by-verb comparison, if we wish, or relating a particular temporal specification, say, to the occurrence of a specific past tense.

15 As Wales (1985) points out, it is not clear that this is the 'simplest' situation for the child, judging by the performance of the youngest children in his sample. A further task had the child and experimenter on opposite sides of the table, with object placing and verbal stimuli as before. This shift appeared to help the youngest children, who tended to perform better in this situation than when they were on the same side of the table as the experimenter.

16 Wales does not unfortunately provide a breakdown of the kind of 'gesture' associated with different categories of deictic. His list of deictic items includes *the* and *a*, as well as *this*, *that*, *here* and *there*. But there is no indication of whether particular subcategories of gesture were more or less likely with particular forms, in view of the argument about the non-spatial basis for the *this/that* contrast developed below.

17 More complex functions of *it*, such as its meaning when referring back to a mass noun which happens to be individualized, are not represented in this sample. Tanz (1977) investigated children's awareness that, when faced with the instruction *give me it*, in the sequence from an adult *Here's some chocolate. Give me it*, *it* means all the chocolate, even if it happens to be in pieces.

18 Tanz points out that one of Huxley's (1970) subjects used nominative forms systematically, for the first time, in sentence-final position in tags (for example, *him did get stung, didn't he*). It will be interesting to see whether Sophie follows this pattern in sample 3.

19 The points usually made about the progressive suffix's phonological salience concern its marking by a separate syllable and its invariant pronunciation. It has been regarded as semantically transparent because,

unlike, for example, past tense, it is applied to actions which are in train in the child's immediate environment.

20 The verbs listed here are included in a category called by Quirk et al. (1972) 'verbs of inert perception and cognition'. The other important subcategory of stative verbs they identify are 'relational verbs'. Examples in this set (*concern*, *contain*, *equal*, *involve*, *sound*) are less likely to appear in the child's vocabulary at around 3;0, with the exception of *have* and *fit*.

21 The first *-ed* suffix appears in *called*, but since this only occurred in apparently formulaic sequences like *what that called*, we have not considered it as a past tense.

22 The semantic classification of verbs into these categories is not of course fixed, but can be altered by the nature of predicates: for example, *run* is atelic in the sentence *he ran towards the park*, but could be telic (accomplishment) in *he ran a half-marathon*.

23 To be more accurate, categories 1–3 all cover irregular verbs; category 1 is for those irregulars which differentiate past and past participle (*took*, *has taken*). It does not differentiate between verbs that form their participles on present-tense stems (*taken*) and those that do so on past-tense stems (*bitten*, *broken*); categories 2 and 3 are for irregular verbs which do not have past form and past-participle distinct (*made*, *has made*). It is also true of category 4, of course, that the same form does duty for both the past form and the past participle (as in *touched*, *has touched*). This causes some problems of interpretation (see note 24).

24 The whole question is complicated by the fact that *-ed* forms could also be considered, formally, as present perfects without auxiliaries, because of the past-tense/past-participle homonymy for regular verbs. Although we cannot logically exclude the possibility, the non-appearance also of *have* auxiliaries with any regular *-ed* marked form over the next year makes this interpretation rather unlikely.

25 This point requires some expansion, in the light of recent accounts of the present perfect, which claim that the two forms are truth-functionally the same, in locating an event at some point prior to speech-time. (See Inoue 1979; Smith 1981; see also McCawley 1981: 354). These accounts attribute the undoubted meaning difference between the two to pragmatic factors which concern the different implications of the forms. Such a view would *expect* past and present perfect forms to have not dissimilar patterns of temporal reference. However, as a matter of fact, it seems to us that whereas present perfects in the adult language *may* refer to remote events, it is rare for them to do so, and it is usual for them to be used for very recent prior events. It is the reflection of this discrepancy (present perfect for recent events, past for recent and more remote events) that we are interested in here, whatever the pragmatic implication of the forms. As a further check on a possible difference in application of the forms, we will also examine the *classes* of verbs to which the two suffixes are attached, to see if there is any difference of this kind.

26 For some systematic ways of distinguishing some of these classes, see Dowty (1979: 57).

27 The issue of the productivity of morphological processes (or indeed any rule) is clearly not independent of the lexical items across which it is distributed. Incidence scores for suffixes like *-ed* and *-en* have to be accompanied by figures about verb-types before we can interpret their significance.

28 There is a three-week gap in the data at this point, while Sophie was away on holiday between 18.4 and 5.5, so the change in frequency of *do*-forms appears rather more abrupt than it might in reality have been.

29 For arguments against the full productiveness of *do*-support, see above, p. 108. We should perhaps note here other pieces of evidence that Sophie is not yet in control of the system, such as the omission of *doesn't* at l. 166, the frequent pronunciation of *didn't* as [dɪnt] (see the discussion on auxiliaries in chapter 1, and her pronunciation of *does* as [duːz].

30 Stephany (1985) takes *wanna* (*want to*) and *gonna* (*going to*) as modals for the child. Although there may well be arguments for treating the child's expression of wishes, desires and intentions as modal (see also Pea and Mawby 1981), we have kept here to a more conservative profile of modality which includes the true modal auxiliaries and some catenatives like *have to*, *have got to*.

31 In the light of the data discussed by Kuczaj and Maratsos (1983), it is interesting to note an example of a question-form using *must* which Sophie produces on 17.4.80, without inversion:

what dress me must wear

The same session shows (a) *can*-initial structures, which have been a regular feature now for over three months, and (b) *do*-initial structures. The discrepant behaviours of three members of the auxiliary category (together with the arguments about *wh* + did structures above) suggests a much more complex and piecemeal acquisition of generalizations about the auxiliary than a casual examination of the data might suggest.

5 SOPHIE AT 3 YEARS 5 MONTHS

1 Smith (1973: 98 ff.) discusses in some detail a wide range of examples of metathesis which occur in Amahl's production. Both the examples cited here from the diary fall into one class of consonant transpositions which are characterized by Smith as involving the movement of a coronal consonant to the right of a non-coronal consonant. Sophie's pronunciations of *nativity* do not of course fit this generalization.

2 Though in fact Sophie's age at this sample, 41 months, falls within one standard deviation below the age predicted by the Miller–Chapman regression equation.

3 This dual function of the unit between catenative and main verb in fact leads Matthews (1981: 184) to reject tree structures (to which the bracketed schema used here is equivalent) as satisfactory representations of constructions such as this, which he calls 'fused constructions'.

4 This is of course an 'adultomorphic' stance, since the positioning of the bracket depends upon arguments like the behaviour of the intermediate unit on passivization, which is irrelevant for the child's grammar at this point. The only way of distinguishing *want* + sequences from *make* + sequences in the child's output at the age of 3½ would be in terms of the use of bare infinitive with the verb in the subordinate clause. It is interesting to note that a *want* + NP + V sequence appears in our first sample, as *me want daddy come down*, and that *make* appears, in a non-causative sense, in both samples 1 and 2. This raises some interesting questions which we shall return to below in the section on valency.

5 To be more precise, we would have to refer here to 'pause following a tone-unit boundary within a child's utterance'.

6 We have assumed, here and throughout, that there will be no difficulty in identifying a tone-unit boundary. In an acoustic analysis of Edinburgh speech, Brown et al. (1980) report some difficulty in identifying such boundaries, and suggest that similar analyses be applied to RP to determine whether there are in fact reliable acoustic correlates that allow one unequivocally to identify tone-unit boundaries in connected speech.

7 There are other inter-tone-unit relationships considered within the system outlined by Crystal (1969: 244 ff.). But such relationships are 'recognised and defined solely on prosodic grounds', and there is no guarantee that 'tonal subordinations' will directly reflect grammatical ones.

8 Crystal notes (1969: 258) that in his data the percentage of clauses coextensive with a tone unit, as a proportion of all clauses in the data, is 46 per cent. The data are of course for adults, but the rather low figure would seem to underline the independence of the two systems.

9 The term used by Bloom, Lahey et al. (1980) to characterize the relative in an utterance like *the man who fixes the door* (used by their subject Gia at 34½ months) is 'object specification'. This seems to be a more useful term for the post-modifying relative on empty NPs.

10 There has been discussion in the literature on the comprehension of relative clauses by children, on the relationship between coordination and relativision. See, for example, Tavakolian (1977).

11 There is in fact an occurrence of *'cos* in sample 2, at l. 271, where Sophie says:

and that one cos look

when she and her mother are identifying the various Mr Men characters. Though it may be possible to argue for a causal relationship here ('that one is Mr Happy also, because if you look at the picture you will see the features that identify him'), the utterance as it stands does not come near our definition of a complex sentence. Such constructions have to be seen as precursors of later causally related clauses, however.

12 It is possible, however, that Sophie's understanding of 'half-term' is that it can be an individual's holiday. Her elder sisters are at different schools and so likely to have a different half-term break to Sophie. So *half-term* becomes for Sophie a brief holiday someone else has. On this reading, the reason she adduces for Sammy's absence is perfectly plausible.

13 There were examples of 'phrasal' coordination in sample 1, but in fixed phrases like 'snakes and ladders'.

14 This is not to deny the importance of coordination, as it develops, as an index of the child's maturing grammatical knowledge. But the scarcity of these constructions in production data suggests that it will be difficult to assess reliably any hypothesis about them. Their infrequent appearance also presumably accounts for the majority of researchers turning to elicitation methods or comprehension for the evaluation of claims about coordination. One further point to make is that we are not given, in the papers cited which deal with production, any account of procedures used for identifying coordinative constructions. It is perhaps this issue that is being skirted when Tager-Flugsberg et al. (1982: 209) refer to the 'well-formed' constructions they counted. All analysts working on spoken language will be at times faced with a decision as to whether an utterance contains a coordination, or two simple clauses, the second of which happens to have an introductory *and*. Nor is it easy (cf. our discussion above about prosodic criteria for segmentation) to resolve the issue.

15 The importance to children of contextual constraints on the syntactic characteristics of coordinations is demonstrated by Jeremy (1978) and Tager-Flugsberg et al. (1982). The latter, in their study of elicited production in English and Japanese, found that even their youngest subjects (3-year-olds) 'respected referential identity/non-identity as a powerful constraint on the use of the phrasal or sentential form of coordinations'. Their study (which is, one hopes, the final chapter in a long, but narrow debate on the relevance of conjunction-reduction accounts of coordination for child language) indicates that syntactic accounts of coordination that rely on the specification of the items that seem to be omitted in cases of 'reduction' are unlikely to be successful. (See Matthews 1981: 211 ff.).

16 This seems to be true. Even if a punctual verb is used in a main clause, a *while* plus durational verb gives the punctual verb a durational (or at least iterative) interpretation:

while Mary sang, George jumped

The use of *while* with two punctual verbs seems odd, because of the durational implication of the connective:

while Mary fell, George jumped

17 This is to exclude from consideration the two occurrences in sample 2 of initial [huːz] (see p. 109).

18 The prerequisites for tag emergence are certainly more extensive than simply the occurrence of polar interrogatives (see below).

19 It is clear from the transcriptions of some of these tags (*doesn't*, *haven't*, *isn't*, *wasn't*) that their orthographic representations are a misleading guide to their pronunciation. Sophie is consistent, in tags and other grammatical contexts, in omitting the fricative preceding the contracted negative in all of them. In all cases but *haven't*, this does not lead to homonymy with other verb-forms. Sophie's form for *haven't* is [hænt], which serves her for *hasn't* also.

20 By way of comparison it is worth noting Todd's (1982) report that Audrey used appropriate pronoun-verb agreement, and pronoun-subject agreement, from 3;2. The examples he gives in his appendix from Audrey at 3;2 include two instances where the subject NP is not a personal pronoun, but where she makes the appropriate tag-pronoun choice:

all the houses are nice, are they
these are too little for me, are they

21 It might be supposed that an analysis of the discourse function of Sophie's tags, and the discourse contexts in which they occur, would prove enlightening. The study by Berninger and Garvey (1982) considers discourse function in detail for three groups of American children, in terms of the specific function of the tag ('information request', 'permission request', etc.) and the effectiveness of the tag at getting the child's interlocutor to respond. Included under the definition of tags, however, are such items as *right*, *OK* and *huh*, which can (perhaps more readily in American English) be appended to matrix sentences as tags. The American children use tags of this kind from quite early on (the youngest children in the study are 2;10), before they use the 'grammatical' tags, and for similar functions. There is thus a continuity of function for tags from quite early in the child's development, although their form changes as the child becomes grammatically more advanced. Assertions for which the child can ask for agreement from his interlocutor via a tag are present late in the third year. Since this is also the case for Sophie (the assertion contexts for an 'agreement request' tag are in sample 2, although not even stereotypic tags are available to her then), it seems very unlikely that we will be able to explain tag emergence in terms of a sudden change in discourse structure.

22 Crystal (1980) maintains that adverbials tend to be ignored also in mainstream grammatical theories of the adult language.

23 *This* occurred in sample 3 in subject position only in *yes/no* questions.

24 Generally, a definite NP as the complement of existential *there* appears to require that the NP referent has already been introduced into the discourse. Sophie does use one existential *there* in this sample – *there's some in*, at l. 108. This could well be stereotypic, however.

25 The full complexity of conditions affecting the use of *come* and *go* is addressed in Fillmore (1975: 50 ff.). An immediate modification to be

made to the statement in the text is that *come* can also be used for motion to an addressee: *is Lily coming to your house?* The deictic centre for *come* can even shift to some non-addressee mentioned in the sentence: *no, she's coming to Harry's.* A problem for the researcher (a problem not restricted to the learning of the meanings of *come* and *go*) is how far to take the complex statement of Fillmore's account as a guide to what the child has to learn, and hence as a framework for investigating acquisition. One plausible, but little used alternative is to examine the meanings of *come* and *go* in child-directed speech and to regard these (probably restricted) uses as a specification of the child's task.

26 Berman actually proposes two potential sources for the 'overextension'. The second source is perhaps less obvious because less direct, but it is still possible. Both conjugations have infinitives which are similar: a prefix li- is added to a stem which includes the root. So *nif'al* has infinite *ləheradem*, for example, and *pi'el* has *ləkabel*. These infinitives are made more alike by children pronouncing the first as *liradem*, and the second as *likabel*, giving the same canonical structure li-CaCeC. The claim Berman seems to make (1983: 65) is that it is this similarity that leads the child to make the overextension. She says: '[the overextension] could be based on the infinitive form of li-CaCeC which children use for both types of conjugations; this is reasonable, since children quite generally use infinitive forms of the verbs and even overextend them somewhat before gaining productive control of the present tense'. Unfortunately, there is no way of telling which of the routes to overextension the child might have followed. As Berman proposes an alternative explanation, however, this is perhaps not so serious a matter.

27 Note, however, that we cannot know whether Sophie has generalized the suffix from a number of examples of a single lexical item (for example, *forgotten*) or from examples in input of a range of lexical items which carry the suffix (*forgotten*, *broken*, *fallen*, etc.).

28 Discussions of the possible range of negative data can be found in Butler, Platt and MacWhinney (1983), Hirsch-Pasek, Treiman and Schneiderman (1984) and Mazurkewich and White (1984).

29 About two-thirds of the *-en* suffixes are on irregular verbs (counting types), whereas of the *-ed* suffixes, only one-third are used with irregulars.

30 The facts relating to phonological conditioning represented in table 5.8 are a further piece of evidence for the similarity of function of *-en* and *-ed* over this period.

31 It is not clear that *been* forms are always to be regarded as precursors of the present perfect. There are contexts where *been* is used which are difficult to interpret in this way, and where *been* seems like a past copula. In the sample for 20.7, for example, Sophie uses it in a complex sentence where past tenses are (in the adult language) required in both clauses, if past is used in one of them:

when he was a baby he been Vin (referring to her father).

6 CONCLUSIONS AND PROSPECTS

1 If mothers generally do behave like Fran, and for children younger than 2;4, the insistence of Gleitman and colleagues (1984) on the stressed and non-contracted nature of pre-subject auxiliaries, and its importance in their explanation of language-learning, is curious. They summarize their views thus: 'in brief, a variety of properties of language-learning, many of them cross-linguistic, suggest that the learner is biased in the initial stage to analyse stressed syllables, and ignore the rest of the waveform; the stressed syllables leap out at the child just as, in visual perception, the figures leap out from the group'. The problem is that it is likely that many auxiliaries *are* cliticized in child-directed speech, and it is not clear, if this is so, how acquisition of these items fits with the view of Gleitman et al.

2 DO is also commonly cliticized, in the present, when it occurs (as it frequently does) with *you*. The normal pronunciation of this, for mother and child, is [dʒuː]. The more general point is that, in considering the extent of the syntactic generalization for question formation, we need to take into account not only the range of auxiliaries used in medial and pre-subject position, but also the range and type of noun phrases which occur as subjects.

3 Similar points are made by Romaine (1984: 78, 257). She also provides an insightful discussion of the development of relative clauses (with data from Scottish children), emphasizing the functional role of these and related structures.

4 British children have a common strategy for ensuring that a referent that is to be identified by a relative clause appears in object position. They introduce the topic in this manner:

Child: You know the man who runs the corner shop?

(An interlocutor may or may not respond with 'yes')

Child: Well, he shouted at me.

Introducing the topic with *you know* avoids having a complex NP with a relative in subject position, as in:

the man who runs the corner shop shouted at me.

5 The data were kindly provided by Jon Miller and Robin Chapman. I am grateful to my colleagues Michael Garman, Michael Johnson, Christine Schelleter and Louisette Stodel for analysing it and discussing it with me.

6 This example is used by Romaine to illustrate this kind of relative, but it is not clear whether it comes from her data. In the genitive example, a more usual substitute for the relative pronoun may be *whose*.

References

Allerton, D. J. (1982) *Valency and the English Verb*. London: Academic Press.

Antinucci, F and Miller, R. (1976) How children talk about what happened. *Journal of Child Language* 3: 167–89.

Atkinson, R. M. (1985) Theories of learnability. In P. Fletcher and M. Garman (eds) *Language Acquisition: studies in first language development* (2nd rev. edn). Cambridge: Cambridge University Press.

Bard, E. Gurman and Anderson, A. H. (1983) The unintelligibility of speech to children. *Journal of Child Language* 10: 265–92.

Barrett, M. (1978) Lexical development and overextension in child language. *Journal of Child Language* 5: 205–19.

Bell, S. (1970) The development of the concept of object as related to infant–mother attachment. *Child Development* 41: 292–311.

Benedict, H. (1979) Early lexical development: comprehension and production. *Journal of Child Language* 6: 183–200.

Berman, R. (1981) Regularity vs. anomaly: the acquisition of Hebrew inflectional morphology. *Journal of Child Language* 8: 205–82.

Berman, Ruth A. (1983) Establishing a schema: children's construals of verb-tense marking. *Language Sciences* 5: 61–78.

Berninger, G. and Garvey, C. (1982) Tag constructions: structure and function in child discourse. *Journal of Child Language* 9: 151–68.

Bloom, L. (1970) *Language Development: form and function in emerging grammars*. Cambridge, Mass.: MIT Press.

Bloom, L. (1973) *One Word at a Time: the use of single word utterances before syntax*. The Hague: Mouton.

Bloom, L., Lifter, K. and Hafitz, J. (1980) Semantics of verbs and the development of verb inflections in child language. *Language* 56: 386–412.

Bloom, L., Lahey, M., Hood, L., Lifter, K. and Fiess, K. (1980) Complex sentences: acquisition of syntactic connectives and the semantic relations they encode. *Journal of Child Language* 7: 235–61.

Bowerman, M. (1979) The acquisition of complex sentences. In P. Fletcher and M. Garman (eds) *Language Acquisition: studies in first language development*. Cambridge: Cambridge University Press.

Braine, M. D. S. (1971) On two types of models of the internalisation of grammars. In D. I. Slobin (ed.) *The Outogenesis of Grammar: a theoretical symposium*. New York: Academic Press.

Bridges, A. (1980) SVO comprehension strategies reconsidered: the evidence of individual patterns of response. *Journal of Child Language* 7: 89–104.

Broen, P. A. (1972) *The Verbal Environment of the Language-Learning Child*. ASHA Monograph 17, December.

Bronckart, J. and Sinclair, H. (1973) Time, tense and aspect. *Cognition* 2: 107–30.

Brown, G., Currie, K. L. and Kenworthy, J. (1980). *Questions of Intonation*. London: Croom Helm.

Brown, R. (1973) *A First Language: the early stages*. London: George Allen & Unwin.

Brown, R. and Hanlon, C. (1970) Derivational complexity and order of acquisition. In J. R. Hayes (ed.) *Cognition and the Development of Language*. New York: John Wiley.

Butler, Platt, C. and MacWhinney, B. (1983) Error assimilation as a mechanism in language learning. *Journal of Child Language* 10: 401–14.

Bybee, J. and Slobin, D. (1982) Rules and schemata in the development and use of the English past tense. *Language* 58: 265–89.

Bynon, J. (1968) Berber nursery language. *Translations of the Philological Society* 107–61.

Campbell, R. (1985) Cognitive development and child language. In P. Fletcher and M. Garman (eds) *Language Acquisition: studies in first language development* (2nd rev. edn). Cambridge: Cambridge University Press.

Campbell, R. and Wales, R. (1970) The study of language acquisition. In J. Lyons (ed.) *New Horizons in Linguistics*. Harmondsworth: Penguin Books.

Chapman, R. (1978) Comprehension strategies in children. In J. Kavanaugh and W. Strange (eds) *Speech and Language in the Laboratory, School and Clinic*. Cambridge, Mass.: MIT Press.

Chiat, S. (1981) Context-specificity and generalisation in the acquisition of pronominal distinctions. *Journal of Child Language* 8: 75–91.

Chiat, S. (1985) Personal pronouns. In P. Fletcher and M. Garman (eds) *Language Acquisition: studies in first language development* (2nd rev. edn). Cambridge: Cambridge University Press.

Chomsky, N. (1957) *Syntactic Structures*. The Hague: Mouton.

Chomsky, N. (1964) Formal discussion. In U. Bellugi and R. Brown (eds) *The Acquisition of Language*. Chicago: University of Chicago Press.

Chomsky, N. (1975) *Reflections on Language*. New York: Pantheon Books.

Chomsky, N. (1979) On cognitive structures and their development: a reply to Piaget. In M. Piatelli-Palmarini (ed.) *Language and Learning: the debate between Jean Piaget and Noam Chomsky*. London: Routledge & Kegan Paul.

Clark, E. (1978) From gesture to word: on the natural history of deixis in language acquisition. In J. Brumer and A. Garton (eds) *Human Growth and Development*. Oxford: Clarendon Press.

Clark, E. and Garnica, O. (1974) Is he coming or going? On the acquisition of deictic verbs. *Journal of Verbal Learning and Verbal Behaviour* 13: 559–72.

Clark, H. H. and Clark, E. V. (1977) *Psychology and Language*. Harcourt Brace Jovanovich.

Clark, R. (1974) Performing without competence. *Journal of Child Language* 1: 1–10.

Clark, R., Hutcheson, S. and van Buren, P. (1974) Comprehension and production in language acquisition. *Journal of Linguistics* 10: 341–58.

Comrie, B. (1976) *Aspect*. Cambridge: Cambridge University Press.

Corrigan, R. (1978) Language development as related to stage 6 object permanence development. *Journal of Child Language* 5: 173–89.

Cromer, R. (1974) The development of language and cognition: the cognition hypothesis. In B. Foss (ed.) *New Perspectives in Child Development*. Harmondsworth: Penguin Books.

Crystal, D. (1966) Specification and English tenses. *Journal of Linguistics* 2: 1–34.

Crystal, D. (1969) *Prosodic Systems and Intonation in English*. Cambridge: Cambridge University Press.

Crystal, D. (1974) Review of R. Brown: *A First Language: the early stages. Journal of Child Language* 1: 289–307.

Crystal, D. (1980) Neglected grammatical factors in conversational English. In S. Greenbaum, G. Leech and J. Svartvik (eds) *Studies in English Linguistics for Randolph Quirk*. London: Longman.

Crystal, D. (1981) *Clinical Linguistics*. Vienna and New York: Springer.

Crystal, D. (1985) Prosodic development. In P. Fletcher and M. Garman (eds) *Language Acquisition: studies in first language development* (2nd rev. edn). Cambridge: Cambridge University Press.

Crystal, D., Fletcher, P. and Garman, M. (1981) *The Grammatical Analysis of Language Disability: a procedure for assessment and remediation* (rev. edn). London: Edward Arnold.

Curtiss, S. (1981). Dissociations between language and cognition: cases and implications. *Journal of Autism and Developmental Disorders* 11: 15–30.

Dale, P. (1976) *Language Development: structure and function* (2nd edn). New York: Holt Rinehart & Winston.

Donaldson, M. (1978) *Children's Minds*. Glasgow: Fontana/Collins.

Dore, J. (1979) Conversation and pre-school language development. In P. Fletcher and M. Garman (eds) *Language Acquisition: studies in first language development*. Cambridge: Cambridge University Press.

Dowty, D. (1979) *Word Meaning and Montague Grammar*. Dordrecht: D. Reidel.

Eliot, A. (1981) *Child Language*. Cambridge: Cambridge University Press.

Erreich, A., Valian, V. and Winzemer, J. (1980) Aspects of a theory of language acquisition. *Journal of Child Language* 7. 157–79.

Fawcett, R. and Perkins, M. (1980) *Child Language Transcripts 6–12*, vols 1–4. Pontypridd: Department of Behaviour and Communication Studies, Polytechnic of Wales.

Fay, D. (1978) Transformations as mental operations: a reply to Kuczaj. *Journal of Child Language* 5: 143–50.

Ferguson, C. A. (1964) Baby talk in six languages. *American Anthropologist* 66 (6, part 2): 103–14.

Ferguson, C. A. (1977) Baby talk as a simplified register. In C. E. Snow and C. A. Ferguson (eds) *Talking to Children: language input and acquisition*. Cambridge: Cambridge University Press.

Ferguson, C. A. and Farwell, C. (1975) Words and sounds in early language acquisition. *Language* 51: 419–39.

Fillmore, C. (1975) *Santa Cruz Lectures on Deixis 1971*. Indiana University Linguistics Club.

Fletcher, P. (1979) The development of the verb phrase. In P. Fletcher and M. Garman (eds) *Language Acquisition: studies in first language development*. Cambridge: Cambridge University Press.

Fletcher, P. (1981) Description and explanation in the acquisition of verb-forms. *Journal of Child Language* 8: 93–108.

Fletcher, P., Peters, J. and Hixson, P. (1982) Sampling situations and language assessment. Paper presented at the Annual Convention of the American Speech–Language–Hearing Association, Toronto, November.

Fodor, J. D. and Smith, M. R. (1978) What kind of an exception is 'have got'? *Linguistic Inquiry* 9: 45–65.

Fourcin, A. (1978) Acoustic patterns and speech recognition. In N. Waterson and C. Snow (eds) *The Development of Communication*. Chichester: John Wiley.

Furrow, D., Nelson, K. and Benedict, H. (1979) Mothers' speech to children and syntactic development: some simple relationships. *Journal of Child Language* 6: 423–42.

Garman, M. (1979) Micro-profile of stage I. In D. Crystal (ed.) *Working with LARSP*. London: Edward Arnold.

Garnica, O. (1977) Some prosodic and paralinguistic features of speech to young children. In C. E. Snow and C. A. Ferguson (eds) *Talking to Children: language input and acquisition*. Cambridge: Cambridge University Press.

Gazdar, G., Pullum, G. and Sag, I. (1980) A phrase structure grammar of the English auxiliary system. *Stanford Working Papers in Grammatical Theory*, vol. 1, pp. 1–124.

Gentner, D. (1982) Why nouns are learned before verbs: linguistic relativity vs. natural partitioning. In S. Kuczaj (ed.) *Language Development: Language, culture and cognition*. Hillsdale, NJ: Erlbaum.

Gimson, A. (1970) *An Introduction to the Pronunciation of English* (2nd edn). London: Edward Arnold.

Gleason, J. B. (1975) Fathers and other strangers: men's speech to young children. In D. P. Dato (ed.) *Developmental Psycholinguistics: theory and applications*. Washington, DC: Georgetown University Press.

Gleitman, L., Newport, E. and Gleitman, H. (1984) The current status of the motherese hypothesis. *Journal of Child Language* 11: 43–79.

Goodluck, H. (1985) Language acquisition and linguistic theory. In P. Fletcher and M. Garman (eds) *Language Acquisition: studies in first language development* (2nd rev. edn). Cambridge: Cambridge University Press.

Gregoire, A. (1939) L'apprentissage du langage: les deux premieres années. Bibliothèque de la Faculté de Philosophie et Lettres de l'Université de Liège.

Griffiths, P. D. (1979) Speech acts and early sentences. In P. Fletcher and M. Garman (eds) *Language Acquisition: studies in first language development*. Cambridge: Cambridge University Press.

Griffiths, P. D., Atkinson, R. M. and Huxley, R. (1974) Project report. *Journal of Child Language* 1: 157–8.

Hakuta, K., de Villiers, J. and Tager-Flugsberg, H. (1982) Sentence coordination in Japanese and English. *Journal of Child Language* 9: 193–207.

Halliday, M. A. K. (1975) *Learning How to Mean: explorations in the development of language*. London: Edward Arnold.

Hamburger, H. (1980) A deletion ahead of its time. *Cognition* 8: 389–416.

Hamburger, H. and Crain, S. (1982) Relative acquisition. In S. A. Kuczaj II (ed.) *Language Development. Volume 1: Syntax and Semantics*. Hillsdale, NJ: Lawrence Erlbaum.

Hart, G. (1982) The development of past time reference. Unpublished PhD Thesis, University of Reading.

Hawkins, J. A. (1978) *Definiteness and Indefiniteness: a study in reference and grammaticality prediction*. London: Croom Helm.

Herbst, T., Heath, D. and Dederding, H. M. (1980) *Grimm's Grandchildren: current topics in German linguistics*. London: Longman.

Hirsh-Pasek, K., Treiman, R. and Schneiderman, M. (1984) Brown & Hanlon revisited: mothers' sensitivity to ungrammatical forms. *Journal of Child Language* 11: 81–8.

Hockett, C. (1955) *A Manual of Phonology*. Indiana University Publications in Anthropology and Linguistics, memoir 11.

Hood, L. H. (1977) A longitudinal study of the development of the expression of causal relations in complex sentences. Unpublished PhD thesis, Columbia University.

Hornstein, N. and Lightfoot, D. (1981) Introduction. In N. Hornstein and D. Lightfoot (eds) *Explanation in Linguistics: the logical problem of language acquisition*. London: Longman.

Howe, C. (1976) The meaning of two-word utterances in the speech of young children. *Journal of Child Language* 3: 29–47.

Howe, C. (1981) *Acquiring Language in a Conversational Context*. London: Academic Press.

Huddleston, R. (1984) *Introduction to the Grammar of English*. Cambridge: Cambridge University Press.

Hurford, J. (1975) A child and the English question-formation rule. *Journal of Child Language* 2: 299–301.

Huttenlocher, J. (1974) The origins of language comprehension. In R. L. Solso (ed.) *Theories in Cognitive Psychology*. Potomac, Md.: Lawrence Erlbaum.

Huxley, R. (1970) The development of the correct use of subject personal pronouns in two children. In G. B. Flores d'Arcais and W. J. Levelt (eds) *Advances in Psycholinguistics*. Amsterdam: North-Holland.

Ingram, D. (1975) If and when transformations are acquired by children. In

D. P. Dato (ed.) *Developmental Psycholinguistics: theory and applications.* 26th Annual Georgetown Round Table. Washington, DC: Georgetown University Press.

Ingram, D. (1976) *Phonological Disability in Children.* London: Edward Arnold.

Inoue, K. (1979) An analysis of the English present perfect. *Linguistics* 17: 561–89.

Jackendoff, R. (1971) Gapping and related rules. *Linguistic Inquiry* 2: 21–35.

Jeremy, R. (1978) Use of coordinate sentences with the conjunction 'and' for describing temporal and locative relations between events. *Journal of Psycholinguistic Research* 7: 135–50.

Johnston, J. and Slobin, D. (1979) The development of locative expressions in English, Italian, Serbo-Croatian and Turkish. *Journal of Child Language* 6: 529–45.

Kaper, W. (1976) Pronominal case errors. *Journal of Child Language* 3: 439–41.

Karmiloff-Smith, A. (1979) *A Functional Approach to Child Language.* Cambridge: Cambridge University Press.

Karmiloff-Smith, A. (1980) Psychological processes underlying pronominalisation in children's connected discourse. In J. Kresinan and A. E. Ojeida (eds) *Papers from the Parasession on Pronouns and Anaphora.* Chicago Linguistic Society.

Keynerès, E. (1926) Les premiers mots de l'enfant. *Archives de Psychologie* 20: 191–218.

Klima, E. and Bellugi, U. (1966) Syntactic regularities in the speech of children. In J. Lyons and R. Wales (eds) *Psycholinguistic Papers.* Edinburgh: Edinburgh University Press.

Kuczaj, S. (1978) Why do children fail to over-generalise the progressive inflection? *Journal of Child Language* 5: 167–71.

Kuczaj, S. and Maratsos, M. (1983) Initial verbs of yes–no questions: a different kind of general grammatical category. *Developmental Psychology* 19: 440–4.

Labov, W. (1971) Methodology. In W. D. Dingwall (ed.) *A Survey of Linguistic Science.* Linguistic Program, University of Maryland.

Labov, W. and Labov, T. (1978) Learning the syntax of questions. In R. Campbell and P. Smith (eds) *Recent Advances in the Psychology of Language: language development and mother–child interaction.* London and New York: Plenum Press.

Lee, L. (1971) *The Northwestern Syntax Screening Test.* Evanston, Ill.: Northwestern University Press.

Leech, G. (1971) *Meaning and the English Verb.* London: Longman.

Leopold, W. (1939–49) *Speech Development of a Bilingual Child: a linguist's record.* Vols I–IV. Evanston, Ill.: Northwestern University Press.

Levelt, W. (1975) What became of LAD? In *Ut Videam: contributions to an understanding of linguistics, for Pieter Verbrua on the occasion of his 70th birthday.* Lisse: Peter de Ridder Press.

Lightfoot, D. (1979) *Principles of Diachronic Syntax.* Cambridge: Cambridge University Press.

Limber, J. (1973) The genesis of complex sentences. In T. E. Moore (ed.) *Cognitive Development and the Acquisition of Language*. New York: Academic Press.

Limber, J. (1976) Unravelling competence, performance and pragmatics in the speech of young children. *Journal of Child Language* 3: 309–18.

Lust, B. and Mervis, C. (1980) Development of coordination in the natural speech of young children. *Journal of Child Language* 7: 279–304.

Lyons, J. (1977) *Semantics* vol II. Cambridge: Cambridge University Press.

McCune-Nicolich, L. (1981) The cognitive bases of relational words in the single word period. *Journal of Child Language* 8: 15–34.

McTear, M. (1985) *Children's Conversation*. Oxford: Basil Blackwell.

MacWhinney, B. (1978) *Processing a First Language: the acquisition of morphophonology*. Society for Research in Child Development Monographs 43.

McCawley, J. D. (1981) *Everything That Linguists Have Always Wanted to Know About Logic*. Chicago: University of Chicago Press.

Macken, M. (1980) The child's lexical representation: the 'puzzle-puddle-pickle' evidence. *Journal of Linguistics* 16: 1–17.

Malan, K. (1983) An investigation of the relationship between maternal speech style and language acquisition. Unpublished MA dissertation, University of Reading.

Marslen-Wilson, W. and Tyler, L. (1980) The temporal structure of spoken language understanding. *Cognition* 8: 1–71.

Matthews, P. H. (1975) Review of R. Brown, *A First Language*. *Journal of Linguistics* 11: 322–43.

Matthews, P. H. (1981) *Syntax*. Cambridge: Cambridge University Press.

Mazurkewich, I. and White, L. (1984) The acquisition of the dative alternation: unlearning overgeneralisations. *Cognition* 16: 261–83.

Miller, J. (1981) *Assessing Language Production in Children: experimental procedures*. London: Edward Arnold.

Miller, J. and Chapman, R. (1981) The relation between age and mean length of utterance in morphemes. *Journal of Speech and Hearing Research* 24: 154–61.

Miller, W. and Ervin, S. (1964) The development of grammar in child language. In U. Bellugi and R. Brown (eds) *The Acquisition of Language*. Chicago: Chicago University Press.

Miller, J. and Yoder, D. (1973) *Miller–Yoder Test of Grammatical Comprehension*. Madison, Wis.: Department of Communication Disorders.

Neiser, U. (1967) *Cognitive Psychology*. New York: Appleton-Century-Crofts.

Nelson, K. (1973) Structure and strategy in learning to talk. *Monographs of the Society for Research in Child Development* 38 (1–2), No. 149.

Nelson, K. (1976) Some attributes of adjectives used by young children. *Cognition* 4: 13–30.

Nelson, K. E., Carskaddon, G. and Bonvillian, J. D. (1973) Syntax acquisition: impact of experimental variation in adult verbal interaction with the child. *Child Development* 44: 497–504.

Newport, E., Gleitman, G. and Gleitman, H. (1977) Mother, I'd rather do it myself: some effects and non-effects of maternal speech-style. In C. Snow

and C. Ferguson (eds) *Talking to Children: language input and acquisition*. Cambridge: Cambridge University Press.
Ochs, E. (1982) Talking to children in Western Samoa. *Language in Society* 11: 77–104.
Olmsted, D. (1971) *Out of the Mouth of Babes*. The Hague: Mouton.
Palmer, F. R. (1974) *The English Verb*. London: Longman.
Palmer, F. R. (1979) *Modality and the English Modals*. London: Longman.
Paul, R. (1981) Analyzing complex sentence development. In J. Miller *Assessing Language Production in Children: experimental procedures*. London: Edward Arnold.
Pea, R. D. and Mawby, R. (1981) Semantics of modal auxiliary verb use by preschool children. Paper presented at the Second International Congress for the Study of Child Language, Vancouver.
Perkins, M. (1980) The expression of modality in English. Unpublished PhD thesis, Polytechnic of Wales (CNAA).
Piaget, J. (1959) *The Language and Thought of the Child*. London: Routledge & Kegan Paul.
Piatelli-Palmarini, M. (ed.) (1980) *Language and Learning*. London: Routledge & Kegan Paul.
Quirk, R. and Greenbaum, S. (1973) *A University Grammar of English*. London: Longman.
Quirk, R., Greenbaum, S., Leech, G. and Svartvik, J. (1972) *A Grammar of Contemporary English*. London: Longman.
Ratner, N. B. and Pye, C. (1984) Higher pitch in BT is not universal: evidence from Quiché Mayan. *Journal of Child Language* 11, 515–22.
Rizzo, J. and Stephens, I. (1981) Performance of children with normal and impaired oral language production on a set of auditory comprehension tests. *Journal of Speech and Hearing Disorders* 46: 150–9.
Romaine, S. (1984) *The Language of Children and Adolescents: the acquisition of communicative competence*. Oxford: Basil Blackwell.
Rondal, J. A. (1980) Fathers' and mothers' speech in early language development. *Journal of Child Language* 7: 353–69.
Ruder, K. (1982) A developmental study of the acquisition of verb meaning – to open. Paper presented at the Annual Convention of the American Speech–Language–Hearing Association, Toronto, November.
Sachs, J. (1983) Talking about there and then: the emergence of displaced reference in parent–child discourse. In K. E. Nelson (ed.) *Children's Language* vol. 4. Hillsdale, NJ: Lawrence Erlbaum.
Sachs, J. and Devin, J. (1976) Young children's use of age-appropriate speech styles in social interaction and role-playing. *Journal of Child Language* 3: 81–98.
Sachs, J., Bard, B. and Johnson, M. (1981) Language learning with restricted input: case studies of two hearing children of deaf parents. *Applied Psycholinguistics* 2: 33–54.
Scott-Goldman, J. (1983) The noun phrase in the written language of deaf children. Unpublished PhD thesis, University of Reading.
Sheldon, A. (1974) The role of parallel function in the acquisition of relative clauses. *Journal of Verbal Learning and Verbal Behaviour* 13: 272–31.

Shockey, L. and Bond, Z. (1980) Phonological processes in speech addressed to children. *Phonetica* 37: 267–74.

Sinclair, H. (1971) Sensorimotor action patterns as a condition for the acquisition of syntax. In R. Huxley and E. Ingram (eds) *Language Acquisition: models and methods*. London: Academic Press.

Slobin, D. (1971) *Psycholinguistics*. Glenview, Ill.: Scott, Foresman.

Slobin, D. (1973) Cognitive prerequisites for the acquisition of grammar. In C. Ferguson and D. Slobin (eds) *Studies of Child Language Development*. New York: Holt, Rinehart & Winston.

Slobin, D. (1985) Cross-linguistic evidence for the language-making capacity. In D. I. Slobin (ed.) *The Crosslinguistic Study of Language Acquisition*. Hillsdale, NJ: Lawrence Erlbaum.

Smith, M. (1926) An investigation of the development of the sentence and the extent of vocabulary in young children. *University of Iowa Studies in Child Welfare* 3, no. 5.

Smith, N. (1973) *The Acquisition of Phonology: a case study*. Cambridge: Cambridge University Press.

Smith, N. (1981) Grammatically, time and tense. In *The Psychological Mechanisms of Language*. London: The Royal Society and The British Academy.

Smith, N. and Wilson, D. (1979) *Modern Linguistics: the result of Chomsky's revolution*. Harmondsworth: Penguin Books.

Snow, C. (1985) Conversations with children. In P. Fletcher and M. Garman (eds) *Language Acquisition: studies in first language development* (2nd rev. edn). Cambridge: Cambridge University Press.

Snow, C. and Ferguson, C. (eds) (1977) *Talking to Children: language input and acquisition*. Cambridge: Cambridge University Press.

Stephany, U. (1985) Modality. In P. Fletcher and M. Garman (eds) *Language Acquisition: studies in first language development* (2nd rev. edn). Cambridge. Cambridge University Press.

Stern, C. and Stern, W. (1928) *Die Kindersprache: eine psychologische und spractheoretische Untersuchung* (4th edn). Leipzig: Barth.

Tager-Flugsberg, H., de Villiers, J. and Hakuta, K. (1982) The development of sentence coordination. In S. A. Kuczaj II (ed.) *Language Development Volume 1: Syntax and Semantics*. Hillsdale, NJ: Lawrence Erlbaum.

Tanz, C. (1974) Cognitive principles underlying children's errors in pronominal case-marking. *Journal of Child Language* 1: 271–6.

Tanz, C. (1977) Learning how 'it' works. *Journal of Child Language* 4: 225–35.

Tanz, C. (1980) *Studies in the Acquisition of Deictic Terms*. London: Cambridge University Press.

Tavakolian, S. (1977) Structure and function in child language. Unpublished PhD thesis, University of Massachusetts.

Templin, M. (1957) *Certain Language Skills in Children*. Minneapolis: University of Minnesota Press.

Todd, P. (1982) Tagging after red herrings: evidence against the processing capacity explanation in child language. *Journal of Child Language* 9: 99–114.

Trudgill, P. and Hannah, J. (1982) *International English: a guide to varieties of Standard English*. London: Edward Arnold.

Uzigiris, I. and Hunt, J. (1975) *Assessment in Infancy: ordinal scales of psychological development*. Illinois: University of Illinois Press.

Wales, R. (1985) Deixis. In P. Fletcher and M. Garman (eds) *Language Acquisition: studies in first language development* (2nd rev. edn). Cambridge: Cambridge University Press.

Wanner, E. and Gleitman, L. (eds) (1982) *Language Acquisition: the state of the art*. Cambridge: Cambridge University Press.

Waterson, N. and Snow, C. (eds) (1978) *The Development of Communication*. John Wiley.

Weist, R. (1985a) Tense and aspect. In P. Fletcher and M. Garman (eds) *Language Acquisition: studies in first language development* (2nd rev. edn). Cambridge: Cambridge University Press.

Weist, R. (1985b) Cross-linguistic perspective on cognitive development. In T. M. Schlecter and M. P. Toglia (eds) *New Directions in Cognitive Science*. Norwood, NJ: Ablex.

Wells, C. G. (1974) Language development in pre-school children. *Journal of Child Language* 1: 157–8.

Wells, C. G. (1975) Language development in preschool children: transcripts. mimeo, University of Bristol School of Education.

Wells, C. G. (1979) Learning and using the auxiliary verb in English. In V. Lee (ed.) *Language Development*. London: Croom Helm.

Wells, C. G. (1980) Adjustments in adult–child conversation: some effects of interaction. In H. Giles, W. P. Robinson and P. M. Smith (eds) *Language: social psychological perspectives*. Oxford: Pergamon Press.

Wells, C. G. (1981) *Learning through Interaction: the study of language development*. Cambridge: Cambridge University Press.

Wells, C. G. (1985) *Language Development in the Pre-school Years*. Cambridge: Cambridge University Press.

Wells, J. (1982) *Accents of English*. Vol. 1. Cambridge: Cambridge University Press.

Wexler, K. and Culicover, P. (1980) *Formal Principles of Language Acquisition*. Cambridge, Mass.: MIT Press.

Wilding, J. (1984) A modality for childhood. Paper presented at the AILA Congress, Brussels, August.

Woods, A. J., Fletcher, P. and Hughes, G. A. (1985) *Statistics in Language Studies*. Cambridge: Cambridge University Press.

Yairi, E. (1981) Disfluencies of normally speaking two-year-old children. *Journal of Speech and Hearing Research* 24: 190–5.

Zwicky, A. (1970) A double regularity in the acquisition of English verb morphology. *Papers in Linguistics* 3: 411–18.

Index